Celia
With fondness
Paul

Questioning BPM?

MK

Meghan-Kiffer Press

Tampa, Florida, USA

www.mkpress.com

Innovation at the Intersection of Business and Technology

Landmark Books by Meghan-Kiffer Press

Cognitive Computing
A Brief Guide for Game Changers

Business Process Management
The Next Wave

Business Architecture
The 21st Century business Platform Built on Cloud Computing

Business Innovation in the Cloud
Strategies for Executing on Innovation with Cloud Computing

Value Networks
And the True Meaning of Collaboration

Smart Process Apps
The Next Breakout Business Advantage

Dot.Cloud
The 21st Century business Platform Built on Cloud Computing

Enterprise Cloud Computing
A Strategy Guide for Business and Technology Leaders

Extreme Competition
Innovation and the Great 21st Century Business Reformation

Business Process Management
The Third Wave

Mastering the Unpredictable
How Adaptive Case Management Will Revolutionize
the Way That Knowledge Workers Get Things Done

IT Doesn't Matter
Business Processes Do

The Real-Time Enterprise
Competing on Time

See more at...

MK

Meghan-Kiffer Press www.mkpress.com

Innovation at the Intersection of Business and Technology

Questioning BPM?

Editors:
Paul Harmon
Roger Tregear

Meghan-Kiffer Press
Tampa, Florida, USA
www.mkpress.com
Innovation at the Intersection of Business and Technology

Publisher's Cataloging-in-Publication Data

Harmon, Paul and Roger Tregear (Eds).

Questioning BPM? / Paul Harmon, Roger Tregear (Eds), - 1st ed.

p. cm.

Includes bibliographic entries.

ISBN-10: 0-929652-54-1 ISBN-13: 978-0-929652-54-2

1. Management 2. Technological innovation. 3. Diffusion of innovations. 4. Globalization—Economic aspects. 5. Information technology. 6. In-formation Society. 7. Organizational change. I. Harmon, Paul II. Roger Tregear. III. Title

HM48.H75 2016

303.48'33–dc22 CIP

Published by Meghan-Kiffer Press

310 East Fern Street, Suite G

Tampa, FL 33604 USA

MK

Meghan-Kiffer Press

Tampa, Florida, USA

Innovation at the Intersection of Business and Technology

Printed in the United States of America. SAN 249-7980

MK Printing 10 9 8 7 6 5 4 3 2 1

Contents

INTRODUCTION

"The single biggest problem in communication is the illusion that it has taken place."

– George Bernard Shaw

Is there another field of human endeavor so beset with problems caused by a lack of agreement about fundamental concepts as we find with Business Process Management (BPM)?

After many years editing a website, teaching and consulting, we know three things about BPM. First, there are always new people asking the same questions others before them have asked. Second, no answers fit all situations, because people from different organizations with different needs have different perspectives. And, finally, the answers keep changing as technology, circumstances, and the things that people seek to do, change as well.

This book provides a forum to ask and answer important questions about BPM, reflecting the many different perspectives. Our first challenge was to decide which questions to ask. The final 15 are briefly summarized as follows:

- How would you describe the scope and limits of BPM?
- How would you characterize the current interest(s) in BPM?
- What role, if any, do you see BPM playing in the execution or achievement of an organization's strategy?
- What role do you think the various BPMS tools are playing in the evolution of BPM and the business process market?
- Is it worth the considerable effort required for an organization to shift to a dual functional and process view?

- How do you see the position of process architecture in the overall 'architecture of architectures'?
- What do you see as the primary components of the return on investment for BPM?
- How do you see BPM and quality management being the same and/or different?
- Where do you see the optimal balance between control and liberty in the management of business processes?
- What impact do you see disruptive technologies having on the management and optimization of business processes?
- Can innovation be a consequence of taking a BPM approach, or is BPM a handicap?
- Who should be responsible for the process work of the future?
- Has the very concept of 'business process' been so disrupted as to make BPM meaningless in the digital economy?
- How can organizations ensure a proper return on modeling?
- Does the future of process work lie with cognitive and dynamic techniques?

No doubt some readers would have made other choices. We look forward to the ongoing discussion of perhaps the most important question "Which questions should we ask?"

We invited process practitioners, vendors, authors, academics and consultants from around the world to answer our questions. They responded magnificently. We have answers from 33 thought leaders from across the spectrum of process views and approaches. In editing this book, we have not changed any of the answers. A brief overview of the range of answers is provided for each question. Apart from formatting and style editing, the answers are as submitted by our authors.

This book will make you think. Answers to the same question will be different, often very different, and occasionally they are quite contradictory. In this book, you will not find a definitive one best answer. You will find different answers argued convincingly by people who believe passionately in their particular BPM worldview. Each of us needs to make our own choices and determine our own answers.

So, will 109 answers by 33 authors to 15 questions define BPM, shed light in dark corners, and resolve all of the disagreements? No, that would be too much to expect. As you will discover in reading this book, there are many things on which process practitioners, vendors, authors, academics and consultants agree and disagree. The differences reflect different perspectives, different lenses through which BPM is observed and practiced. We don't suggest that resolving these differences is a necessary objective. The BPM world can be seen through different lenses and a finite set of different perspectives of BPM is becoming increasingly clearer. Discussions about BPM will become much easier as we continue to develop cleaner language that uses a minimal vocabulary for which we have a genuinely shared understanding.

Our hope is that this book helps, not to define the critical one right answer, but to give added clarity to the important different answers.

We thank our authors. This is their book and its value comes from their robust views, intelligent debate and powerful insights. The book would not have been possible without the excellent coordination of Paul Heidt, the superb editing of Karl Craig (www.karlcraig.com), and the design brilliance of Rachael Shea (www.shea.space). Our thanks to each of you for making us all look good.

We also acknowledge with gratitude our own organizations, BPTrends and Leonardo Consulting, in whose company we have been able to continue our own search for both the questions and the answers.

Paul Harmon
Roger Tregear
Editors

AUTHORS AND EDITORS

DR. ROGER M. ADDISON

is an internationally respected practitioner of Human Performance Technology (HPT), performance consulting, and founder of Addison Consulting. Roger is a past president of ISPI and received ISPI's highest award, Member for Life. He is the recipient of numerous other ISPI awards, including the Gilbert, the Rummler, Service and Outstanding Communication. Roger has presented and worked in North America, South America, Asia, Europe, Africa and the Middle East. Roger is a coauthor of *Performance Architecture—The Art and Science of Improving Organizations.*

rogeraddison@earthlink.net

DR. AHMAD ALIBABAEI

is an assistant professor at the Shahid Beheshti University of Medical Sciences in Iran. He is also an associate dean in the faculty of Health, Safety and Environment. Ahmad earned his PhD in industrial engineering with a focus on Business Process Management in 2010. He was an academic visitor to the Queensland University of Technology BPM group in 2008 for about 8 months. He has more than 12 years' experience in IT and management as a manager and consultant. He also founded Zeus Advanced Systems Consulting Company in 2012, which provides IT and management consultancy services. Dr. Alibabaei has served as a track chair, member of scientific committees, and reviewer in many international conferences, such as AMCIS and ECIS.

babaei@gmail.com

TALAL ALSUBAIE

has extensive knowledge in BPM, IT and software development. He has considerable experience in process and project management, and BPM automation. Talal holds the degrees of Master in Information Systems and Bachelor of Computer Science from King Saud University. He worked in for Saudi Arabian government agencies in the field of BPM and IT for 11 years, specializing in process modeling and improvement. At the Saudi Food and Drug Authority, Talal established the BPM department tasked with operating both the business and technical aspects of BPM. Based in Riyadh, Saudi Arabia, Talal is currently the Managing Director of Modprex, a company specializing in software solutions supporting process analysis and publishing.

t.subaie@gmail.com

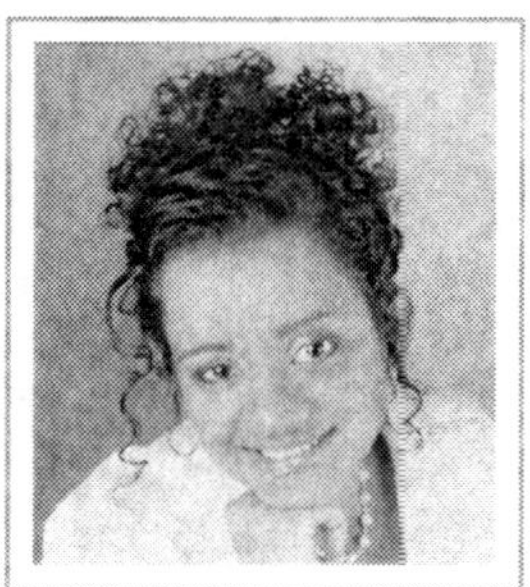

DR. WASANA BANDARA

is a tenured Senior Lecturer at the Information Systems School, Science and Engineering Faculty, Queensland University of Technology, Brisbane Australia. She coordinates the Master of Business Process Management (BPM) and conducts research in BPM and information systems (IS). She has researched a broad range of topics such as process modeling, enterprise systems, shared services, and IS/BPM education. More recently, her research has focused on BPM and ICT for development, in particular on people-oriented aspects of BPM. In addition to research in her discipline areas, she has a passion for scholarly investigation into and the teaching of research methods. She has published over 75 refereed articles in leading IS and BPM outlets, and has received institutional, national and international awards in recognition for her academic excellence (for both research and teaching). For more information, see Dr. Bandara's personal web page www.wasanabandara.com.

w.bandara@qut.edu.au

JIM BOOTS

worked worked at Chevron Corporation for 30 years in a wide array of functions, including sales, total quality management, business development, supply chain management, business management, ecommerce management, health safety and environment management, enterprise architecture, and Business Process Management (BPM) program development. He was the primary force behind building Chevron's BPM foundation from 2005 to 2010. He also is a principal ITCMF professional at the Innovation Value Institute with responsibilities that include a role as Lead Architect of the BPM Critical Capability. He is author of the book *BPM Boots on the Ground: How to Implement Strategic Business Process Management: Lessons Learned from one of the World's Largest Organizations.* Jim now runs his own BPM consultancy known as Global Process Innovation.

jimboots.gpi@gmail.com

ROGER BURLTON

is the President of Process Renewal Group and cofounder of BPTrends Associates. He is the author of the pioneering *Business Process Management: Profiting from Process* and the collaborative effort *Business Process Manifesto*, now available in 14 languages. He developed and delivered the first Business Process and Business Architecture management classes in the world in 1991, certified today by universities in North America, Europe, Australia, and South America. He is recognized as a world leader in transforming companies from traditional hierarchical organizations to process-managed ones. He has led numerous initiatives to implement new process-centric business models, governance frameworks, and process management capabilities for global corporations. He continues to chair the most prominent business process conferences in the world, which he has done on over forty occasions.

rburlton@gmail.com

INDRAJIT DATTA CHAUDHURI

is a Senior Consultant with Leonardo Consulting. With 10 years of experience in business process analysis and improvement, he helps clients to improve process performance. He is a specialist process and business analyst with extensive international experience. He has consulted and trained in business process modeling, analysis, and management across many industry sectors.

i.chaudhuri@leonardo.com.au

FRED A. CUMMINS

is a former HP and EDS Fellow currently doing business as Agile Enterprise Design, LLC. He has developed solutions or functioned as a technical consultant across multiple industries, including manufacturing and distribution, financial services, transportation, insurance, healthcare, and government. He has been co-chair of the Business Modeling and Integration task force at the Object Management Group for 15 years and, most recently, was a leader in the development of the Case Management Model and Notation specification and the Value Delivery Modeling Language specification. Fred has authored three books, and he is currently writing the second edition of his last book *Building the Agile Enterprise with Capabilities, Collaborations and Values* (Elsevier, 2016). He is currently an independent consultant focusing on business analysis, design and transformation.

fred.a.cummins@gmail.com

GABY DOEBELI

is a long-time member of Australia's Business Process Management (BPM) and Business Architecture community. She founded and chaired the Brisbane BPMLink Community and has participated in many of Australia's BPM roundtables run by Prof. M Rosemann.

Gaby has a Masters in Information Systems, and her thesis focused on the application of BPM governance. Her findings are widely presented and documented in Australia and the U.S. Over the last seven years, she has further operationalized these in a number of organizations as part of business transformation programs, including enterprise resource planning systems implementations. Her roles, spannings across Enterprise Architecture (EA) and BPM, have included Business & Process Architect, Process Design Adviser, Senior Integrated Systems Adviser, Internal Business Improvement Consultant, Six Sigma Black belt, Quality Facilitator and Internal Auditor. Gaby is currently engaged by Brisbane City Council, the largest local council in Australia, where she received an award as the best architect in the Business and Systems Efficiency transformation program.

Gaby.Doebeli@onthenet.com.au

MELISSA DOHERTY

is a highly experienced professional with extensive experience in Business Process Management (BPM), business improvement, enterprise architecture, and ICT system implementations. As the Process and Innovation Manager at Brisbane City Council, the largest local government in Australia and the country's fastest growing city, Melissa is responsible for embedding BPM in the organization. Her role includes managing a team that provides expert advice and improvement services to process owners, all divisions and projects in the Council's BPM standards, methodology and practices.

Prior to her current role, Melissa led the Business Architecture Team, in the Enterprise Architecture Group, in the Council's Information Services Branch. Here she led the establishment of BPM in Council and worked on building stronger relationships between business areas and ICT. Throughout her career, Melissa has held roles at the Department of Immigration and Border Protection (federal government department), Optus (telecommunications), and CSG International (a software vendor, formerly ADC Telecommunications). These roles have given her a diverse range of experiences in different industries. Melissa has exceptional experience driving business process thinking that has resulted in the delivery of ICT solutions, improved customer outcomes, organization efficiencies, and achieving strategic outcomes. Melissa holds a Bachelor of Business from the University of Queensland, along with certifications in ITIL, and Business Architecture from BPTrends.

Melissa.Doherty@brisbane.qld.gov.au

PETER FINGAR

is regarded as one of the original promulgators of BPM, beginning with the publication of the seminal book coauthored with CSC's Howard Smith, *Business Process Management: The Third Wave* (www.mk-press.com). As a former CIO and college professor, Peter has been working at the intersection of business and technology for over 40 years. His recent books include: *Cognitive Computing: A Brief Guide for Game Changers; Business Process Management: The Next Wave; Business Innovation in the Cloud;* and *Dot. Cloud: The 21st Century Business Platform Built on Cloud Computing*. He joined forces with Jon Pyke, founder of the Workflow Management Coalition, and Andy Mulholland, Global CTO of Capgemini, to pen the influential book, *Enterprise Cloud Computing: A Strategy Guide for Business and Technology Leaders.* His books have been published in Chinese, Korean, Japanese and Russian. Peter delivers keynote talks across the globe, and is speaking this year in Asia, Europe, and the Americas (www.peterfingar.com).

peter@peterfingar.com

DENIS GAGNÉ

has been a driving force for over a decade in the majority of international BPM standards in use today. He is a member of the Workflow Management Coalition Steering Committee, chair of the Business Process Simulation Working Group, and the coeditor of the XPDL 2.2 process definition standard. For the Object Management group, Denis is the Chair of the BPMN Interchange Working Group, and a member of the Business Process Model and Notation and the Case Management Model and Notation team. Denis is CEO and CTO of Trisotech, and the driving force behind www.BusinessProcessIncubator.com, a free online resource providing access to BPM, change management, process improvement, Lean and Six Sigma resources.

dgagne@trisotech.com

IAN GOTTS

is a serial tech entrepreneur whose passion and energy are infectious and inspiring. He is founder and CEO of Q9 Elements, a software company with a suite of Cloud process solutions that promise to "Make work easier, faster and more valuable for millions of people." Ian was founder and CEO of Nimbus for 15 years, a software company with a process knowledge and governance solution that was acquired by TIBCO Software in 2011. Prior to Nimbus, Ian was at Accenture where, as an Associate Partner, he led the Program Management Group.

Ian is the author of eight books, and a prolific blogger with a rare ability to make the complex seem simple. This makes him a sought after and entertaining conference speaker. Oh, and he's powered by Duracell. Further information at www.iangotts.com.

igotts@q9elements.com

CAROL HAIG

is principal of Carol Haig & Associates, a performance improvement consulting firm. For more than 30 years, she has helped organizations in a range of industries to improve employee performance. Carol is co-author of the award winning *Performance Architecture—The Art and Science of Improving Organizations* and the co-author of the *Performance Architecture* column for BPTrends. Carol has served as Director on the executive board of ISPI, and received ISPI's awards for: Outstanding Instructional Product; Outstanding Organization; the Performance Improvement Award of Excellence; Distinguished Service; the Communication Award; and named Member for Life. She is a regular presenter at ISPI's annual conference. She is also a licensed ham radio operator, WE7TBD.

carolhaig@earthlink.net

ANDREAS HAVLIZA

joined Leonardo Consulting in 2010 after 10 years working as a consultant in Europe and Australia. As a Consulting Principal, he is based in Perth and responsible for the Leonardo Team in Western Australia. His previous position was as a Senior Expert in BPM with IDS Scheer AG in Germany. Andreas' specialist experience and expertise are in governance, risk and compliance management (GRC) and BPM. As a project manager for GRC and BPM projects, Andreas has led and coordinated project teams in various industries, including finance, banking, insurance, logistics, utilities and semiconductors. While working for IDS Scheer, he was the GRC solution owner in Germany, Austria and Switzerland. In this role, Andreas was responsible for the alignment of GRC-related topics within those three countries.

a.havliza@leonardo.com.au

ERIC HERNESS

is an IBM Distinguished Engineer and is the CTO for the IBM business focused on Business Process Management and Operational Decision Management. Eric is also the Chief Architect for BPM. He leads the team of architects that define product architecture and technical direction for this business, and works with many large clients and business partners on all things Smarter Process.

Eric has deep experience in BPM, Cloud, rules, events, integration, application servers, connectivity, and object technology. He has had key lead architectural roles in WebSphere and IBM Middleware going back over 20 years.

Eric joined IBM in 1985. He has a bachelor's degree in management information systems from the University of Wisconsin at Eau Claire, as well as a master's in business administration from the Carlson School at the University of Minnesota.

EricHerness@kmtel.com

CLEMENT HURPIN

graduated from a leading Canadian business school with a trilingual (French, English and Spanish) business administration degree and joined the Leonardo Consulting team in July 2012. During his time with Leonardo, Clement has gained experience in a wide range of business process analysis approaches, tools, and techniques. He has worked on projects involving process modelling, improvement (through the application of the BPTrends methodology) and automation (involving among other things data modelling, use case definition, workflow and report design). His successes during those projects saw him promoted to the established position of Consultant in 2014. He firmly believes in process-based management and provides support to build process capability within client organizations.

c.hurpin@leonardo.com.au

LEANDRO JESUS

is co-founder and director at EloGroup, a business transformation company that delivers consulting services, technology solutions, and accelerates technology startups. He earned his master of science in industrial engineering at Federal University of Rio de Janeiro, with complementary studies at Carnegie Mellon University. Leandro is Vice-President at the Association of Business Process Management (ABPMP) Brazil chapter, the largest one in the world, which annually influences 15,000+ BPM professionals in Brazil. He is author/co-author of Rethinking Management through Processes (2014), and Establishing the Office of BPM (2011).

leandro.jesus@elogroup.com.br

PETER MATTHIJSSEN

is managing consultant and trainer at BiZZdesign. As a Lean Six Sigma black belt and BPM expert, he builds change capabilities in organizations around the globe. With his master's degree in industrial engineering and management (University of Twente), and over 15 years of experience in the field, he helps organizations in private and public sectors to work smarter and get better results from their processes. Peter is the author of numerous books and publications on BPM and Lean management; for example Thinking in Processes (2011), and Working with Lean (2013). He speaks on a regular basis at international conferences on business design and change, like IRM-UK and Building Business Capability.

p.matthijssen@bizzdesign.nl

MATTHEW MORGAN

is Head of Process Excellence at Bridgewater Associates, an investment manager with US$169 billion in assets under management. Before joining Bridgewater, Matthew led global business improvement at Parsons Brinckerhoff, an engineering company with 14,000 employees and US$2.6 billion in annual revenues. There, he developed and deployed a new process improvement function where none had previously existed, and a global business management system to drive continual improvement and process standardization across the many business units overseeing the firm's 150+ offices worldwide. Previously, Matthew worked as a strategy consultant at McKinsey & Company and as a Lean Six Sigma professional and operations leader at Starwood Hotels. A former army intelligence officer, Matt has written nine books on Afghanistan, terrorism, and related topics. He graduated with a BS from West Point and MBA from Harvard Business School.

mmorgan@mba2007.hbs.edu

GILLES MORIN

is a founder of BPMPLUS Inc. and a BPM coach, expert and trainer. He is also a Canadian partner for BPTrends Associates. Gilles has more than 30 years' experience in leading business units and businesses transformation programs, and consulting. He worked in vice-president and general manager positions in flagship public and private organizations in the financial and business services industry. He also played key leadership roles in starting new consulting practices in change management and BPM.

In the past 15 years, he has led several BPM transformational initiatives, including: BPM driven IT transformations; implementation and management of four BPM-performance centers of expertise; incubation of BPM programs and BPMS team; process-driven business architecture projects; and process governance and change management programs.

gilles@bpmp.ca

CHRIS POTTS

is a corporate strategist, speaker and writer, specializing in strategies and processes for enterprise investment. He works as a practitioner and mentor, helping executives and managers worldwide to drive the best possible outcomes from the changes in which they invest. He delivers keynote speeches and intensive workshops, and has been a visiting lecturer at New York University, City University in London, and the IT University in Copenhagen. Chris is also the author of the world's only trilogy of business novels, *The FruITion Trilogy (FruITion, RecrEAtion* and *DefrICtion).*

cdpotts@dominicbarrow.com

ALAN RAMIAS

is a Partner of the Performance Design Lab (PDL), a consulting, coaching and training company that specializes in organizational performance improvement. He is also an instructor with the BPM Institute. He brings 30 years of consulting experience in analysis, design and implementation with organizations in Asia, Europe and North America. He is a co-author of the books *White Space Revisited: Creating Value through Process and Rediscovering Value: Leading the 3-D Enterprise to Sustainable Success.* Before becoming a management consultant, Alan was an instructional designer, training manager and organizational development manager at Motorola. Alan joined The Rummler-Brache Group (RBG) in 1991, and led improvement projects, became a Partner and Managing Director of Consulting Services at RBG, and was responsible for selecting, training, and overseeing RBG's consultant teams.

aramias@thepdlab.com

PROFESSOR MICHAEL ROSEMANN

is Professor and Head of the Information Systems School at Queensland University of Technology. A disruptive thinker with a digital mind and a passion for innovation, Michael's work is focused on creating exciting future worlds. He is the author/editor of seven books, 250 refereed papers, Editorial Board member of 10 international journals, and co-inventor of US patents. Michael is a prolific researcher of global prominence and his projects have received funding both from government and from industry partners such as Accenture, Australia Post, Brisbane Airport Corporation, Infosys, PricewaterhouseCoopers, Rio Tinto, SAP and Woolworths.

m.rosemann@qut.edu.au

RON ROSS

is co-founder and Principal of Business Rule Solutions LLC, Executive Editor of Business Rules Journal, and Chair of the Business Rules & Decisions Conference. At Business Rule Solutions, Ron engages in presentations, consulting services, publications, the Proteus® methodology, and RuleSpeak®. Ron is recognized as the 'father of business rules'. He is the author of nine professional books, including *Building Business Solutions: Business Analysis with Business Rules* with Gladys S.W. Lam (2011, An IIBA® Sponsored Handbook), and the ever-popular *Business Rule Concepts* (2009, 1998).

RRoss@BRSolutions.com

PHIL SHORT

leads the IT operations for the Canadian division of a large privately owned global CPG company, and supports other major business change initiatives in the global organization. He adapted his formal engineering education to the modern business environment and has a track record of delivering pragmatic solutions to complex business problems, including a successful SAP ERP implementation, and establishing an enduring business process governance organization. He is continually looking to drive enhanced business performance through the appropriate use of BPM and supporting technologies. Phil has also presented at several international BPM and IT conferences on topics such as business process architecture and business process governance.

phil.short@yahoo.com

ANDREW SPANYI

is widely recognized as a major contributor to process management. He is a member of ABPMP's Advisory Board and an instructor with BPM Institute.org. He was formerly an adjunct faculty member at Babson College. He is the author of dozens of articles and several books emphasizing the importance of cross-functional collaboration and a customer-oriented, process based focus—titles include: *More for Less: The Power of Process Management; Business Process Management Is Team Sport: Play It to Win!* and *Operational Leadership*. Contact Andrew at www.spanyi.com

or andrew@spanyi.com.

JAMES TAYLOR

is a leading authority on applying decision management, business rules and predictive analytic technologies to improve business performance. He is the CEO of Decision Management Solutions, a full service consultancy. He works on the *Decision Model Notation* (DMN) standard and is a faculty member of the International Institute for Analytics. James is the author of *Decision Management Systems: A Practical Guide to Using Business Rules and Predictive Analytics* (2012) and co-author of *The MicroGuide to Process and Decision Modeling in BPMN/DMN* (2014) with Tom Debevoise and Smart Enough Systems: Smart (Enough) Systems (2007) with Neil Raden. James also blogs at www.JTonEDM.com and can be reached at

james@decisionmanagementsolutions.com.

PROF.DR.IR. WIL VAN DER AALST

is a full Professor of Information Systems at the Technische Universiteit Eindhoven where he is the scientific director of the Data Science Center Eindhoven. Since 2003, he has held a part-time position at Queensland University of Technology. His personal research interests include workflow management, process mining, Petri nets, business process management, process modeling, and process analysis. Wil van der Aalst has published more than 180 journal papers, 18 books, 400 conference/workshop publications, and 60 book chapters. He one of the most cited computer scientists in the world and his ideas have influenced researchers, software developers, and standardization committees. In 2012, he received the degree of doctor honoris causa from Hasselt University in Belgium. He also served as scientific director of the International Laboratory of ProcessAware Information Systems of the National Research University, Higher School of Economics in Moscow.

w.m.p.v.d.aalst@tm.tue.nl

PROFESSOR JAN VOM BROCKE

is head of the BPM group in Liechtenstein. He is Professor of Information Systems, the Hilti Chair of Business Process Management, Director of the Institute of Information Systems, and Vice-President of the University of Liechtenstein. He has over 15 years of experience in BPM research, teaching, and practice, and he is a co-founder and co-director of international Master and PhD programs on IS and BPM (see: http://www.bpm-education.org). Jan has published more than 300 papers in renowned outlets, including *MIS Quarterly (MISQ)*, the *Journal of Management Information Systems (JMIS)* and the *Business Process Management Journal (BPMJ)*. He has co-authored and co-edited 25 books, including the *International Handbook on Business Process Management*, and the books *Green BPM – Towards the Sustainable Enterprise,* and *BPM – Driving Innovation in a Digital World.* Jan is an invited speaker and trusted advisor on BPM serving many organizations around the world.

jan.vom.brocke@uni.li

DR. STEPHEN A. WHITE

is sometimes described as the father of BPMN. Steve has over 25 years of process modeling experience, ranging from modeling pilot workload to commercial business processes, and has been involved in most aspects of business process modeling software, from product management, design, consulting, training, and technical writing. In the last few years, he has been active in the development of business modeling standards, was the primary editor of the BPMN 1.0 and BPMN 2.0 specification.

sawhite@bpmadvantage.com

PAUL HARMON, EDITOR

is a co-founder, Executive Editor and Senior Market Analyst at Business Process Trends—www.bptrends.com—a popular website providing free information on trends, directions and best practices in business process management. He is also a co-founder, Chief Methodologist and Principal Consultant of BPTrends Associates, a professional services company providing executive education, training and consulting services for organizations interested in understanding and implementing business process management. Paul is the author of some 15 books, including *Business Process Change*, 3rd ed. Morgan Kaufman, (2014).

npharmon@gmail.com

ROGER TREGEAR, EDITOR

delivers BPM education and consulting assignments worldwide. Based in Canberra (Australia), Roger spends his working life talking, consulting, thinking and writing about the analysis, improvement and management of business processes. He works around the world, especially in Australia, New Zealand, U.S.A., Saudi Arabia and other Arab States. Working across many industries, Roger has delivered successful projects in many sectors including: hospital healthcare, university education, fresh fruit supply chain, banking, finance, government administration, and regulatory administration. He is a regular columnist for BPTrends, author of *Practical Process* (2013), and co-author of *Establishing the Office of Business Process Management* (2011). He also contributed the chapter *Business Process Standardization* in *The International Handbook on Business Process Management* published by Springer in 2010. A new book, *Reimagining Management*, will be published in 2016.

r.tregear@leonardo.com.au

QUESTION 1

WHAT IS BPM?

There are many ways of characterizing business processes and their management. Many elements can be included under the broad term 'business process management', ranging from process modeling, process improvement, and capability maturity improvement, through to human performance management, process automation and business architecture. Some focus narrowly on analysis of specific flows of activities; others emphasize holistic management aspects.

How would you describe the scope of BPM? What are the limits on BPM? Would you discriminate between BPM and some more generic term like business process improvement?

OVERVIEW

More of our authors chose to respond to this question than any other, a reflection on the confusion that has surrounded the term 'Business Process Management' (or just BPM) from when it first came into widespread use in the early years of this millennium. From the very beginning, two groups have claimed the term. The software vendors like to use BPM to describe software tools that capture and, in some cases, manage the execution of business processes. At the same time, business people have argued for a broader use of the term, to refer to an effort to coordinate all of the process activities within an organization. The business people, however, have also divided, with some using process broadly to include the management of almost all of the technologies and practices that can impact process performance within an organization, while others prefer to limit the scope of BPM in various ways.

Most of our authors have come down on the side of business management, but they differ in what exactly they include within the scope of the term 'process'.

....

AHMAD ALIBABAEI

Assistant Professor, Shahid Beheshti University of Medical Sciences

Different management techniques arise from time to time, each promising many advantages. For each of these techniques, the literature shows some degree of success, but also many failures. One prominent management technique, widely adopted in recent years, is Business Process Management (BPM). Andrew Spanyi (2003, p.25) has defined BPM as: "the deliberative, collaborative and increasingly technology-aided definition, improvement and management of a firm's end-to-end enterprise business process."

However, defining the scope of BPM is not easy since almost every activity in an organization is undertaken to improve a business's performance. BPM includes every initiative that is initiated to improve a business process with two qualifications:

- Every BPM initiative should be based on organizational strategies. In process thinking, having a global view instead of a local view is very important. An effort for improving a process, or fixing a problem in a process, is called BPM when it can be aligned with an organization's strategy. In other words, if a process effort is narrowly focused on a department improvement goal, there is always a possibility that it will not have a considerable effect on business goals. The goals of a BPM initiative should be defined based on strategic goals.
- BPM should not be confused as ad hoc initiatives. Business process improvement projects may be ad hoc initiatives, in which case they

are really not part of an overall BPM effort.

Based on these definitions, even a process automation project, if it is aligned with the organization's strategy, can be considered as a BPM initiative. Similarly, other organizational improvement efforts—such as Six Sigma, business process improvement, etc.—can be part of the Business Process Management.

Some other organizational activities—like defining business models, strategic planning, and designing organizational structure—are not necessarily part of the BPM initiative. The outputs of these programs can be used as inputs for Business Process Management initiatives. In such cases, these ad hoc activities are not, in themselves, included in BPM, even though the outcomes of these initiatives can affect the strategies or the structure of the organization. BPM is one of the concepts that should be implemented during the design of business models. Business modeling in an organization includes the design of the processes that will run the business; therefore, it should be included within the scope of BPM.

In strategic planning, process redesigning and improvement is usually considered as one of the actions undertaken to help achieve strategic goals, since one of the competencies that can generate competitive advantage in the organization is having agile processes. Process maturity and process capabilities can also play an important role in defining organizational strategies. Transforming an organization from a functional perspective to a process perspective usually requires changes in the organization structure.

In summary, BPM seeks to establish and embed a management culture of continuous business improvement that is aligned with an organization's strategies, and is controlled by suitable governance mechanisms.

DR. WASANA BANDARA

Senior Lecturer, Queensland University of Technology

As a community of 'BPM advocates', we seem to believe that we have come a long way. Yet, many of the initial challenges of BPM that were raised years ago—such as; "it's hard to get buy-in for BPM?", "people do not understand 'process'", "they don't care about processes and only bother about their own functions"—still remain very much live issues, which can significantly hinder the progress of the planned BPM work. None of us would argue that these issues are unimportant, or resolved, and nor would any argue that the blockages caused by these are trivial. It is common to blame the other parties for their ignorance, narrow mindedness and unwillingness to see things the same way as BPM advocates. But whose responsibility is it to create the correct awareness? Have we thought deeply about the liability we create in not addressing this sustained blockage in the discipline?

The shared terminology (and comprehension) used in a discipline is vital for its positioning, scoping and growth. It is understandable that each of us may have different areas of emphasis when answering the simple question "what is BPM?" But the question to think about is: do the term(s) we use accurately illustrate the aims, scope and principals of our discipline to the people with whom we are trying to communicate?

Let's take 'BPM—Business Process Management' as an example. We have created numerous definitions of BPM, with a common essence that it is viewed as a (holistic) management practice (that may apply various methods, systems, etc.) that is 'process centric'. Agree? Let us try to understand why this could be contributing to the issues mentioned above.

The very 'process-centric-ness' we emphasize could be the first bullet we shoot ourselves with. For many, 'process' means a set of tasks, which are granular in nature—like a set of documented procedures people encounter in their role/task definitions. Our 'process-centric' emphasis may be perceived by the non-converted (and those whom we need to win over) as BPM being only related to those granular operational tasks. This is, perhaps, further fueled by the way we train people and actually conduct BPM. Many BPM project work and training programs undertaken in organizations look solely at the details of a single process; typically, with an internal focus on time/cost/quality metrics. Hence, even with so-called BPM training and experience, people end up having a limited understanding of BPM as an area that looks at single processes in depth.

However, BPM as a discipline is much more than the analysis and improvement of a single process. It is how we integrate this single process's existence within a portfolio of processes that work together to deliver valuable products/services to customers, while adhering to internal policies and controls, through the support of human resources and IT systems. Improving processes often requires change to some or all of these aspects across the organization, both horizontally (with other processes within the organization and beyond) and vertically (across the organizational layers).

Successful BPM creates an organization-wide movement. It creates an aspiration to continuously review and transform the organization to better meet customer needs, while remaining a viable organization. But, in the course of (over)emphasizing the process centeredness, we (often) fail to communicate and emphasize that the real jewel is in the integrated-ness of the processes, both across the organization and its ecosystem.

Positioning our work as wholly 'process-centric', often automatically builds a barrier to other groups to resonate with and support BPM. It must be recognized that distinct organizational teams apply their own 'language' and perspective to progressing corporate objectives. For example, HR people advocate that the organization must be 'people-centric' to be continually effective. IT people advocate that being 'systems-centric' is the answer. 'Service-centric' is another term often used. This is essentially the same as what we mean by being 'process-centric', in that we first define the customer requirements for a 'service or product' (and how to measure attainment of this), then we design a process to best deliver this (and how to measure the process performance, and enablers, to that end). For each, the centralism they are in is the most important aspect to them. Hence, when we approach these organizational groups with our sole 'process-centeredness', it is natural that we encounter resistance and struggle to get their support and buy-in. What we need to do is to see how we can make our unique contributions—that is, how to offer our specialized set of BPM values and outcomes within these other 'centralisms'. Given that we do deeply consider and integrate people, systems, products/ services in our BPM work, this challenge can be overcome with the right positioning and by communicating the value of BPM work;—showing how the process view will help integrate the different aspects of people, systems, policies, et cetera, to achieve a common goal.

Also, how often (or rarely) do we make an effort to explain how BPM is different to (or, indeed, complementary to) any other management paradigm? Our key contribution is how we use a process-centric view to bring together core elements of other management disciplines, to provide an integrated view of how the organization delivers value to its customers and sustains itself. BPM should be positioned as an overarching strategic management paradigm that enables real-time monitoring of the organization's performance in product/

service delivery. BPM needs to interface with strong IT management, HR management, FI management, change management, et cetera, to be effective in delivering better organizational outcomes. BPM doesn't exists in isolation separate from other management practices; instead, the purpose of BPM is to mediate the interaction with these other management disciplines and provide a consistent and useful way of measuring organizational performance. We often fail to communicate this and, instead, try to promote BPM as a new/different paradigm, superseding counter management practices.

The term 'business' in BPM poses a different kind of issue; it communicates that BPM is only relevant to 'businesses'. The scope of BPM is beyond mere business, and it has been proven that BPM can bring immense positive impacts to government[1] and not-for-profit organizations,[2] and even for individuals' private processes.[3] Have we shot ourselves (again!) by limiting the scope with the terminology we use? Who is at fault when people in public service state "BPM is not for us—we are not a business", and cannot see its relevance? This is clear evidence that the true concept of BPM (or similar label) is not yet widely understood.

Figure 1: The wrong labeling or terminology used in BPM can distort meaning

It is important to pause and think if we are doing justice to the discipline's current and future status and scope with the terminology we currently use. At the very least, we need to be mindful about how this terminology resonates with those from other management backgrounds. We should clearly communicate that business process management is not limited to the intricacies of low-level processes, nor is its aim to replace other established management disciplines. We need to think beyond mere process centralism. Processes and process-centric management, which BPM is all about, are the means to achieve integration and not the end in itself. We fail to communicate that. BPM is not just for profit-oriented businesses—it is for all organizations. It is time to pause and think of the discipline-wide branding/labeling we have been using, as the discipline's progression (or even future existence) will depend on how we label and communicate what we offer.

References

[1] McAdam, R., and Donaghy, J. (1999) "Business process re-engineering in the public sector", Business Process Management Journal (5:1), pp.33–52.

[2] Peterken, H., Bandara , W., (2014) "Business Process Management in International Humanitarian Aid", in the Handbook on Business Process Management 2, Second Edition J. vom Brocke and M. Rosemann (eds.). Berlin, Heidelberg: Springer, pp.761–786.

[3] Brambilla, M. (2013, January) "Application and simplification of BPM techniques for personal process management". In Business Process Management Workshops (pp.227–233). Springer Berlin Heidelberg.

Acknowledgements

I'd like to thank Ms Islay Davies and Mr Paul Mathiesen for their detailed input and insights to the discussion presented here.

JIM BOOTS

Owner, Global Process Innovation

It is appropriate to define the scope of BPM as encompassing all activities, artifacts, and tools that specifically have processes as a primary focus. This includes:

- Process improvement
- Process automation

- Process execution
- Process reengineering
- Process architecture
- Process simulation
- Process modeling
- Process engagement
- Process stewardship
- Process governance
- Process performance measurement
- BPM technology

Figure 2 is a simple representation of the breadth of BPM—that is, everything under the umbrella and anything else one can think of wherein process is a primary focus.

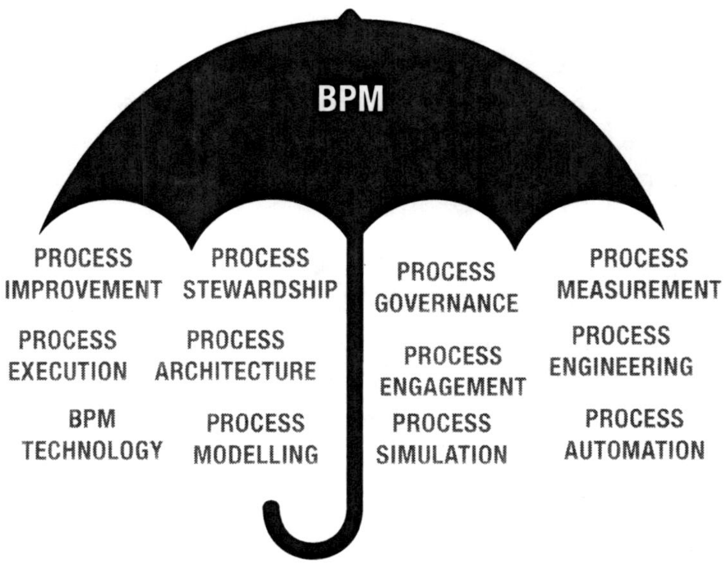

Figure 2: The BPM umbrella

Perhaps the more interesting question is: what are the limits of BPM? The key to discerning the limits of BPM is to think of processes as assets. With that acceptance, a natural next question is: what are other assets of interest to an organization, and are they managed distinctly from processes (even though there may be important inter-relationships between assets)? Yes, it is possible to list the assets, including processes, used by organizations to produce their products and services. These assets could be listed exhaustively, with careful definitions, but that is beyond our need here. It is good enough to say that the primary assets of interest used by an organization in the course of doing its work are:

- People (i.e. workers)
- Processes
- Information (including data, plans, policies)
- Equipment (e.g. machines, tools, computers, servers)
- Software (including applications)
- Inventory and real estate
- Financial assets

In turn, it is not difficult to match disciplines with each asset type: 'people' are addressed in the disciplines of leadership, management science, and human resources; 'processes' are addressed in Business Process Management; 'information' in information management, and so on. These disciplines each contain particulars that may be of somewhat limited interest to others. Yet, each discipline can impact the organization in dramatic ways if not handled properly.

So, to answer the question raised, the conceptual limit for BPM per se is the process asset itself, comprised of activities, performed by roles and resources, producing materials and/or information in contribution to desired organizational outcomes. Processes exist in both the human world of manual and mental activity, and the machine world of numeric or material analysis and transformation, as well as combinations of human and machine.

Note that processes and information are paired assets. Process steps produce information, and information feeds process steps. Yet processes and information are still distinct assets—often with complex many-to-many relationships—and each is managed by its own discipline. In fact, all assets have complex relationships. For example, 'information' is used by 'people' following 'processes' and, quite likely, using 'software'. In actual work practice, all asset types interact with most of the other asset types, yet each can be distinctly identified, described, and managed– although, management of any asset will need to take into account dependencies with other assets.

Thinking about assets this way, we gradually begin to realize that the intelligent combination of assets delivers sustainable value in the form of organizational capabilities. Said another way, organizational capabilities are enabled by assets. Indeed, it is management's responsibility to weave together a somewhat dynamic set of constrained assets into organizational capabilities, which, woven together themselves, produce the know-how-dependent outputs necessary for the organization to be successful.

Ultimately, when there is an organizational need that must be addressed, such as a performance issue, management will be interested in having a clear understanding of the particulars of assets that underpin the capabilities that produce the said performance. The specialists associated with each asset discipline (e.g. HR, BPM, IM, financial management) might be expected to characterize the quality, evolution, and assignment of the asset.

Further addressing the limits of BPM, it is worth making the point that the group that supports the BPM discipline within an organization typically does not have within its scope of accountability the performance of specific organizational processes (other than those associated with the BPM discipline itself). Managers across the organization have accountability for the performance of specific processes under their control—for example, an operations manager is accountable for the performance of operations-related processes. Presuming that sufficient funding is provided to the BPM manager to grow and sustain BPM capability, the manager of the BPM discipline is accountable for providing tools and resources to: (a) all managers so they can effectively manage the processes they are accountable for; and (b) other specialists so they can optimize interactions between their assets and the process architecture, or implement process improvement or automation methodologies.

This conceptualization of the limits of BPM as a discipline and a capability is consistent with enterprise architecture thinking. The discipline of enterprise architecture has the potential to provide further optimization of assets as it peers orthogonally through organizational capabilities to distill common needs and synergies within and between asset types. In most organizations, however, the maturity level of enterprise architecture hardly extends beyond the assurance that each asset discipline exists and is functioning to an acceptable level. In the case of BPM, most organizations have very little going on (and that sadly remains acceptable to management!). Deep understandings of cross-asset-type interactions tend to exist only on a transient, case-by-case basis driven by a particular need. A much more holistic understanding of an organization's enterprise architecture—accompanied by graphical representations and insightful statistics—is likely to be commonplace within 10 to 15 years. Already, many BPM software packages go far beyond capturing process information, and are serving to some degree as capability management systems, although, generally, only across a limited scope of processes. There is nothing to prevent further extension of this concept into a comprehensive enterprise architecture/capability management platform.

Unfortunately, in 2016, managers at many companies have not come to understand the broad scope of Business Process Management. Usually at best, a manager is a robust supporter of process improvement programs (e.g. Lean Six Sigma), and does not conceive BPM as being anything more than that. In such cases, sometimes impressive tactical improvements can be achieved through process improvement efforts—but a strategic step-change in performance achieved via broad-based organizational capability will remain out of reach.

A key question for your organization if you are undertaking a BPM initiative: what are the understanding levels and mindsets of key decision-makers (especially the top person) in your organization with regard to BPM? The answer to that question will be an important factor in laying out the milestones for your BPM initiative. If leaders understand the strategic potential of BPM, then a BPM initiative is more likely to achieve strategic impact. Management achieving such understanding should be an important and visible milestone early in the BPM initiative.

....

FRED CUMMINS

Business Systems Architect, Agile Enterprise Design, LLC

Business collaboration management should subsume Business Process Management

The scope of BPM is too narrow. 'Business process improvement' is even narrower. Instead, we should focus on 'business collaboration management'.

Generally, BPM is expected to focus on repeatable business processes. However, repeatable business processes have been defined and automated.

The work that has not been automated is the work of knowledge workers. Many repeatable business processes are viewed as supporting knowledge work, but the activities typically delegate the responsibility to determine the details of appropriate actions to knowledge workers. The repeatable activities are at a higher level of abstraction, and may restrict the knowledge workers from the most efficient or effective sequence of actions and collaborations. In addition, this means that specific actions of the knowledge worker are not recorded, and the collaboration that occurs and the information exchanged between knowledge workers are not defined nor recorded.

Much of the work of knowledge workers is recurrent, but each occurrence involves initiative, judgment, planning and coordination that is adapted to the particular situation. I will refer to these as adaptive processes. Furthermore, there are ad hoc activities and collaborations (emergent processes) that may have some commonly-occurring activities, but each situation involves different objectives, roles, actions and expertise. These processes are more characteristic of management activities and ad hoc committees or task forces. Nevertheless, both adaptive and emergent processes have commonly occurring, fine-grained actions that can be predefined and used when appropriate.

Automation has focused on repeatable processes because they can be programmed. The repeatable processes define and control what actions are taken by the computer and by people. People are typically engaged when there is knowledge work of limited scope—particularly work assigned to one person. Current technology has enabled a much more interactive relationship between people and computer systems—smart phones, tablets and web-based applications enable interactions with people anytime, anywhere. This support is no longer driven by the flow of control from activity to activity, but by the flow of information/deliverables between participants and changes to the state of the subject as reflected in shared data—the case data.

The expanded scope of BPM practice should include all collaborations. Collaborations are people engaged in roles, performing activities and exchanging deliverables to achieve a shared result. Business collaborations include committees, task forces, projects, exchanges with customers and business partners, and much of the work of managers. Collaborations often delegate to other collaborations to meet the requirements of certain activities. A collaboration will produce one or more deliverables that may be an end product or inputs to other collaborations.

When we look at the operation of the enterprise, it occurs in a network of collaborations. If we look only at repeatable processes, even if we include adaptive processes, we still don't understand the way the business actually works unless we look at commonly occurring collaborations.

Value Network Analysis as described by Verna Allee, is a practice that deals with understanding collaborations. The analysis includes tangible (formal) and intangible (informal) deliverables to clarify the way the business actually works, and explores ways to improve business operations. Often, fundamental problems are not understood until the dependencies and flows of intangibles are understood.

Business Process Management is not an appropriate name for a practice that analyzes, develops and improves the network of collaborations. The expanded scope needs a new name to legitimize the scope of work that should be included. It would be appropriate to call this expanded practice 'Business Collaboration Management'. This expanded scope calls for specialization of skills, and the enterprise-level analysis calls for working at the management level to describe and improve the general design of the business from a network-of-collaborations perspective.

VDML (Value Delivery Modeling Language) provides a modeling capability that is essential to this expanded scope. It has been recently adopted by OMG (Object Management Group). In VDML, the enterprise is a network of collaborations, which include: interactions with customers and business partners; organization units (people working together); members of communities (people with shared interests); and capability methods—the abstraction of people working together to perform a service. The VDML abstraction is more suited to the level of interest of managers, and provides a better view of the network of collaborations. Business Collaboration Management should comprehend this network of collaborations.

At the operational level, there are potential specializations for management of repeatable processes, adaptive processes and emergent processes. People who develop and improve repeatable business processes continue to have an important skill. This is the domain of BPMN (Business Process Model and Notation from OMG). The development and improvement of adaptive process models is a new discipline that requires a considerably different way of thinking about and modeling processes. This is the domain of CMMN (Case Management Model and Notation from OMG). Participants in CMMN adaptive processes will be involved also in defining reusable elements and process patterns, but these will be configurable fragments of processes. CMMN can also be applied to emergent processes, but these will likely involve specialists in each application domain to manage specification of the emergent activities and events.

Adaptive and emergent processes represent a very large domain to be addressed by Business Collaboration Management. In addition to operational knowledge work, automation should be applied to initiatives and other undertakings to develop or improve the way the business works, including substantial business transformation initiatives. These all involve collaboration—sometimes with project management facilities, and sometimes with less formal approaches. Furthermore, executives are often involved in multiple collaborations that should be supported by facilities that at least improve collaboration of participants and raise alerts regarding events.

Business Collaboration Management should include collaborations to address concerns that require specialized attention: implementation of policies, security assurance, accountability, and risk mitigation. Many of these concerns are often relegated to IT people as technical issues. They are, in fact, business issues, and IT people should only provide support. The following paragraphs provide brief discussions of these concerns.

Business collaboration specialists must collaborate with other business experts to identify and ensure compliance with business policies. Business policies include those based on government regulations. Policies must be applied to relevant collaborations. VDML-level analysis should support identification of the collaborations affected by a policy. Repeatable processes and adaptive processes must enforce policies or provide guidance for compliance. All collaborations may require reviews and approvals for certain actions to enforce policies.

Security of collaborations involves restricting access to information and automation. Collaboration specialists must collaborate with security experts. Roles must be filled by persons who have appropriate authority to perform the associated activities and have access to the associated information. Activities must be performed in an adequately secure environment. Data must be retrieved, added, deleted and changed with appropriate access controls, and communicated with appropriately secure communication protocols.

Collaboration specialists should also consider the environments and media in which activities are performed and data is stored, communicated, and viewed to ensure security and regulatory compliance. With the use of cloud computing, these specialists should ensure that data in the cloud is not violating export regulations in the communication of restricted data.

Collaboration specialists should collaborate on the definition of roles, not only from the perspective of process design, but also from the perspective of assignment of roles to people. These role assignments should not just be ad hoc for assigning people to processes, but should be persistent designations of the capabilities and authority of individuals.

Basic accountability requires capture of actions taken and the person responsible for the action. Accountability can be strengthened by preventing the action until authorized, or by requiring that two persons agree on the action. Additional measures might involve restricted access to areas in which certain actions can be taken, or requiring that the decision-maker order a desired action be performed by another person.

Another level of accountability involves identification of the person granting authority, which may include assignment of persons to roles and delegation of authority to a surrogate.

Finally, processes can be the basis for identification of risks as well as the mitigation of risks. Collaboration specialists should collaborate with risk management experts. For example, a critical process may be disrupted by the need for a key person or resource. The risk might be mitigated by raising an alarm, by assigning resources from another source, or by initiating an alternative process. Other risks should be assessed and reported, and then processes must be defined for action when such an event occurs. For example, storm damage, a fire, or a strike may stop operations. Mitigation of the effects should also consider the impact on downstream operations and customers. This requires the broader understanding of the network of collaborations and dependencies. That broader understanding can be provided by a robust VDML model of the business.

In summary, there is a need for a new business discipline that subsumes BPM, and provides a more comprehensive understanding and contribution to the development, management and optimization of all forms of collaboration. That discipline might be called Business Collaboration Management. It includes consideration of the network of collaborations through which the work and the management of the business is accomplished, and it includes collaboration on related concerns, such as implementation of policies, information security, accountability, and risk mitigation.

ROGER BURLTON

President, Process Renewal Group

The 'M' in BPM represents 'Management'. Process modeling and process improvement have been around for more than a century. What's new is the need to sustain the assets produced by process efforts. These assets require a mechanism in place to look after them, keep them current and leverage them for a set of purposes, such as performance tracking, risk mitigation, and capability development. I feel any time work is performed by anything or anyone that we are talking about processes, resources, business results and stakeholders.

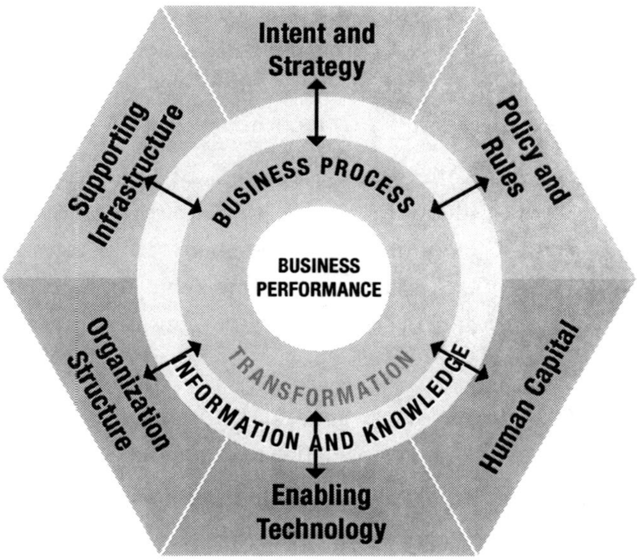

Figure 3: Burlton Hexagon

This means that all knowledge or resources used to conduct, guide, or enable processes must be in the scope of Business Process Management. It is much more than workflow and modeling, and more than a technique—it is a means to an end. It is a means that must be evaluated, changed, monitored, and constantly adapted as part of end-to-end modern management systems and modern business models. The Burlton hexagon from Process Renewal Group and BPTA shows the issues that must be addressed. All are part of the scope, and BPM is the management of them,—nothing less.

....

GABY DOEBELI

Enterprise Architect, Brisbane City Council

I would describe the scope of BPM as being one that can vary from organization to organization. Some use BPM as a management practice enterprise-wide, top-down approach and as a strategic tool and method of prioritization of performance improvement initiatives across the business. Other organizations work bottom-up, applying incremental and ad hoc business process improvement efforts across the enterprise. The senior leadership team has the role to set the scope of BPM supported by the necessary infrastructure and governance to allow the practice to be applied and embedded in their business. The team further sets the BPM vision and strategies for the management capability and ensures the scope is well defined, objectives are identified, and execution efforts are monitored.

BPM-driven organizations often put in place a BPM Centre of Excellence with the overall responsibility to manage the implementation of the BPM infrastructure and to build and monitor capability. BPM roles and responsibilities are defined and assigned, and methods and tools provided to run BPM efforts, like business process improvement, business process design, or re-engineering.

The scope of BPM defines the target and the goal for the BPM Centre of Excellence, and it might range from transforming an organization from a functional to a matrix managed organization, and creating a performance improvement focused culture, or support mainly business-process improvement projects in improving processes and automating them. As with all initiatives, the larger, broader and more complex, the more effort is required and the more expensive it is to implement.

The limits of the BPM practice are often other management methods and how they are applied, the level of integration and alignment of key principles with the ones of BPM, and the readiness of the culture to embark on a business process management journey. The limitations can be minimized by: having a strong governance structure that sets the direction and enables business process change decision-making from an end-to-end perspective; when roles and responsibilities are assigned to process stakeholders to be performed and to contribute to the BPM journey; and when methods and tools are in place to improve processes and monitor end-to-end process performance. These elements integrated and aligned with other management practices—like strategy and performance management, portfolio and program management, financial management, and human resource management—will enhance the outcome of BPM.

I would not discriminate between BPM and some more generic terms, like business process improvement (BPI). Many organizations treat business process review, BPI, business process design and re-engineering (BPR) as methods to manage and improve business processes. These methods are used to review process performance and understand the current state, as well as to analyze and identify options to improve the way of delivering an organizations services and products to their customers.

With this, I like to conclude that the scope of BPM in some organizations is limited to doing BPI, while others use it as a management practice across the enterprise integrated and aligned with other practices and disciplines.

....

PETER FINGAR

Managing Principal, Meghan-Kiffer Research

To understand the scope of business process management, we can start by looking at the scope of a business process as defined in Business Process Management: The Third Wave—"A business process is the complete and dynamically coordinated set of collaborative and transactional activities that deliver value to customers." Oh my, that definition covers all of what it means to be a business; it's how work gets done, including the work of innovation. It's how the 'potential energy' of capabilities is released as kinetic energy with BPM. Thus, BPM includes all of the items from the above question: modeling, process improvement, capability maturity improvement, human performance management, process automation, and business architecture.

Processes are dependent on, and supportive of, the intelligence and judgment of humans. People perform tasks that are too unstructured to delegate to a computer, or that require personal interaction with customers. People also make sense of the rich information flowing though the value chain, solving problems before they irritate customers, and devising strategies to take advantage of new market opportunities. What's really emerging in the BPM world, and expanding its scope, is the advent of cognitive computing, which we'll discuss more in Question 15. For now, let's consider:

- "Artificial Intelligence is likely to change our civilization as much as, or more than, any technology that's come before, even writing"—Miles Brundage and Joanna Bryson, Future Tense.
- "The smart machine era will be the most disruptive in the history of IT"—Gartner, The Disruptive Era of Smart Machines is Upon Us.
- "Without question, Cognitive Computing is a game-changer for businesses across every industry"—Accenture, Turning Cognitive Computing into Business Value, Today!

As reported in the book Enterprise Cloud Computing, from a business model perspective, our business becomes a "mediator" between supply and demand. We no longer are 'sellers' to our customers; we become 'buyers', going to the ends of the earth to bring the greatest value to our customers. Our customers become 'prosumers', helping us to create maximum value across the entire value delivery system.

Yes, you can innovate, but your competitors soon catch up with you. So winning is a matter of 'punctuated equilibrium', where you set 'the pace of innovation'. Innovate and disrupt. Then innovate and disrupt again … and again. In this new world, everything is customer driven, and customers are the only assets you have in the brave new world of total global competition.

So, there you have it. Choreography in the Cloud is the future of building customer-driven value delivery systems in twenty-first century businesses. Just a few years ago, value-chain dominance by an 800-pound gorilla orchestrating everything was the key to competitive advantage. Today, it's process collaboration, cooperation, and choreography. Can your company teach elephants to dance? Certainly not without cognitive computing driving this new scope of BPM (Cognitive BPM).

As we explain in the book The Chief Operating Officer (COO) Revolution: Reinventing Customer-Facing Processes for Moments of Truth, the person who has been mostly responsible for process management inside the enterprise, the COO, must now pivot. While traditional back-office functions will certainly not go away, COOs must pivot and also focus on the front office. The primary role of the modern COO should be that of delivering customer experiences that delight! And that great experience is what CMOs are obsessing over.

The design point of products and services, especially those in information industries like banking, insurance, entertainment, and retail, has shifted from the product to overall user experience. User experience is now primary to customer loyalty and competitive advantage. Connecting the CMO and COO may not be the most intuitive suggestion, but it's a modern one. It's a connection that business leaders must understand and capitalize on. The new dominating roles of customers, communities, and capabilities in the digital enterprise are elaborated on in Lewis and Scott's new book, the Cognitive Enterprise. The scope of BPM will never be the same and will be driven by cognitive, prescriptive analytics. Prescriptive analytics ingests hybrid data (a combination of structured and unstructured data) and business rules to predict what lies ahead and to prescribe how to take advantage of this predicted future right here, right now, with next-best-action at customer moments of truth!

....

LEANDRO JESUS

Co-Founder & Director, EloGroup

First of all, I believe we should understand BPM from an outside-in perspective. From my point of view, many definitions still fail at explaining this.

An organization's main purpose is to create value to its customers through the delivery of products and services that satisfy customer needs. This applies for any kind of organization, both profit and non-profit. Customer centricity is crucial to all businesses in the twenty-first century.

Considering this, 'management' is about improving and sustaining organizational performance so that a business can deliver better products and services to its customers, creating value in a consistent and balanced manner.

Process orientation refers to understanding how work is performed in order to create value to customers. It puts emphasis on collaboration, shared responsibilities, and the articulation of people and resources (materials, information, infrastructure, etc.) to achieve organizational goals. Therefore, it puts processes as a key element to a management system.

BPM is, thus, a management discipline that aims at improving and sustaining organizational performance, based on process orientation, so that an organization can deliver better products or services to its customers.

That means BPM is about management: a better way of management. A management style that puts customers in first place and emphasizes the need of collaboration and integration in order to create value for customers. And, of course, which is increasingly empowered by emerging technologies (but not limited to them).

When we think of BPM as a management system based on processes, we can understand it as composed of 3 main elements:

- Projects execution. The execution of diverse projects aimed at changing the way work is conducted and reaching significant performance gains. Projects rely on process orientation, and begin with the understanding and analysis of the current situation. They usually lead to the design and implementation of new work practices, which may refer to changes in workflows, rules, involved technologies and infrastructure, organizational structure, and people´s responsibilities, as well as changes into customer experience throughout the process. In this sense, project execution allows for the transformation of the business, putting new and better processes in place.
- Day-by-day (or routine) management. Establishing a continuous cycle for the measurement, evaluation and improvement of work practices, based on process orientation, in order to sustain organizational performance. Rather than one-off initiatives, day-by-day management is a routine that needs to be incorporated into each manager's role.
- Strategy deployment. The definition of goals for day-to-day management and of a portfolio of prioritized projects for transforming work practices. Strategy deployment usually runs on an annual basis and relies on well-defined process architecture.

The figure below illustrates those elements and main relationships between them.

We may note that BPM elements communicate with business strategy by receiving inputs from strategic plans and reporting results from the portfolio. In the same sense, they interface with processes execution, gathering measures and promoting the required changes (based on projects or action plans) in order that processes can be well performed.

Besides that, we may also note that those elements, when combined, form a life-cycle in which: (a) ideas and demands are prioritized based on strategy and become projects that are part of a portfolio; (b) projects are conducted and put new work practices in place; (c) information gathered from execution is monitored and controlled; and then (d) provide ideas and demands back for the portfolio.

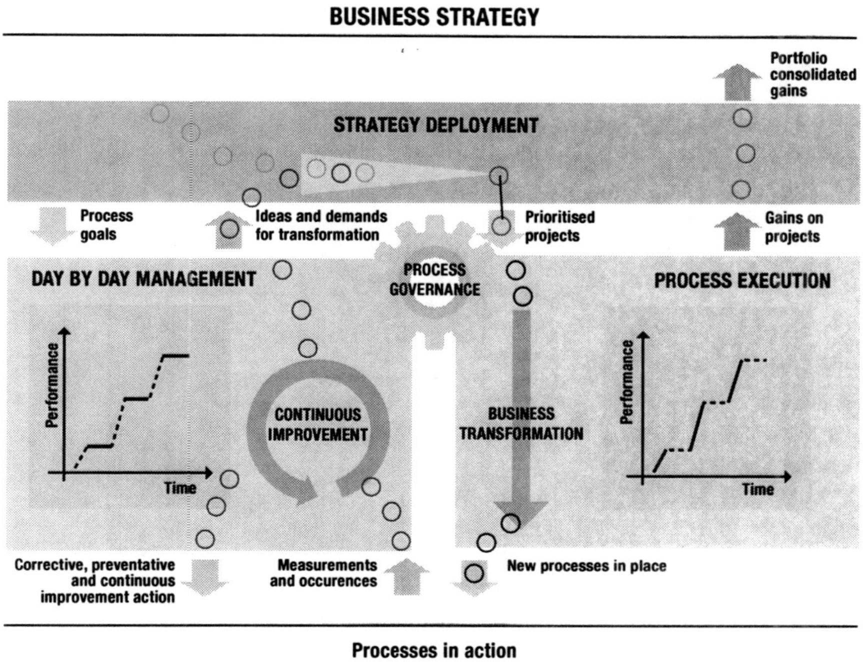

Figure 4: BPM main elements—project execution; day-by-day management; and strategy deployment

Based on process orientation, with a clearly defined process governance, this life cycle allows the management system to be continuously refined towards better organizational performance, thus creating more value to customers.

....

PETER MATTHIJSSEN

Managing Consultant, BiZZdesign

The scoping of BPM is always interesting. There are many discussions about BPM in relation to, for example: business analysis; process modeling; process control; lean management; business process engineering; BPMN; BPMS; business architecture. In my opinion, discussions about which approach or technique is best are not very useful. It is more interesting how different approaches and techniques can support each other. We look at BPM as:

"a management discipline

with processes in a central role,

with one goal: better results"

Based on this broad definition, BPM can be seen as a kind of umbrella, covering and connecting all kind of other disciplines. The figure below illustrates the scope of BPM, in our vision.

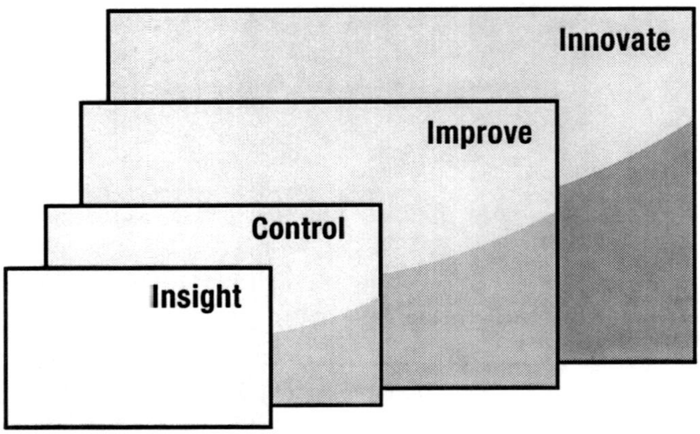

Figure 5: Scope of BPM

- The basis of BPM is 'insight'; what kind of processes do we have and how do they interconnect? Typically, process architecture has a place here.
- The next area is process control. How do we ensure that the daily performance of our processes is at the right level? Typically, process ownership, process instructions, key performance indicators (KPIs), and governance have a place here.
- When process performance is not at the right level, improvement is needed. What causes our process to under-perform? Project-based improvement techniques are used to bring together the right people, collect information, find (root) causes and implement improvements. Lean and Six Sigma are widely used process-improvement methods.
- Sometimes we need or want to do different things, or do things in a different way. In this case, we might need to design 'new processes', or redesign existing ones. Business process engineering (BPE) and

business process re-engineering (BPR) techniques and approaches support practitioners in these design processes.

In my opinion, the power of BPM is the way it connects different disciplines. BPM treats processes as important, central assets of the organization. A process perspective provides a powerful view on the organization, connecting tasks, people, IT, projects, organizational structures, etc. This central role is illustrated in the 'Process Flower'. The many BPM techniques and tools are there to improve process performance.

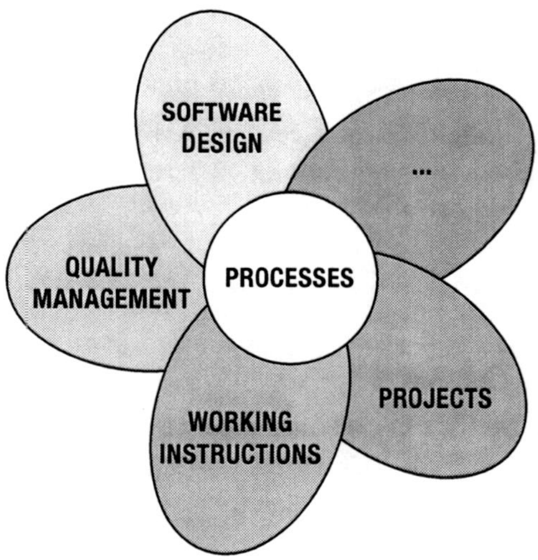

Figure 6: Process Flower

But BPM is bigger than just techniques and tools. BPM is about process thinking, and process thinking is about value thinking, and value thinking is about customer thinking. A favorite quote of mine is one I borrowed from Bert Kersten (Professor at Nyenrode Business School): "Large organizations don't need customers, they can be busy with themselves." And it is so true! I see it every day; people being busy with internal projects, organizational structures, performance indicators, IT issues. But where is the customer? Organizations have become so large and complex, that most employees and management never even come close to a customer. Customer contact is delegated to a small group of employees, supported by CRM systems and big data analytics. How can we talk about customer value and quality if the customer is that far away?

BPM is also there to keep track on customers and their needs. I know from personal experience how easy it is to get lost in all available tools, models and approaches that BPM supplies. However, it's important to always keep track of the customer impact for everything you do. This isn't always easy; it often requires asking ourselves and our environment some basic questions:

- Who is our customer?
- Why are we doing this?
- Does the customer want to pay for this?
- Which problem do we solve?
- What if we just stop doing this?
- How would we organize this process on a much smaller scale?
- So, next to all the tools and techniques, BPM is also about common sense; it's about observations in 'the real world' and asking basic questions like those above.

....

MATTHEW J. MORGAN

Head of Process & Metrics Excellence, Bridgewater Assoc.

At its best, business process management, or BPM, is a holistic approach to management. It includes disciplines such as business architecture, process modeling and governance, process improvement, and process automation. It leverages, but does not include, other disciplines like program and project management, information technology, change management, and leadership.

In some organizations, the group responsible for BPM has a narrower scope than all of the disciplines listed above. An example of such a relatively narrower scope could be focusing only on process modeling. In this case, other parts of the organization focus on other responsibilities, such as business architecture, process improvement, or process automation. Alternatively, the BPM group in some organizations focuses on process automation, or business process management suite technology, as defined by its role in the organization. Often, especially in large organizations, various disciplines of BPM thus operate in silos, separated both from each other and from a function called 'BPM'.

This often occurs due to the vertical, organization-structure oriented management of many companies, in which there are few horizontal connection points that allow different groups to share awareness or effectively collaborate on related activities. In addition, different business units can undertake initiatives or new programs independently. Executive sponsorship creates constraints around the design and scope of new programs and, due to the different perspectives and authority of different sponsors, can prevent the alignment of different BPM-related activities and functions to one another.

In best-practice organizations, these various BPM activities are organized and integrated under a central programmatic oversight (or at least coordinating through a stakeholder committee with all relevant participants). The reality often does not align with this best practice. The irony is that one of the aspirations of BPM is to create a process-driven approach to management to prevent or avoid the very siloed approach to management that allows for the emergence of various uncoordinated BPM-related entities in organizations.

I view BPM as a fundamental enabler to create and implement business transformation. In my experience, overseeing new enterprise-wide process excellence programs at a multi-billion-dollar engineering and project management company and then at a multi-billion-dollar investment management company, my core responsibility was to develop and deploy a new capability in process management and process improvement where one previously did not exist.

....

CHRIS POTTS

Corporate Strategist, Dominic Barrow

For people more familiar with other management approaches, BPM can represent both an unusual perspective and, potentially, a very different scope. This can limit people's understanding and appreciation of BPM as a complementary and valuable management approach. A vital challenge for BPM specialists, therefore, is to demonstrate how BPM's scope complements, while differing from, other business management approaches.

In the context of business, 'management' is the organization and coordination of activities in order to achieve defined objectives.[1] Among alternative approaches to business management, a significant differentiating factor is the primary unit of organization. For example, an activities-oriented approach to business management treats discrete business activities as the primary unit of organization. In contrast, a services-oriented approach treats a service as the primary unit of organization, and coordinates activities within services. BPM, being process-oriented, treats a business process as the primary unit of organization, and coordinates activities within processes.

For business managers used to taking, for example, an activities-oriented or services-oriented approach to management, BPM offers two fundamental challenges. The first is to perceive how the enterprise performs from the perspective of the processes in which it appears (i.e. from the external stakeholder's perspective). The term 'outside-in' has become a popular and useful expression for this perspective, distinguishing it from 'inside-out' or 'inside-in'. The second fundamental challenge that comes with BPM is how to 'manage' activities that are outside an enterprise's control, but are within the processes in which the enterprise appears, and are essential for the enterprise to succeed (for example, the activities that a customer undertakes in choosing and buying a product). These external-but-essential activities may be considered out-of-scope for many management approaches, but are central to the scope of BPM.

An enterprise that efficiently organizes and co-ordinates its internal activities will, nevertheless, struggle if it is out-of-sync with the external processes in which it wants to be valued. A term that has been coined by enterprise designers to describe such situations is an 'awkward' enterprise,[2] characterized by inconsistencies in how the enterprise behaves when appearing more than once in an external stakeholder's processes. An awkward enterprise may, for example, demonstrate apparently different values between its brand proposition and service, and between various services. Were an awkward enterprise's priority to invest in improving the efficiency of its 'internal processes', it risks getting better at being awkward.

BPM's overall value proposition, orientation and scope is, therefore, concerned with how coherently, rather than 'awkwardly', the enterprise appears in its stakeholders' processes. Given that those processes evolve over time, BPM also has in its scope the enterprise's investments in process-related innovations. Where an innovation enhances the enterprise's value within a process, BPM acts an agent of change. Conversely, if an innovation would damage the enterprise's value in a process, BPM acts as an agent of stability.

The best evidence of an enterprise that has mastered the scope of BPM is that it efficiently creates value by staying in-sync with external processes. Where it is valuable, possible, and legitimate to do so, a BPM-savvy enterprise also influences the architectures of the processes in which it appears.

References

[1] www.businessdictionary.com

[2] See INTERSECTION, Guenther M, Elsevier Inc., 2013

....

ALAN RAMIAS

Partner, Performance Design Lab

My roots in BPM go back to the work Geary Rummler did at Motorola in the 1980s. So, naturally enough, I continue to think about processes with the lens that he provided in his book Improving Performance: How to Manage the White Space on the Organization Chart (Rummler, Geary A., Jossey-Bass, 2nd ed., 1995). That model, shown in Figure 1, posits that every organization consists of three levels of performance, and that the role of leadership is to set goals, design and manage at all three levels, keeping them aligned and capable of producing desired results. For people who had never before recognized the importance of the process level (or even realized it was there), this simple model was a revelation.

In my opinion, the model holds up well as a framework for BPM, but I would suggest a few minor modifications to make its application to BPM a little more obvious. Figure 2 contains the following changes to the model:

- The word 'Goals' is changed to 'Planning', because in another of Rummler's models (i.e. the management system) it is clear that goal-setting is only one part of the key responsibilities of management in what he called "Performance Planned."
- The 'Job/Performer Level' contains two classes—people and technology—because today's processes are virtually all executed by some combination of human and electronic performers. The Level 3 cells are labeled as "performance" planning, design and management, which means addressing all necessary elements (work environment, tools, resources, training, etc.) at the performer level to enable desired performance.

- Process improvement is implied by 'Design', but I added a loop back from Process Management to Design, meaning that when it becomes clear from performance data that performance is inadequate, one goes back to the Design stage. To achieve lasting improvement, though, redesign may be required at any level, or any combination.

With this model in mind, what is BPM? It is the planning, design and management of the process level of an organization. The process level is connected to the other two levels and mediates between them. For example, at the organization level, strategic and operational plans are created and cascaded down to the performer level in the form of goals, standards, and directions, along with the allocation of resources required to perform the work. When explicitly recognized and carefully designed, the business processes in the middle translate and organize those goals and standards into process performance language for teams and individuals who will do the actual work. As performance happens, the process level mediates in reverse, with individual and group activities and achievements monitored and reported upward through the process layer to the organization's leaders. When performance improvement is needed, the process level that is most useful in identifying what has to change and what the specific improvement targets should be.

So with this model in mind, BPM includes: process performance planning, goal setting and standards setting, process design and improvement, process ownership; performance monitoring, performance diagnostics, decision-making and corrective action.

As for the limits of BPM, this model also helps answer that question. The process level is important but it's not everything constituting an organization. If a company decides, for example, to restructure, the resulting design activities are aimed at the organization and performer levels. But a restructuring that includes examining key processes and altering them to make the restructuring goals achievable and the performers capable for doing their work in the altered structure—that's process-driven reorganization. So, BPM is not everything, but it should be core to any strategic change or improvement an organization may wish to make.

••

PROFESSOR MICHAEL ROSEMANN

Head of Information Systems School, Queensland University of Technology

Business Process Management is dedicated to the value-driven design, management, execution, ongoing monitoring and improvement, and modernization of flows of activities. BPM needs to consider process-relevant strategies, plans, resources, existing and emerging technologies and, in particular, a variety of internal and external stakeholders.

As such, BPM provides a 'process-centered view'. This is a beneficial lens if processes are broken (operational efficiency issues), or process performance is a core element of deriving competitive advantages. However, if corporate opportunities and challenges are not primarily process-related (e.g. data quality, product features, brand value, compliance issues), BPM's contribution to corporate performance is limited (first limitation).

BPM can be seen as the over-arching term comprising a number of process-related approaches that are more limited in their scope. This includes, in particular, reactive approaches dedicated to overcoming process-inherent problems, such as: the existence of non-value-adding activities (Lean Management); variation (Six Sigma); general quality problems (Total Quality Management); manual labor (workflow management); or bottlenecks (Theory of Constraints). These approaches tend to be focused on the process analysis stage of the process lifecycle. Other approaches targeting different stages of the lifecycle are: business process modeling, process risk assessment, process costing, process monitoring or process mining. While the plethora of BPM approaches provides fertile ground for a comprehensive set of tools, techniques and methods, we still observe a lack in the overall integration of these. For example, as of today, an efficient, tool-supported approach that capitalizes of the potential of process mining and uses these data to inform activity-based costing or Six Sigma is still missing (second limitation).

Business Process Management can be seen as a framework under which these and other approaches can be integrated and orchestrated to a company-tailored way of managing business processes. In particular, and in addition to all previously mentioned approaches, this includes enterprise-wide capabilities, such as: process-centered strategy management, process governance, methodology design and maintenance, BPM capability and capacity development, and process-centered cultural change.

Related current limitations in this context are the lack of meta management frameworks allowing the integration of BPM with other management philosophies that are centered on different corporate artifacts, such as the internal resources, intellectual property, customers, or data (third limitation).

....

RON ROSS

CEO, Business Rules Solutions

BPM often overreaches. Understanding, modeling, and managing a business require a balanced view of six basic questions, as follows. (Yes, I have a Zachman bias.)

If your business does nothing but manufacture or produce physical widgets (forget all the meta-data about those widgets), you will probably emphasize question 2 (i.e. process) above the others. Your overall approach and architecture will reflect that. You will naturally gravitate toward BPM.

That tendency has at least three basic risks, even for organizations that do fall into the nothing-but-widgets category (most don't):

- Your metrics will largely focus on process productivity (e.g. throughput, bottlenecks, and latency) rather than strategic goals and alerts centered on external risks. E-suite executives, however, tend to be much more focused on the latter.
- Your mindset will be procedural, rather than declarative, which can cause you to embed business rules in process flows rather than externalize them. As a result, your process models will be unnecessarily complex and your overall solutions un-agile.
- Your approach will fall short of addressing the operational business knowledge that underlies the processes. Such knowledge ranges from simple meta-data, to the business logic that underlies operational business decisions.

Fewer and fewer business problems these days fall into nothing-but-widgets category. Even for widget-centric businesses, at least three needs are increasingly urgent:

- Ensuring the quality of meta-data.
- Demonstrating compliance-based actual rules, rather than the artifacts and effects that IT systems produce.
- Retaining, teaching and repurposing basic operational business knowledge.

These are not strengths of common BPM practices.For all the non-widget-centric business activity in the world—which includes just about every conceivable form of white-collar work—these needs become paramount. And, make no mistake, the future lies with automation of white-collar work.

What would I do to correct the shortcomings of BPM? Become more why-centric, rather than how-centric. That shift has several essential features:

- Understanding business strategy as something distinct from business processes (and BPM). Business goals and business risks should be drivers of business process design—not the other way around. Be strategy-driven, not simply process-driven.
- Designing core metrics around business goals and business risks—the things that concern C-suite executives the most.
- Realizing that for white-collar work, the 3-D world of widgets has vanished, and that tolerances and quality can be expressed only in terms of business rules.
- Treating business rules as a first-class citizen, externalized from process models.[3]
- Identifying operational business decisions (based on encoded business rules) as a crucial focal point in re-engineering business processes.
- Including a Why Button as part of every business solution. Pressing the Why Button leads immediately to the business rules that produced the results you see from any process.[4]

Table 1: Zachman Architecture Questions

	Interrogative	Basic Business Question	Kind of Model
1	What	What inventory of things needs to be managed to support business activity?	Structural model (e.g., concept model,[1] data model)
2	How	How do transforms of things in business activity need to take place to add value?	Process model
3	Where	Where does business activity occur?	Network model
4	Who	Who collaborates with whom to undertake business activity?	Interaction model (e.g., organizational chart, use case)
5	When	When does business activity take place?	Temporal model (e.g., schedule, event model, milestone model)
6	Why	Why are results of business activity deemed appropriate or not?	Strategy model (e.g., Policy Charter,[2] constraint model

References

[1] Refer to Refer to Business Rule Concepts: Getting to the Point of Knowledge (4th ed) by Ronald G. Ross, 2013, Chapter 1 and Part 2. http://www.brsolutions.com/b_concepts.php

[2] Refer to Building Business Solutions: Business Analysis with Business Rules by Ronald G. Ross and Gladys S.W. Lam, 2nd ed. (Sept, 2015), an IIBA Sponsored Handbook, Chapter 4. http://www.brsolutions.com/b_building_business_solutions.php

[3] Refer to the Business Rules Manifesto, now in almost 20 languages: http://www.businessrulesgroup.org/brmanifesto.htm

[4] Refer to: Ronald G. Ross, "The Why Engineer™," Business Rules Journal, Vol. 14, No. 11 (Nov. 2013), URL: http://www.BRCommunity.com/a2013/b727.html

PHIL SHORT

IT Director, Mars Canada

This is largely down to interpretation, but I take it literally and consider BPM to be a strategic approach to define and understand the organization's business process assets as a management tool. It assists in optimizing its operational performance and achieving its strategic goals. BPM professional practice has been established over time to provide a methodical approach to applying those tools, holistically and effectively, to how work gets done across an organization. Along with this professional practice has evolved various methodologies, each with a slightly different focus and vocabulary but, in essence, it is the organization that chooses BPM and then a methodology that best fits its culture to help realize its benefits.

First, to be clear about what BPM is, requires the definition of a business process. In its simplest form it is 'how work gets done', from a high level abstract Business Process Architecture, down to detailed activities with a series of work instructions for specific tasks. One of the key things to remember is that work gets done in all organizations, regardless of whether it uses a formal BPM practice or not—so, all organizations have business processes. Products are made, orders are taken, product is shipped, cash is collected, services are provided, even in the most simplistic and poorly managed organizations. So, there is no magic about business processes themselves. Business Process Management is a conscious decision by an organization to use the understanding of their business processes, or how the work gets done in their organization, to better achieve operational and strategic objectives. How they go about this is where the plethora of methodologies, tools and techniques come in, and the subject of BPM gets very murky. For many organizations, starting BPM is prohibitive because the supposedly high cost of introducing it. My personal view is that BPM costs nothing; it is just the recognition by an organization's leadership that by understanding how work gets done, you can start to make changes to become more efficient, more agile, and more customer-centric. These lead to better growth, profit, and employee engagement to name but a few benefits.

So, there is a question: 'Can you have business process improvement without BPM?' You could argue that any work done on any business process is considered Business Process Management. It is, however, very difficult to get proper benefit from such initiatives when they are, for instance isolated to a single business function, or a particular computer application. Although valuable to smaller parts of the organization, I would not consider them to be BPM. Most organizations spend some time looking at getting better or fixing things that are not working well. Without a BPM approach, they are more likely to fire an employee, change computer programs, or reorganize a department to fix a problem. These will, at best, create some local improvements and, at worst, improve one area of the organization to the detriment of another.

If, however, an organization creates a strategy to use BPM to better manage their organization, then small business process improvements, process modeling, and re-engineering initiatives could and should happen as the organization builds this business process management capability—but they will have a cross functional awareness. As these initiatives get bigger and start to cross functions, they ultimately become a go-to tool in any business changes they undertake to meet operational and strategic objectives. This evolution of maturity is reflected in Table 2.

Table 2: Bearing Point process maturity model

STRATEGY	
Siloed	-Reactive to market conditions within 1-2 years, typically chasing a competitor -Integration within functions -Driven by cost and efficiency
Tactically Integrated	-Adapt/react to market dynamics within 12 months -Some cross-functional integration to solve pains -Initial entry into point-to-point integration with partners
Process Driven	-Adapt/react to market dynamics within 3-6 months -Enterprise-wide process leadership is established -The business process is the foundational element of the enterprise
Optimized Enterprise	-Adaptive to market dynamics within weeks -Enterprise organized completely around processes -Optimized processes + execution yield competitive advantage
Intelligent Operating Network	-Predictive capabilities and market leadership -Continuously adaptive to market dynamics in near real-time -Enterprise and its partners are organized around processes -Competitive advantage is driven and shared by partners

CONTROLS	
Siloed	-Local and functional level authority/ autonomy -No enterprise-wide standards or governance -No formal value measurement program
Tactically Integrated	-Hierarchical mgmt. Structure -Independent functional department decision -Limited enterprise-wide standards or s
Process Driven	-Formal process leadership establishes priorities -Business cases drive projects -Process metrics tied to individual and team performance
Optimized Enterprise	-Process teams responsible for overall performance -Relevant process metrics institutionalized as main performance measures
Intelligent Operating Network	-Inter-enterprise process teams own performance
PROCESS	
Siloed	-Static business processes -Functional silos -Geographic silos -Department focused -Informal communications within departments
Tactically Integrated	-Limited process reengineering and cross-functional/process coordination (often manual, one-time efforts) -Systems drive baseline process definitions
Process Driven	-Fully transitioned from functional to process focus, including management structure, execution teams, and performance evaluation -Targeted BPO
Optimized Enterprise	-Total process integration across the enterprise -Commitment to continuous process improvement program -Outsource non-core business processes (reduce cost and increase quality)
Intelligent Operating Network	-Total process integration across the ecosystem -Key processes flow seamlessly across firewalls

PEOPLE	
Siloed	-Subject matter experts -Culture is adversarial, mutual distrust -No formal change management procedures -I'll do my job, you do yours
Tactically Integrated	-Cross-functional/process team members (usually led by IT) -Limited understanding of cross-departmental process needs and dependencies
Process Driven	-Process leaders define, deploy, enhance, and maintain core processes -Functional teams focus on high quality execution
Optimized Enterprise	-Lean organization focused on optimizing process definitions and execution -Ongoing process training for employees
Intelligent Operating Network	-Partner selection includes process & cultural attributes -Ongoing process training for employees and partners
IT	
Siloed	-Independent systems -Islands of automation -Integration only within functions -Legacy enterprise system(s)
Tactically Integrated	-Leverage ERP systems for cross-functional integration -Point-to-point partner integration -IT leads cross-functional initiatives (system focused)
Process Driven	-IT supports process leadership team in initiatives -System and instance consolidation to streamline processes and info mgmt
Optimized Enterprise	-Utilize Business Process Management (BPM) solutions to automate process execution, monitoring, and control across the Enterprise
Intelligent Operating Network	-Utilize Business Process Management (BPM) solutions to automate and monitor process execution throughout the ecosystem¬¬

So, it comes down to the strategic intent of the organization. In my early work as an IT professional, I was introduced to the concept of 'process-based change', and to the idea that before you do an IT project, you need to understand why the organization is asking for the change. To do this, you have to understand which work the IT capability will support. By modeling the business processes, the context of the IT capability, and how it interacts with the work in general, becomes apparent. At the time I started using this approach, the organization did not have what I would consider a BPM strategy; but my work on modeling and designing better business processes at the micro and macro level of the organization were still beneficial.

The limitations of this approach—and the reason I argue that, in isolation, they are not BPM—is that there are instances where you have a process that crosses functional boundaries, and one functional head supports the business process approach, and the other does not. At this point, the process work becomes sub-optimal. True value only comes when the business looks at its processes from end-to-end and where all executives and functional heads have bought in and support the initiatives.

In summary, business process work almost always has value because it looks at the work being done and optimizes that. I only consider it Business Process Management, however, when the organization recognizes and implements a strategy to understand and use the management of its business processes assets to achieve its operational performance and strategic objectives.

....

JAMES TAYLOR
CEO, Decision Management Solutions

Should BPM include decisions or not?

When initiating a BPM project, or setting up a BPM competency, organizations often wonder if they should include decisions and business rules in these BPM initiatives. The answer, as it so often seems to be, is both 'yes' and 'no'.

Why 'yes'?

Fundamentally, decisions matter to processes. If decisions are identified explicitly as distinct from but integrated with processes, then the resulting processes are simpler, smarter, and more agile:

- Simpler because the complexity of the decision-making can be modeled and managed outside of the process model, keeping the process cleaner and more streamlined.
- Smarter because the decision-making can be continually and systematically improved without changing the process. More smarts—in the form of analytics, for instance—can be applied to the decision-making to improve the decision and indirectly the process(es) of which it is part.

- More agile because decision-making and process flow can be changed independently, increasing the flexibility of response when change it required. If the decision-making is implemented in a Business Rules Management System (BRMS), then this agility can be further increased by taking advantage of the BRMS to make rapid, safe changes to decision-making logic.

This last point brings up a critical issue for many BPM projects. Decisions allow business rules to be applied within the process (making decisions that impact the outcome of the process), not just to the process (controlling routing and escalation, etc.). Extensive use of business rules to manage the decisions within a process is much more valuable than simply using business rules to define some of the process.

Why 'no'?

Decisions are not processes. They should be modeled differently, have different approaches to reuse, consume and transform data differently, and require somewhat separate technology. As such, lumping them together can be dangerous. It is better and more effective to consider decisions and processes as peers, collaborating to deliver business value. If decisions are included in BPM without thinking, then there is a real danger that decision-making will not get the focus it deserves, and that decision-making technology, like business rules and advanced analytics, will be underutilized.

Very process-centric organizations might find it most effective to consider decisions and processes as peers within an overall process framework—that is, consider them as separate but related concepts, and always use both when tackling a business process project. This is hard, however, so it is generally better to think of Business Process Management and Decision Management as parallel cooperating threads at both a project and competency level.

Many BPM projects include a focus on decisions, and a growing number of BPM competency efforts include a focus on decisions. A better approach is to establish both under an umbrella of operational effectiveness, or something similar. This allows for projects and efforts that are more or less completely BPM focused, more or less decision focused, or balanced between the two as necessary. It allows for sharing and overlap without subsuming one within the other.

PROFESSOR JAN VOM BROCKE

Hilti Chair of Business Process Management, University of Liechtenstein

BPM represents a holistic management approach that provides capabilities to sustain organizational competitiveness in today´s fast-changing business environment. Rosemann and de Bruin's (2005) BPM maturity model distinguishes between six core factors: i) strategic alignment; ii) governance; iii) methods; iv) IT; v) people; and vi) culture. The model has become an established framework to assess the BPM maturity of organizations, and it can also be used to determine the scope of BPM according to six core elements of BPM (vom Brocke & Rosemann, 2015a, 2015b):

STRATEGIC ALIGNMENT is a factor that emphasizes the importance of aligning BPM with the overall strategy of an organization. It calls for tightly linking organizational priorities and business processes in order to continuously improve and innovate business. Strategic alignment is required in all lifecycle phases of organizational processes, from process design via process execution, to process monitoring and process redesign.

- Governance is a factor that emphasizes establishing appropriate accountabilities. That means roles and responsibilities need to be clearly defined in all phases of managing business processes in organizations. Furthermore, decision-making on processes needs to be designed in an appropriate way, so suitable key performance indicators that give guidance towards managing processes need to be defined.
- Methods refer to a factor that emphasizes tools and techniques that facilitate the management of organizational processes throughout the process lifecycle. Such methods include tools related to process analysis, process design, process modeling, process execution, and process improvement. For example, Lean management and Six Sigma are specific methods appropriate for eliminating waste and improving quality in organizational processes.
- Information technology is a factor that emphasizes the significance of IT solutions for managing business processes efficiently. Most prominently, enterprise resource planning systems and workflow management systems play a key role in designing, implementing, executing, and monitoring business processes.
- People refer to a factor that emphasizes the need to consider process management skills and knowledge in BPM. Everyone involved in

the management of organizational processes should continuously enhance their qualifications in the area of BPM and apply appropriate skill sets to increase business performance. Therefore, organizations need to monitor the competence requirements of their human resources to successfully manage their business processes.

- Culture is a factor that emphasizes the need for a common value system that supports process improvement and process innovation. It calls for an environment that facilitates efficient and effective business processes. If there is a lack of values and beliefs that support a process-centered organization, cultural resistances are likely to occur, and BPM projects are likely to fail. While culture cannot easily be changed, it is still highly important for the success of BPM initiatives to ensure a BPM-facilitating cultural environment.

The six core elements of BPM help to scope BPM initiatives. They can be used to assess the status quo of an organization, and to derive specific strategies on how to further develop the BPM capabilities of an organization in line with specific strategic objectives. While single BPM projects might fall primarily in only one or a few capability areas, the framework is useful to reflect the alignment with all other elements.

References

Rosemann, M., & de Bruin, T. (2005). Towards a business process management maturity model. In: Proceedings of the 13th European conference on information systems, Regensburg, Germany, May 2005.

vom Brocke, J., & Rosemann, M. (Ed.). (2015a). Handbook on Business Process Management: Introduction, Methods and Information Systems (International Handbooks on Information Systems) (2 ed. Vol. 1). Berlin et al.: Springer.

vom Brocke, J., & Rosemann, M. (Ed.). (2015b). Handbook on Business Process Management: Strategic Alignment, Governance, People and Culture (International Handbooks on Information Systems) (2 ed. Vol. 2). Berlin et al.: Springer.

QUESTION 2

WHO CARES?

There is considerable interest in business processes and in process management. These interests are apparent in many different parts of an organization: in strategy, operations, IT, risk management, HR, and in other areas.

How would you characterize the current interest in BPM? In what ways, if any, do you see organizations benefiting from a BPM approach?

OVERVIEW

When you ask about who is interested in BPM, the answer you are given very much depends on who you ask. As you will see when you read the answers below, if you ask someone from IT, they will describe the needs for IT and automation that drive an interest in BPM. If you ask someone who is primarily working with organizations that use Lean or Six Sigma, they will talk about how these practitioners are hoping that BPM can supplement or extend their practices. All respondents, however, agree that there is a growing interest in BPM, driven by the challenges organizations face, and their hope that the management of processes will help them deal with those challenges. Most of our authors emphasized a vertical view of the organization, and stressed that BPM was of interest to senior management as a way of dealing with strategic initiative, and of interest to middle managers as a way of providing new insights into how the organization works. It was also seen as a help in integrating new technologies, and as a way to automate new sets of activities. Less common were respondents with a vertical emphasis who pointed out how BPM is spreading from its core concerns with improving basic business practices, and was being used by government and even international agencies as a way of defining and standardizing approaches to health, to international development, or responding to emergencies. Whatever you emphasize, our authors suggest that BPM holds out a growing hope to a wide variety of possible users.

....

DR. WASANA BANDARA

Senior Lecturer, Queensland University of Technology

BPM can (and should) be applied beyond commercial settings where profit is a focus, to now also address key global challenges, and point to a new area of focus for the BPM discipline: BPM for Development (BPM4Dev).

A clarification of what the term 'development' means is first warranted, for it can have a wide range of conceptions. Economic, political, and/or social level development has long been the focus of many authors and institutions.[1] Environmental issues have also gained massively increased focus with the growing interest of 'sustainable' development: "development which meets the needs of the present without compromising the ability of future generations to meet their own needs."[2] These issues are not limited to developing countries, but are an important focus for the developed world too: "today the wealthy world spends around a third of its income on internal poverty relief".[3]

An understanding of development priorities can help with identifying BPM's potential in supporting these initiatives. While priorities can be diverse, reviewing a sample of popular frameworks,[4] a common thread is observed across the themes of: economic growth and poverty reduction; quality education and access to educational services; access to high-quality health services; equality and inclusion; environmental protection; global integration and partnership.

A country's economic growth and poverty reduction efforts depend heavily on a well-functioning trading system; where (innovation driven) product and services from private sector and efficient administration support from the public sector play a major role.[5] These are both existing core focus areas of BPM. While the private sector is already applying BPM for efficient processes, the public sector (especially in developing nations) is lagging behind with many process issues across all layers of government. An efficiency government system will have significant impact on overall economic and social growth factors in a country, especially with its contributions to B2G, G2B, C2G and G2C services.[6] Innovative BPM efforts in government assist to crowd out the private and non-government sectors for activities (that they may be more capable of providing) to provide sustainable interventions to improve the wellbeing of the communities.[7] Transparency (one of the most fundamental values that BPM brings) can also play a major role in controlling corruption,[8] a well-known impediment to growth in many developing contexts.[9]

Quality education and access to educational services relates to better and equitable access to quality education. Education is paramount for sustainable development, as it provides the essential capabilities to build all other development efforts upon. BPM can be applied in the education sector[10] to improve sector-wide quality and service; for example, to establish procedures to ensure quality and equity of education (i.e. with nationwide standardized teaching practices) and promote continuous evaluation. Furthermore, the current BPM body-of-knowledge can be embedded into the training and development curricula of other sectors to promote improvement and innovation.

Access to high-quality health services encapsulates the provisioning of quality, equitable and accessible health services, with the aims of reduced mortality rates, disease control, and prevention management. BPM is already a well-established practice in the health sector in the developed-country context. It been applied to: (i) enforce standard and compliant processes to reduce errors (i.e. for patient safety); (ii) reduce waste within processes (i.e. wait time, inventory, and resources); (iii) monitor, predict, and improve care processes in real-time (and not post-patients' treatment); and (iv) automate non–value-added administrative tasks (i.e. scheduling, capturing quality, and compliance metrics) allowing clinicians to focus on patient care and to reduce administrative paperwork.[11]

The increased level of transparency and compliance that BPM brings can be applied to create more democratic processes and, when relevant, offer unique process variants to cater for the special needs of the underprivileged and support equality and inclusion.

Environmental protection is primarily concerned with reversing the loss of environmental resources for ecological sustainability. Processes can be redesigned to make dramatic reductions in the use of resources, and contribute to the efficient utilization of scarce resources.[12]

BPM can provide support to establish global integration and partnership with standardized and effective processes to interact and collaborate. BPM can play a valued role in forming global networks for development, coordinating support efforts across regions, and engaging multiple stakeholders (i.e. private and public sector, NGOs, local communities) to create multilateral organisms of cooperation and value creation for the underprivileged.

Discussions of BPM's potential for the developing context has already commenced, describing its value and necessity in developing nations,[13, 14] and BPM's role for global sustainable development.[15]

Case studies demonstrating the power of process improvement and innovations for development are sprouting. Supply chain process innovations to deliver access to basic human needs—such as food, water and medical treatment in the developing context—is an example of this. The portable water supply model known as the 'Community Mixed Water Supply' (CMWS) in Dhaka, Bangladesh, is an example of such. The majority of people living in the large cities of developing countries are poor and lack access to clean water. Sometimes, the reasons are not the physical availability of water, as many cities in developing countries are in areas of heavy rainfall or close to rivers. The CMWS integrates available local water resources, local communities, and complementary actors (such as NGOs, civil societies, government and private sector) to a single water supply process, which manages water as an economic and social good, while adhering to institutional and political rules and regulations. The CMWS addresses the immediate problem of inadequate water supply and the development of a long-term supply, and demonstrates how profitable private sector engagement can be utilized to empower poor local communities and support the access to basic human needs, such as water, food, and shelter.[16]

Process management is also gaining popularity in humanitarian relief chains to better streamline: time consuming processes (i.e. bidding, customs clearance); relief supplies applied through in-kind donations (usually after a disaster occurs—which can congest the relief chain, particularly if unsolicited); and transportation capacity management of large shipments.[17, 18] The 'Sahana' (meaning 'relief') project, developed by the Sahana Software Foundation of Sri Lanka (now deployed across the globe), is an excellent example of technology-driven improvements in humanitarian relief processes. They develop free and open source software, and provide services that help solve concrete problems and bring efficiencies to disaster response coordination between governments, aid organizations, civil society, and the survivors themselves.[19]

Another compelling example is the 'Narayana Hrudayalaya' hospitals in India, which standardized complicated heart procedures (one of the most complicated and expensive medical procedures) enabling the health system to serve a high volume of patients while maintaining high-quality standards.[20] The founder, Dr Devi Shetty, who believed that "poor people in isolation are weak but together they are very strong," leveraged economies of scale to provide affordable healthcare, proving that "you don't need to be rich to avail healthcare." The Wall Street Journal has given him the title of the 'Henry Ford of heart surgery.'[21]

Though BPM's role (or even 'duty') for development is apparent, likely challenges also need to be recognized. All trials we currently face in our discipline (some questioned by this book) will remain, and those more specific to the developing domain will arise. One is the mere notion of 'BPM'. Due to cultural differences and lack of awareness, BPM can be perceived by many as only a developed world concept and less suited for the Third World. People used to current (thus far, unchallenged) systems and organization hierarchies that have functioned for years in these developing nations are very likely to resist change and reject the BPM mindset.

Another reason could be the lack of forces to drive BPM in the developing world; especially the appropriate BPM capabilities and leadership.[22] While digitally disruptive processes are creating a new wave of process innovations, and technology can indeed be an enabler for poverty reduction,[23] developing nations may not have the infrastructure to support some technologies. And as we have already experienced, systems solutions that fail to underpin a deep(er) understanding and appreciation for the underlying processes are bound to be unsuccessful.

Despite these challenges, BPM in the developing context can open new opportunities for practitioners, consultants, educators, researchers, and BPM adopters/users (in this case the stakeholders in the developing nations), with new directions. For example, to succeed with BPM in a developing country context may require higher macro level BPM capabilities beyond firm (or even inter-firm) level (that we have to date), opening new opportunities for BPM capability building in a different magnitude. Concepts of 'reverse innovation' (an innovation seen first, or likely to be used first, in the developing world before spreading to the industrialized world),[24] 'constraint-based innovation' (innovation that relies on creative improvisation rather than scientific and technological breakthroughs),[25] and/or those that focus on what the poor have—in terms of tangible assets (e.g. labor) and non-tangible assets (e.g. house-hold relations and social capital)—rather than what they do not have, could create new strides in BPM innovations of the future.

References

[1] Such as the World Bank, Asia Development Bank (ADB), Inter-American Development Bank (IDB), UNESCO, and the Organization for Economic Co-operation and Development (OECD), to name a few.

[2] For example UNESCO's Millenium Development Goals (MDGs) Saith, A., From Universal Values to Millennium Development Goals: Lost in Translation. Development and Change, 2006. 37: p.1167–1199, Sida's Global intervention prioritization

Swedish International Development Corporation Agency (Sida). Global Development Interventions. 2012; Available from: http://www.sida.se/English/where-we-work/Global-development-interventions/

World Bank's framework for successful development World Bank. About Development. Available from: http://go.worldbank.org/N174APV2T0.

[3] For instance, the establishing a good procurement process with supporting policy mandating to comply with it, will discourage bribery corruptions. IT-enabled process improvements further increase transparency.

[4] Brundtland, G.H., Our Common Future: Report of the World Commission on Environment and Development. 1987, Oxford.

[5] The Challenge Network. Factors affecting economic and social development. Available from: http://www.chforum.org/library/xc123.shtml.

[6] Saith, A., From Universal Values to Millennium Development Goals: Lost in Translation. Development and Change, 2006. 37: p.1167–1199.

[7] Swedish International Development Corporation Agency (Sida). Global

Development Interventions. 2012; Available from: http://www.sida.se/English/where-we-work/Global-development-interventions/.

[8] World Bank. About Development. Available from: http://go.worldbank.org/N174APV2T0.

[9] Dethier, J.J., M. Hirn, and S. Straub, Explaining Enterprise Performance in Developing Countries with Business Climate Survey Data. World Bank Re-search Observer, 2011. 26(2): p.258-309.

[10] Dubey, S.K. and S. Bansal, Critical Success Factors in Implementing BPR in a Government Manufacturing Uni—An Empirical Study. International Journal of Business and Management, 2013. 8(2): p.17.

[11] National Commission of Audit. What should governments do? [cited 2015 Aug 9]; Available from: http://www.ncoa.gov.au/report/phase-one/part-a/2-2-what-should-governments-do.html.

[12] Bardhan, P., Corruption and Development: A Review of Issues. Journal of Economic Literature, 1997. 35(3): p.1320–1346.

[13] Medosh, M., Getting the Faculty ready for growth through process improvement, in Tertiary Education Management Conference (TEMC), I. Dobson, R. Sharma, and M. Conway, Editors. 2013: Hobart, Australia.

[14] Kemsley, S. Business Process Management in Health Care. Available from: http://www.fortherecordmag.com/news/100314_exclusive.shtml.

[15] Watson, R., Preface, in Green Business Process Management: Towards the Sustainable Enterprise, J.v. Brocke, S. Seidel, and J. Recker, Editors. 2012, Springer: Berlin, Heidelberg.

[16] Isaksson, R. and H. Wiklund, On the use of process management in the Third World. Total Quality Management, 2002. 13(4): p.419–426.

[17] Bandara, W., et al. Building essential BPM capabilities to assist successful ICT deployment in the developing context: observations and recommendations from Sri Lanka, in SIG GlobDev Fifth Annual Workshop. 2012. Orlando, Florida, The United States of America: Association of Information Systems.

[18] Brocke, J.v., S. Seidel, and J. Recker, Green Business Process Management: Towards the Sustainable Enterprise. 2012, Berlin, Heidelberg: Springer.

[19] Akbar, H.M.D., et al., Community water supply for the urban poor in developing countries: The case of Dhaka, Bangladesh. Habitat International, 2007. 31(1):

p.24–35.

[20] Balcik, B., et al., Coordination in humanitarian relief chains: Practices, challenges and opportunities. International Journal of Production Economics, 2010. 126(1): p.22–34.

[21] Peterken, H. and W. Bandara, Business Process Management in International Humanitarian Aid, in Handbook on Business Process Management 2, J.v. Brocke and M. Rosemann, Editors. 2014, Springer: Berlin, Heidelberg. p.761–786.

[22] Sahana Software Foundation. SAHANA. Available from: http://sahanafoundation.org/about-us/

[23] PricewaterhouseCoopers - PWC. Global healthcare case studies and best practices. Global healthcare case studies and best practices: Process Improvements in Hospitals [cited 2015 Aug 2nd]; Available from: http://www.pwc.com/gx/en/healthcare/bending-the-cost-curve/index.jhtml.

[24] sociovigil.in. Dr. Devi Shetty—The Henry Ford of Heart Surgery. 2013 [cited 2015 Aug 2nd]; Available from: http://sociovigil.in/dr-devi-shetty-the-henry-ford-of-heart-surgery/.

[25] Urquhart, C., S. Liyanage, and M.M. Kah, ICTs and poverty reduction: a social capital and knowledge perspective. Journal of Information Technology, 2008. 23(3): p.203–213.

[26] Govindarajan, V., Reverse innovation: create far from home, win everywhere. 2012: Harvard Business Review Press

[27] Thompson, L., Less is more: Emerging economies as innovators. Organization for Economic Cooperation and Development. The OECD Observer, 2013(297): p.28.

[28] Moser, C.O.N., The asset vulnerability framework: Reassessing urban poverty reduction strategies. World Development, 1998. 26(1): p.1–19.

Acknowledgements

I'd like to thank Mr Rehan Syed, Mr Danny Morales Rubio and Ms Kanika Goel, who are conducting dedicated studies on process management efforts in the developing contexts and whose work has contributed to this paper.

MELISSA DOHERTY

Process and Innovation Manager, Brisbane City Council

To many, not much appears to have changed with BPM in the many years that the practice has been formalized. To me, even over the last 15 years, much has changed in the BPM landscape. Perhaps that's just how I view BPM as a practitioner and represents my increasing capabilities in this practice. Perhaps I see the evolution of technologies to support BPM as the catalyst that keeps moving us forward.

I do recall sitting in a conference, perhaps five years ago, with an experienced c-level executive who had been in the workforce for the best part of forty years. They made the comment to me that BPM was nothing new; it was the same stuff they'd seen for decades, just packaged in a different way. A fair point?

There certainly seem to be many different perspectives of what the practice of BPM is about. Clearly different parts of an organization expect different outcomes from BPM programs. The 'strategy people' want to know that a project is going to align with over-arching organization objectives; the 'change management group' want to be assured that a change will be successfully embedded; the 'IT group' want to assure you're aligning to their architecture; and 'the HR people' want to be assured that the affects to people in the organization are understood. And that's the tip of the iceberg—nothing is ever quite that simple. Sometimes, these different areas don't understand why you're interested in their domains at all! Why do these BPM people want to learn about our business? Who do these BPM people think they are?

Navigating through these expectations, particularly if they all converge on one project, can be difficult. I find it very strange that, as a practice, BPM still has not quite worked out its identity. We talk about BPM being a management practice—but if we can't define ourselves consistently is there any chance of this being taken seriously? Or is this to the BPM practices' benefit? Is it a bonus that we can be whomever it is we need to be?

The most common definitions and approaches of BPM certainly seem to still be in the incremental improvement sphere: Lean and Six Sigma, and BPI, as well as the usual expectation that BPM is all about 'workflow'. I can't be the only BPM practitioner who is regularly reminded how far the BPM practice has come when I have to explain that there's more to BPM than a picture of a workflow diagram.

The reality, though, is that BPI projects make up the bread and butter of BPM work. And this continues to be an area of big interest, especially when the objectives of enterprise process management, process governance, and embedding BPM through an organization can be seen as too ambitious an objective.

The differing expectations of what BPM can deliver certainly give the practice more areas of impact and influence. The significant areas of interest, certainly in my experience at present, are in the following areas:

- BPM to maximize the value of technology investments.
- BPM as a means to deliver automation and innovation.
- BPM driving to remove silos, improve collaboration and integration.

I have also been heartened by the increasing interest in managing the performance of process. The desire to track process performance to targets, and the need to be able to report and ensure processes are meeting business outcomes in a business-as-usual environment. This is encouraging, as it's my belief that BPM being embedded into an organization in this way will do nothing but improve the ability to deliver innovative change and improvements. It also is the way to demonstrate continued value from BPM investments and to ensure the embedding of process change programs.

There also seems to be continued interest in the integration of BPM with other practices, including change management and enterprise architecture. There certainly is some overlap between these practices—even confusion where each of these practices stops and another starts. But this is exciting, and certainly a big step forward to achieving a holistic approach to BPM and it finding its place as a management practice that is integrated into an organization.

A question that should be asked, however, is whether BPM is branching too far into the domains of other practices. Are we perhaps, as BPM practitioners, our own worst enemy? We are in the business of efficiency and improvement. By nature we're always looking for innovation and change; it makes sense that we continue to do the same in our own field of expertise.

I do believe, however, that the continued pushing of boundaries in the BPM practice, the emphasis on collaboration and building organization maturity as a whole, brings nothing but positive outcomes to an organization. A better understanding, not just of what we all contribute to a process, but of how different practices can contribute to improve it and organization outcomes is a great thing. BPM, if nothing else, has the capability to bring all the elements of an organization together.

....

ANDREAS HAVLIZA
Consulting Principal, Team Leader, Leonardo Consulting

INDRAJIT DATTA CHAUDHURI
Senior Consultant, Leonardo Consulting

CLEMENT HURPIN
Consultant, Leonardo Consulting

The current interest for BPM is strong and it should rise more and more in the years to come. The process idea has come a long way; it is now widely accepted by management science (as proven by countless papers and dedicated university departments) as well as industry. As mentioned in the Harvard Business Review,[1] "the question for top management is no longer whether your organization's processes need to be improved, but rather which ones, how much, and when." The interest for BPM rises as it appears to be a viable answer to the challenges organizations are facing these days.

Major challenge faced by organizations number 1: complexity. With more software available, with more off-shoring, more suppliers, more revenue streams, more platforms, etc., the average organizational landscape has drastically changed in the past decade, and not necessarily for the simpler. For example, with more technologies from different vendors, one may be in need of more integration and/or customization.

Facing that challenge, organizations turn to BPM and, through this approach, it is possible to highlight where products and services come from and where they should go; it can identify where the issues are and actions can be triggered. In the case of a process requiring multiple stakeholders with multiple hand-offs, BPM seems like a good way to handle the complexity. The process can be modeled from end-to-end and gaps, risks, and opportunities can be identified, and then presented to decision-makers in an easily-understood manner. BPM can be a truly efficient weapon against complexity.

Major challenge faced by organizations number 2: the rise of data. Data is everywhere—on phones, laptops, and tablets—being relentlessly produced by ourselves. Data has come from being an edge over the competition, to a necessity. If not collected and used, chances are companies will face big problems in the not-so-long run. But data itself is not enough; it needs to be contextualized data. This is where BPM is of interest. Data can be put in the context of a process—where the data is collected, where it is used—which provides many benefits: a simple way to understand the data; a basis for process improvement; a better use of the data to drive performance, et cetera. With the rise of data mining, we have seen the emergence of process mining, a very interesting subset of it, giving much welcome insights on the behavior of processes. BPM is again in the spotlight because of its potential to leverage the collected data.

Major challenge faced by organizations number 3: flexibility. Companies today must be able to make process changes in days or weeks, not months or years. With an ever faster changing environment, companies must change, and change fast. The product development cycles (build to market) are now dramatically reduced, and customers expect their orders to be fulfilled within the week. In this case, companies turn more and more to process. With well-structured process improvement projects, major process changes can be achieved within a very short period—looking at weeks, not months. This flexibility also allows for a more opportunity-based change,[2] where the trigger for change is not pain, but opportunity.

More than ever, BPM can be seen as a holistic view of the organization—the functional departments are no longer the only way. BPM has taken boardroom meetings by surprise and can now be used as a strategy enabler. The time of local optimization is over; change can happen at every level, big and small.

So, what drives BPM these days to overcome the challenges pointed out above? It's worthwhile looking at recent BPM engagements with similar underlying drivers. WA industry is highly resource-driven—with the big mining and oil and gas companies all being active in WA's north—and there are three major drivers for BPM in Western Australia these days:

THE FIRST DRIVER is the need to support cost-cutting exercises. With most commodity prices falling, there is a huge demand to reduce operational costs and to optimize workflows. The overarching goal is to be able to produce more with less. Two ways this optimization is being achieved can be recognized:

- The first is the classic, process optimization. Projects are created in order to optimize process flows. The concentration is on time and involved resources. Both areas are targeted to be reduced. In these projects, processes are optimized and are supposed to stay in-house. There is no appetite to outsource the process (for various reasons). The only goal is to reduce time and resources being consumed by the process in focus.

- The other way to achieve a reduction in overall costs is to make use of outsourcing. The outsourcing of processes. To be able to outsource processes, organizations are aware that they have to be packaged in some way or no efficient outsourcing would be possible. The packaging includes process standardization; variants of processes are standardized and streamlined before being outsourced to low-cost countries. Dependent on the BPM maturity within an organization, these activities are either part of an enterprise-wide BPM strategy—but, more often than not, it can be discovered that an ongoing BPM strategy is not necessarily in focus. Business Process Management is often understood as a tool to get somewhere, but not fully understood and recognized as a management discipline. It follows that an interest in BPM is indeed given but, unfortunately, often only because of a very special need—in this case, the vehicle to achieve a reduction in costs.

THE SECOND DRIVER of Business Process Management is the requirement to document processes (for various reasons), such as compliance demands, or the simple need to capture an as-is process in order to optimize it. More often than not these process documentations are, unfortunately, just a one-off modeling exercise and not really part of an organization-wide BPM strategy. They are an important step of improvement, but do not, by themselves, result in better performance. All those programs to model the world do not provide any satisfactory return on investment.

But it can be observed that more and more organizations are leaving this path and do see BPM in a more holistic way—sometimes because they themselves have discovered that one-off exercises aren't sustainable and do not avoid rework (costs!) at a later stage. These organizations have become aware of the fact that a BPM framework is required to make BPM activities sustainable. The aspect 'change', which is often the driver for BPM activities, must be accompanied by aspects like architecture, governance, change, measurement, and ongoing support to achieve positive results based on BPM in the long term.

THE THIRD DRIVER OF BPM is the need for automation. Although BPM is a management method, many companies consider process discovery, modeling, and analysis as a pre-work for automation. When process modeling is done only for automation without much consideration to the bigger picture in the context of the entire organization, there is a risk of automating a sub-optimized process only to do wrong things faster. However, when done in the context of entire organization, and taking steps to optimize the entire end-to-end process, automation can add significant value to the operations.

References

[1] https://hbr.org/2012/10/when-it-comes-to-operational

[2] https://hbr.org/2012/03/look-to-it-for-process-innovation

....

ERIC HERNESS

CTO & Chief Architect (BPM), IBM

The current interest in BPM remains diverse and quite widespread across many industries. The benefits of BPM also remain pretty consistent if we look at them from a high level and from a business perspective. Within the details, there are certainly some changes going on that are driven by business climate and technology evolution.

While the interest in BPM changes shape over time, the core benefits continue to be largely the same. How those benefits are derived is evolving, however.

INTEREST IN BPM APPROACH

It remains the situation that organizations have two general sources of interest in BPM. The first is the IT organization, where they think about process automation and are obviously influenced a lot by the technology. They are interested in BPM because of the kinds of requirements they are getting from their business stakeholders. As those requirements trend towards needing visibility to processes, ongoing process improvements and increased rates of change, the BPM technologies available today—via BPMS and BRMS offerings—become appealing and, in fact, cost effective from an IT standpoint.

The second source of interest comes from the business strategy and business operations part of an organization. These efforts are focused on understanding and improving the business itself, and processes become a means to that end. This constituency has many new things to think about in the world of business. The twenty-first century business is much more dynamic and involves more and more participants that are not a part of the classic organizational structure. Suppliers, partners, marketers and other business relationships are the norm when looking at modern value chains and the processes that make them go.

TRADITIONAL VISIBILITY REMAINS IN DEMAND

Visibility is a classic benefit of the BPM approach. Organizations are continuing to benefit from this type of visibility. The conceptual idea of seeing the business run through dashboards that show the process and status of key business transactions will always deliver value. Proper visibility can deliver value to business stakeholders managing individuals as well as teams, and visibility can also provide value to those taking a broader look at how processes contribute to value chains and strategic business objectives.

Another interesting observation I have seen on visibility starts with the IT constituency. In IT-driven process automation projects, visibility is often placed second in priority to getting a process automated and executed in a BPMS. An interesting phenomenon I have seen here is where business stakeholders are now compelled to see what is going on with these processes. To that end, I see IT organizations being asked to provide exports of data to common formats to allow business stakeholders to roll their own visibility. I take from this a couple of things. First, automating processes becomes a catalyst for further understanding by business and, thus, is value delivered by BPM.

Second, perhaps it is time to re-evaluate and re-invigorate industry efforts around BAM (business activity monitoring) and the role it should have in an overall BPMS. We sit here today, in the era of big data, and have access to a lot more technology that we can leverage to slice, dice and evaluate data to provide business with not only better visibility, but also new insights. More benefits from the BPM approach are contained within this idea of providing further visibility.

NEW INSIGHTS ARE SOUGHT AFTER

Meanwhile, while this more longstanding and traditional visibility quest is going on at some organizations, others are moving beyond visibility, in the traditional sense, and looking for much more pro-active notification of interesting changes in process behavior. Mobile device ubiquity among business stakeholders becomes the platform for this. These stakeholders might pull information in various forms for viewing and understanding what is going on with the process in which they are interested. Mobile footprints demand that this is done in a more creative presentation style.

More importantly, those mobile users want exceptions and threshold breaches to be pushed to them. The mobile technology platforms are making this easier with each turn of the technology crank. This actually improves the value of BPM to business, and creates more active and precise feedback for further improvement. Mobile is an accelerator to the BPM value story.

IT AS CHANGE AGENT FOR BUSINESS

Another interesting benefit from the BPM approach I have seen is an IT initiated conversation with business about how well processes are designed. Let me explain in more detail. An IT-led process automation project occurs to support some business stakeholders. Those business stakeholders will embrace the system and begin leveraging it. Growing pains often occur with the underlying technology platform, as organizations embrace the new system and IT teams figure out how to tune and manage the platform. That all sounds normal.

In some situations, the IT organization realizes that no end of tuning the IT system can support the way that the business is currently operating. Maybe it is queries for work assignments that are just too complex to process efficiently. Maybe it is integrations to systems that are just not capable of providing the right information back to the business process participant. In reality, the real problem is that sometimes the business process itself is extremely convoluted or inefficient and, thus, the IT materialization of that process also suffers. Brave IT executives then can step forward and suggest process improvements are the best way forward, not only from an IT automation perspective, but also for the business. Picking up on the example above, this could mean restructuring work assignment and teams or reevaluating existing systems and applications that are being used to support the end-to-end process.

The good news is that there is a stronger set of technology available to enable and support that type of business change.

FINAL WORD

Organizations continue to benefit from the BPM approach. New ways of benefiting are being demanded by business. This is due, in part, to the speed of business, the nature of the business organization, and diversity of process participants. The evolution of the technology platform that supports BPM offers ways to address these new opportunities. The technical platform also, through technologies like mobile, offers additional possibilities. These are exciting times to be in a business role and engaging with modern BPMS-enabled business processes.

....

GILLES MORIN

Founder, BPMPlus, Inc.

I have been promoting BPM and educating clients, partners and colleagues in my part of the world for the past six years. I have to say that at the beginning, the market was not receptive. I have noticed a major shift in interest over the past three years. Here are examples of the new signals I have from the market:

- Lean niched consulting firms are being asked about BPM by their clients.
- BPM is still confused with BPMS, but BPMS and case management are getting more traction, and are strong BPM demands catalysts.
- The acquisition of architectural tools like Casewise, and Sparx Enterprise Architect leads to BPM awareness.
- The words transformation, customer experience, digitalization, process, and BPM are used more and more in the same sentence!
- Public sectors leaders are now seriously looking at intelligent BPM platforms and case management solutions as a way out of legacy processes, systems and thinking.
- Quite a few organizations are still caught in the 'get your unit costs down' mood—yet, a few leading ones are starting to inquire about BPM and customer experience after several failed attempts to tackle CeX.
- The word processes is regularly on decision-makers' minds. They ALL face overwhelming challenges and are looking for more efficient and effective ways to take them on.

So, what drives these new interests, beside technology vendors' sales pitches? In fact, the simplistic answer is it depends if you are 'vision driven' or 'pain driven'. Let's be frank, most organizations are pain- and short-term driven. I would venture to say that, at most, one organization in ten is vision driven. The "boss wants it" is probably the most powerful driver—and the simplest! Unfortunately, we are not all that lucky.

In pain-driven organizations, financial drivers dominate—followed closely by technology drivers and, lastly, market and customer drivers. I have to say that within the financial services industry, the 'customer experience hype' is picking up. Here are some common drivers:

- Lean has migrated from the manufacturing world to the service world—putting processes to the forefront of the lever to deliver value. Service industry managers use Lean as a way to kill waste (cut costs) and to refocus key resources on value creation. They have been progressing along that route for years and realize that they are missing key capabilities to continue their value-creation pattern—governance, end-to-end improvement, reuse patterns, capabilities management (e.g. Burlton's Hexagon), etc.
- Repeating budget cuts and resource crunches, compounded by accelerated knowledge-workers retirement and diminishing IT budgets, stretch organizations thin and force leaders to think outside the box and realize that they should have documented their knowledge-based processes.
- Business leaders wanting to get out of the 'death by a thousand cuts' or 'siloed' behaviors.
- CIOs have identified 'lack of process knowledge' as one of the top barriers for them to deliver better value, and are facilitating BPM program incubation.
- Board members, citizens, owners are putting more pressure on service delivery organizations to not only lower their costs, but also to increase quality of service, value creation and customer experience. Linear thinking in such a high-pressure context is simply not working!
- Decision-makers and leaders are starting to realize that IT and making changes to their organigram ARE NOT the answer to all business performance problems. BPM is seen as a way to leapfrog your way out of legacy thinking!
- Benefits at stake are high along the process route—minimum performance gains of the order of 20–30% are common and well documented, giving credibility to BPM.
- Technology has evolved and is being democratized. Technology is shifting from an IT focus to business—and business is starting to

notice it and expect different answers from IT. The vendors 'siren song' is more appealing than ever!

- Most public organizations and mature insurance industry players struggle with obsolete mission-critical applications and legacy processes. Business architecture is seen as a way to make new IT execution strategy less risky and to increase value delivery.

A growing interest in BPM will continue to rise, fueled by the alignment of red novae like IoT, cloud, Mobile, Big Data, social media, software manufacturing applied to services—and this is not a fad! Brace yourself for more pressure to think, act on and deliver value differently!

....

PROFESSOR MICHAEL ROSEMANN

Head of Information Systems School, Queensland University of Technology

Current BPM is going beyond a focus on operational efficiency, the center of attention for most of the first wave BPM approaches. Of course, gaining from incremental improvements and further streamlining business processes in search of cost savings will always be of interest to organizations and a long-lasting driver for BPM. However, in an age when digitization, and not automation, provides new forms of value for the customer, BPM would be underutilized if operational efficiency were its only contribution to organizational performance.

The digital economy has empowered citizens with the provision of intuitive, personalized, and hyper-connected technologies and applications. This has not only enabled the integration of citizens into extended corporate value chains but, even more, allowed citizens to become co-designers, and valuable resource providers (e.g. Airbnb, Uber), in new emerging digital value chains.

As a consequence, organizations increasingly explore how BPM can help them to understand and design such citizen-centered processes. In such processes, the traditional focus of BPM (i.e. having business processes with a number of customer touch-points) is flipped around. Instead, such digitized, citizen-centered processes are capturing end-to-end customer experiences covering multiple providers. Corporate touch-points are activities along this process where companies have an opportunity to enrich such processes.

Obviously, this current interest in BPM has a much stronger outside-in perspective and is grounded in a view of how corporations can take part in these customer processes. This view is complemented by the first set of systems—such as digital identity solutions, or vendor relationship management systems—which truly put the citizen, and not the corporation, at the core of the analysis.

In light of these developments, BPM provides tremendous value as it sensitizes the organization for the context during which its services and processes are consumed. It facilitates the up-stream and down-stream expansion of services along business processes. Moreover, such a citizen-centered view on business processes facilitates the identification of additional touch-points. An example is Tesco's virtual store in South Korea. Here, identifying customers' idle time while waiting at subway stations triggered the idea of virtual walls featuring frequently sold items that can simply be ordered via a QR-code based app. A narrow, classic process view restricted to the boundaries of the organization would have not allowed this opportunity to be identified.

....

PROFESSOR JAN VOM BROCKE

Hilti Chair of Business Process Management, University of Liechtenstein

During the past decades, BPM has proven largely supportive of productivity growth and efficiency improvement. However, most of today's organizations are increasingly concerned about keeping up with digital transformation. While digital innovation offers huge business potentials, it also challenges organizations to master substantive and partly disruptive changes. Against this background, current interest in BPM increasingly focuses on how BPM can help organizations to increase their innovation capabilities. The figure below illustrates both 'modi' of BPM, to improve and to innovate.

AMBIDEXTROUS BPM

It is timely to question if the BPM tools we have developed are sufficient to address contemporary organizational and societal problems. In particular, the current set of BPM capabilities need to be enhanced to capitalize on fast emerging digital affordances (Schmiedel & vom Brocke, 2015). BPM needs to further develop its conceptual and methodological basis to focus stronger on exploration in addition to its rich set of exploitative, problem-driven capabilities, also referred to as 'ambidextrous BPM' (Rosemann, 2014).

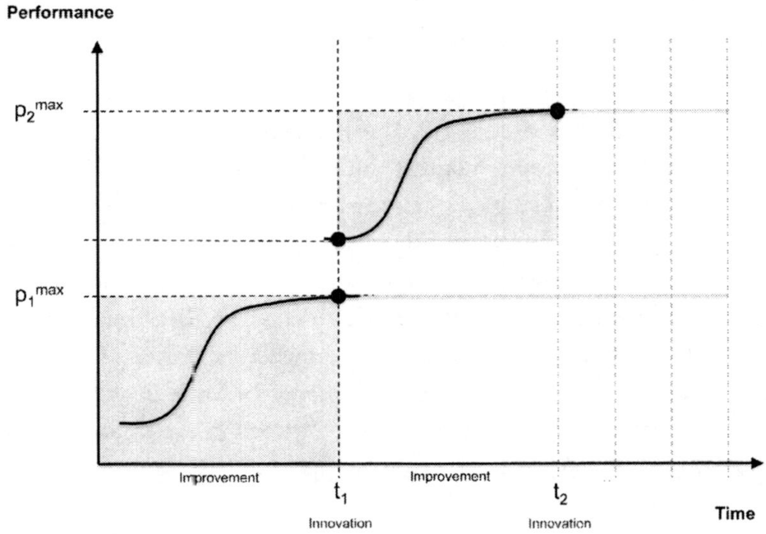

Figure 7: Improvement and innovation in BPM (vom Brocke & Rosemann, 2014)

Contemporary BPM combines both perspectives: exploitation aiming for improvement and exploitation aiming for innovation. Given a certain technological frame, BPM provides an integrated set of methods, tools, and techniques to continuously improve business processes in order to meet business targets (process effectiveness) in the most economical way (process efficiency).

The technological frame, however, sets the boundaries (viz., a logical limit) for improvements (referred to as p1max in Figure 7 above). To increase performance beyond this point, new technology can afford radical process change. Such technology is referred to as 'disruptive technology' (Bower & Christensen, 1995), and information systems to date have particularly proven to be a facilitator of process innovation (Markus & Silver, 1995). BPM also concerns identifying and evaluating the action possibilities originating from existent or new technologies, so as to capitalize on affordances that emerge in relation between systems, users, and the context in which information systems are used (Leonardi, 2011). As changes in technology and processes create new risks, BPM also requires us to evaluate alternative process designs and decide upon the right time to implement the next innovation.

This view of BPM is in line with the two roots and objectives of BPM as outlined by Hammer (2010): process improvement, and process re-engineering. While the continuous improvement and management of existing processes will remain highly important, the focus will shift to reacting to and resolving existing process shortcomings. Exploitation relates to more efficient and effective better use and, typically, incremental change by utilizing tools, management approaches, and techniques within the well-defined set of process boundaries. Such a view, however, neglects the exploration potential of BPM. Exploration-oriented BPM operates under the paradigm of innovation of processes, services, products, and business models by applying techniques of creative and abductive thinking, design, and communication (vom Brocke et al., 2015).

MULTI-DEXTROUS BPM

Apart from improvement and innovation, several organizations value BPM as a means to foster regulatory compliance, business continuity, risk mitigation, and sustainability, among others. Against this background, there are even more than the two objectives of improvement and innovation—so we may need to prepare for a 'multi-dextrous approach to BPM' research and practice, which I would like to propose here.

The potential BPM can offer for organizations is to build capabilities to better understand and further develop their processes, and this potential can serve multiple purposes. Even in one organization, such purposes can considerably differ between business areas, and they do change over time. BPM therefore needs to be sensitive towards different organizational objectives (vom Brocke et al. 2016), and following a multi-dextrous understanding, their identification is an essential first step of every BPM initiative (vom Brocke et al. 2014). In multi-dextrous BPM, identifying the purpose of BPM, and adjusting its scope and objectives accordingly, is an integral BPM capability, also referred to as strategic alignment (vom Brocke, Rosemann, 2015).

Against this background, we need to better understand which of the BPM tools can suit which purpose. Also, further tools need to be developed to complement the BPM body of knowledge to support today's organizations.

References

Bower, J.L., Christensen, C.M. (1995). Disruptive Technologies: Catching the Wave, Harvard Business Review, January–February 1995

Leonardi, P.M., When Flexible Routines Meet Flexible Technologies: Affordance, Constraint, and the Imbrication of Human and Material Agencies, MIS Quarterly (35:1) 2011, pp.147–167.

Markus, M.L., and Silver, M.S. A Foundation for the Study of IT Effects: A New Look at DeSanctis and Poole's Concepts of Structural Features and Spirit, Journal of the Association for Information Systems (9:10) 2008, pp.609–632.

Rosemann, M. (2014). Proposals for Future Bpm Research Directions. In C. Ouyang and J.Y. Jung (Eds.), (Vol. 181, pp.1–15). Cham: Springer International Publishing.

Schmiedel, T., & vom Brocke, J. (2015). Business process management: Potentials and challenges of driving innovation. In J. vom Brocke & T. Schmiedel (Eds.), BPM - Driving Innovation in a Digital World (pp. 3-16). Heidelberg: Springer.

vom Brocke, J. Rosemann, M., (2014). Business Process Management. In: D. Straub, R. Welke, Wiley Encyclopedia of Management, Vol. 7, Management Information Systems. 3rd Ed., 2014.

vom Brocke, J., Seidel, S., Tumbas, S (2015). The BPM curriculum revisited. BPTrends, Class Notes April 2015, 1–7.

vom Brocke, J., Zelt, S., Schmiedel, T. (2016), On the Role of Context in Business Process Management, International Journal of Information Management, forthcoming

Womack, J.P.; Jones, D.T., Lean Thinking: Banish Waste and Create Wealth in Your Corporation. 2003.

QUESTION 3

IS BPM A STRATEGIC TOOL?

An organization exists to deliver on one or more value propositions that are often defined by statements of strategic intent (vision, mission, values and the like).

What role, if any, do you see BPM playing in the execution or achievement of an organization's strategy? To what extent is BPM valued by management as a strategic tool?

OVERVIEW

Taking the view of BPM as a management philosophy, our authors are in general agreement that it and organizational strategy are closely coupled. BPM approaches are generally seen as a toolset that underpins the execution of strategy. Business processes are seen to be a natural way of expressing the execution of strategy, and strategy failure is seen to reflect process failure. Several authors also express a more profound role for BPM in the discovery, testing, and documentation of strategic intent. If BPM is closely coupled to strategy, it cannot be successful if the strategy is deficient. A vague generic strategy cannot be mapped to business processes and, therefore, cannot be effectively managed. Taking a BPM approach forces clarity about strategy. It is also inherently customer-focused. Profound discussions result from the exercise of linking strategic intentions to their operationalization via business processes, from connecting the abstract to the practical. At this strategic level, our authors agree that BPM is a critical and fundamental organizational capability

••

TALAL A. ALSUBAIE

Managing Director, Modprex

It is not news that most strategies fail. The literature is full of such discussions and reasons for strategic failure. Rather than trying to answer the question of why strategy fails, I would like to describe a model that I developed with my colleagues Mr. Abdullah Alhaqbani, and Mr. Bassam Alkharashi. Our model proposes a new way of thinking about strategy execution using BPM as the main tool.

Most organizations aim to execute strategy through various projects and programs, with little focus on how processes affect strategic objectives. The figure below illustrates the new model we are proposing for the execution of strategy, which we believe is mainly achieved by three functions.

BPM is one of the main methodologies for the execution of strategy, and process performance directly affects strategic outcomes. Therefore, by improving organizational processes, you are improving your strategy. However, strategy should directly impact the priority of process improvement projects, taking into account what processes should be improved at present, what processes should be improved later, and what processes may not be improved at all. This type of prioritization cannot be achieved unless we link our strategic objectives to our value chains so that we are able to take a closer look at which value chains or processes are affecting our strategic objectives.

Innovation, on the other hand, helps to provide solutions to BPM challenges and problems. These solutions change the way processes operate, work to help obtain better results and, in the end, achieve strategic objectives. In addition, linking the strategy and objectives to the innovation architecture focuses the ideas that the organization generates on specific strategic themes that we call innovation zones. These zones bring together different ideas and suggestions from the organization's employees, customers, and stakeholders to change the organization's business model—for example, dramatically changing existing services, or even introducing new services or opportunities.

These new innovation ideas affect the way the organization operates by making some changes to its processes and value chains.

The project management office (PMO) helps the proper execution of initiatives and process-improvement projects. Most process improvement projects struggle with implementing the to-be processes. The PMO will play a major role in implementing change. Those to-be projects will impact IT, HR, and infrastructure, if needed. However, from the innovation side, PMO will have a list of initiatives and programs cascaded into projects changing the organization's as-is processes or adding new ones to fulfill the new services introduced by innovation zones.

Closing the gap and executing the strategy requires the collaboration of different departments and roles to achieve strategic objectives. Strategy prioritizes the process improvement projects, and defines the gap(s) we need to close between the as-is and to-be processes. In addition, strategy will guide the innovation zones to develop better ideas in targeted areas. Finally, the PMO assures the proper execution of the process improvement and the business transformation projects based on time, budget, and quality.

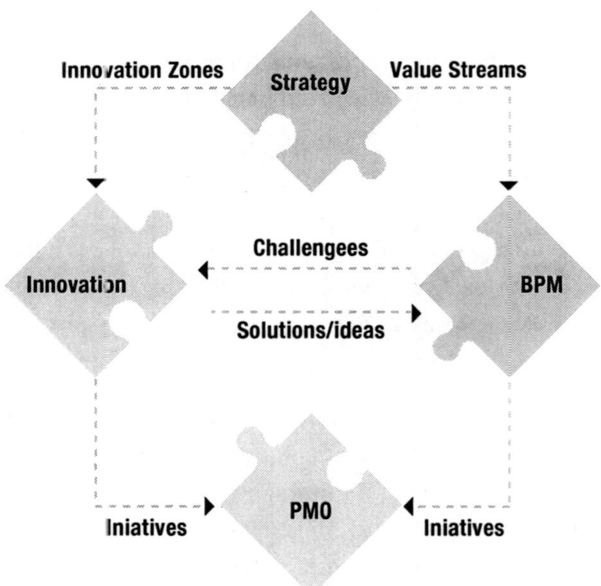

Figure 8: Executing strategy

JIM BOOTS

Owner, Global Process Innovation

Generally, BPM will not be on the nameplate of an organizational strategy or initiative. Rather, BPM is well suited to be the primary underpinning—the toolset, if you will—of an organizational strategy.

First, let's briefly consider what we mean by strategy by imagining what could have been strategy statements by well-known organizations that have achieved notable successes with their apparent strategies.

- Walmart's (apparent) strategy: Deliver the lowest prices on consumer goods (in part) by optimizing the supply chain and leveraging clout with suppliers.
- Apple's (apparent) strategy: Deliver high-end and exciting consumer electronics via consumer research, design innovation, and strict quality control across the supply chain.
- ExxonMobil's (apparent) strategy: Create the most efficient global refining system via strategic capital investments over a multi-decade period.

Whether or not any of these organizations explicitly adopted BPM to achieve their strategies is moot. But there is little doubt that process thinking and process management played a significant role in the execution of these strategies.

Let's take the Walmart example further. With a focus on the supply chain, where does process come into play? The discipline of supply chain management (SCM) is rife with processes ultimately designed for optimization. SCM processes include: inventory targeting; production and distribution planning; and sales and operations planning. Each of these processes requires a lot of data rigor and cross-functional coordination. Additionally, Walmart would have developed detailed processes for negotiating with suppliers, and sharing information and process expectations with them.

Similar cases for deep process thinking could be made for the Apple and ExxonMobil examples. Inevitably, there is a lot of process underneath most successful strategies. The real issue is whether an organization is going to commit to a robust approach in dealing with its processes—that is, a BPM approach. Too often, strategic failure results not from poor strategies, but from poor execution of strategies. In other words, strategic failure is most often a process problem.

Strategy, in essence, is the first step for going from *what* we want to achieve (i.e. objectives) to *how* we will achieve them. Without strategies for realization, objectives are just wishful thinking. Without processes, strategies are hollow shells with no substance.

Shifting gears a bit, let's consider an organization that has adopted a strategy of operational excellence (OE). OE evokes many appropriate desirable concepts such as: efficiency, reliability, product consistency, high equipment utilization, incident-free operations, and standardization. Does anyone seriously think these things can be achieved in a complex organization without careful attention to processes?

Publishing a strategy to the workforce is only the very beginning of a strategic effort. Management must continuously lead a discussion about how the strategy applies in every part of the organization. For example, OE applied to the manufacturing function can lead to a vast array of process-related activities such as:

- Carefully documenting start-up, shutdown, and routine operating procedures so hazards are avoided.
- Training and mentoring new personnel until they can prove their practical knowledge.
- Establishing measurement systems and analysis practices that uncover abnormal operations.
- Establishing behavioral and/or value-based reinforcement systems so employees are motivated to follow procedures.

Each of these has many process details in them. And, if disasters like the Challenger Space Shuttle, the BP Deepwater Horizon explosion and oil spill, or the 2008 Global Financial Crisis have taught us anything, it's that the devil is often in the details. It is only rigorous attention to processes where the details are properly addressed.

Unfortunately, many management teams do not reliably demonstrate the ability to push strategy down into operational details. They recognize the connection, but they either don't know how to operationalize strategy, or they don't have the fortitude to see it through until an initiative's elements are embedded in the organizational culture. So, the results are often inadequate. Execution of the strategy is a failure.

Typically, the management teams that 'get it' when it comes to seeing a strategy through to the point of sustainable advantage recognize that it will be a multi-year effort. Every incident, every performance issue, every missed operational target is looked at as an opportunity to make execution of the strategy more robust by building the principles of the strategy into the way the work gets done in the organization. If a manufacturing line fails, questions are asked: Why? What in the process specifically went wrong? Are there actions we can build into our operational practices to avoid this outcome next time? What specifically needs to change, and who needs to do it? What impacts will the change have beyond the immediate area, and have we addressed the consequences? Are there measures we can put in place to give us forewarning of a potential failure like the one we had? And so on.

The answers to these questions, when they come, must be embedded into the fabric of the organization. This is the real difference between good organizations and truly excellent ones. Good ones identify some needed changes and they cascade expectations about them. Truly excellent ones develop solutions supported by data, test changes for effectiveness, document changes in a universally accessible process architecture, train personnel in the new ways, reinforce critical behaviors, and ensure (e.g. through periodic audits or measurement) that the new strategy-aligned practices are the *modus operandi.*

These points are not exclusive to an operational excellence strategy. They apply to other strategies as well, such as technology leadership or customer intimacy. Employees at leading technology companies do not sit in a quiet room and wait for the next idea to occur to them. Rather, they create and use all kinds of processes associated with research, analysis, collaboration, prototyping, testing, scale-up, commercialization, intellectual property protection, etc.

There are either good or bad strategies and there are, distinctly, either good or bad executions of strategies. It should be clear that process management—whether or not it is called that by managers—is essential to good execution of strategies. Of course, BPM also can be applied to the creation of strategies. What is your organization's process for developing strategies? How do you know the process is an effective one?

If your management thinks strategy is important, then BPM also should be considered important. Without attention to processes, strategies are at risk of being poorly decided and badly executed.

....

ROGER BURLTON

President, Process Renewal Group

The challenge with this question is the use of the term 'organization'. It has multiple meanings depending on who uses it and hears it. In my mind, it implies a reporting structure and functional point of view, and implies that business processes fit within such a structure when it may or may not. This is especially true when we take a portion of a corporation organizationally where its processes are typically portions of an end-to-end value creating business process. We do not call our approach 'organization process management', but use the word 'business'. In many modern examples, the value created is based upon several organizations collaborating on a holistic process that spans all of them. This is the business.

The strategic intent on the scope of the work chosen is not itself business strategy, but the ends that we are supposed to strive for. To bring it all to life, we have to decide how we will accomplish the ends. That means that business processes are a critical element in how the intent will be accomplished and sustained. Many processes will need to be changed to realize the intent (vision, goals and objectives). This is strategy, and process design is a core element of it. Taking an end-to-end approach will require an end-to-end process management perspective. To use a purely organizational structure approach will surely lead to a set of sub-optimized activities that may not connect or deliver aligned capabilities.

This reality can be seen in the structure of many reference frameworks, such as the APQC models, which are functionally and organizationally oriented. Business processes cross these areas when one looks at the higher-level value creating work of the business. We have been involved with modern challenges that involved many organizations that worked together to take on a process which involved all of them working together to satisfy the service recipients. The 'organization', in this case, was all of them—with a shared strategic intent, and a single end-to-end process as the strategy.

Business processes are a natural way of breaking down the delivery of outcomes, whereby organization charts are not. Business processes assure alignment of measurable results towards the goal and ensure the strategy is broken into manageable portions. Unfortunately, most organizations today do not use business processes architected for value creation as the vehicle to build the strategy, although more are realizing the benefit now than in the past.

GABY DOEBEL

Enterprise Architect, Brisbane City Council

Many organizations apply business process management (BPM) in various ways. In some organizations, the term BPM is used for business process improvement (BPI), where the focus predominately stays on improving operational processes. This approach is often termed a bottom-up approach, and BPI efforts are often of a more *ad hoc* nature and scoped with a particular business function.

Other organizations define BPM as a management practice, including: business process architecture design; BPI; business process re-engineering (BPR); business process automation (BPA); and other process management methods and tools. These organizations usually have a BPM vision and mission statement that translates into strategic initiatives and objectives. In this scenario, BPM is treated the same as other disciplines and/or functions—like finance, human resource and project management—where the practice has input into the strategic and performance management process, and can also be used as strategic tool to assist in the design, change, and performance improvement of capabilities. This type of BPM approach is positioned and applied from top down, and its scope usually spans enterprise-wide across all functions and delivery areas.

An enterprise-wide, top-down BPM approach requires a robust governance and decision-making structure that is of dual nature with clearly defined BPM and functional roles and responsibilities. This matrix management model requires strong relationships, integration and alignment across functions and business areas. Key BPM principles are applied throughout the different functions, and disciplines and made a part of the business's DNA—and, as a result, the practice becomes more sustainable.

Ultimately, it is the processes of an organization that deliver products and services to customers and stakeholders; therefore, it is feasible to place a strong focus on the BPM practice that includes the lifecycle management of processes. Processes in an organization are often structured into core (delivery) and non-core (support/management) processes. These are defined as part of a process architecture and communicated to the business providing transparency of delivery, ownership, and decision-making and, therefore, can be used as a key input into the prioritizing and selection of strategic changes and/or business improvement initiatives.

Furthermore, in process centric organizations, processes are managed as an asset where core processes create and deliver customer and shareholder value. Therefore, they are managed to maximize customer value and financial returns, and non-core processes that perform supportive or management functions are managed to minimize risks and control costs. The BPM practice focus is on adding value to achieving strategic outcomes, and uses the process architecture as an input to prioritize BPI efforts. Examples of such a BPI initiative would be to reduce the cost of work performed, or to bring the products and services quicker to the customers. These organizations use BPM as a strategic tool, and the BPI component as the method to implement.

In my experience, operational management often places a lot of emphasis on BPI to reduce cost, minimize effort, and reduce rework in their business area. There seems to be less value placed on moving towards a process-centric organization where BPM is embedded into the organizational design, and the necessary infrastructure is in place to run the practices as a strategic tool.

In conclusion, BPM is often used on a more operational and transactional level rather than on a strategic level, as the efforts, cost, and commitment required are far greater and, usually, a long-term strategy.

LEANDRO JESUS

Co-founder & Director, EloGroup

We, as process professionals, often cannot demonstrate that BPM should be treated as a priority. Our initiatives thus end up disconnected from strategic plans, relegated to bureaucratic activities and not perceived as value adding.

To change this situation, it is vital to demonstrate how processes, in fact, contribute to strategy. Leaders are heavily involved in defining and monitoring strategy. Everything that is directly linked to strategy turns out to be, naturally, part of their agenda.

We suggest one can emphasize the BPM relevance to strategy by establishing a better connection between process architectures and strategic planning techniques. If we define a process architecture as 'a set of interconnected processes that a business must perform in order to realize its strategy and deliver value to their customers', this connection may sound simple. In practice, however, it's often not dominant.

Just to be provocative, is your existing process architecture, in fact, used by leadership in strategy formulation and deployment? If the answer is negative, it is very likely that the architecture is just a document prepared by a team of consultants or a BPM Office, and known by just a few employees. It is not, however, a legitimate management tool.

A legitimate process architecture must define key business processes that, in fact, will be analyzed into strategy. Strategic planning techniques must then rely on process architectures.

Let's consider, for example, a company that discusses its strategy and formulates goals using a strategic map with four basic perspectives: financial, customer, internal processes, learning and growth. How can we 'connect' the process architecture with the strategic map? See the figure below:Purposely, the architectures' primary processes are correlated to the internal process perspective of the strategic map. Objectives from the internal process perspective can then be aligned naturally with primary processes, objectives and goals. The ones responsible for this perspective's objectives and goals are, naturally, process managers (owners), and strategic projects set for the perspective will, therefore, be process-transformation projects. Leadership will then start defining strategic priorities based on a common understanding of legitimate processes.

Unfortunately, however, most strategic maps are not built considering this connection. On the contrary, objectives from the internal processes perspective end up being inaccurately filled with generic terms, such as 'improve the various processes', 'achieve cost efficiencies', 'implement quality management standards', among others. Generic objectives do not allow managers to focus their decisions: in which processes should they act primarily in order to deliver a better value proposition to customers? Which process goals are really critical to achieve market growth and financial gains?

The imprecise use of strategy maps causes leaders to not take prioritization decisions based on processes. On the contrary, these maps give the impression that one should act on all processes, interchangeably. As a result, leaders frequently do not see a process architecture as a tool that directly supports them in their decisions.

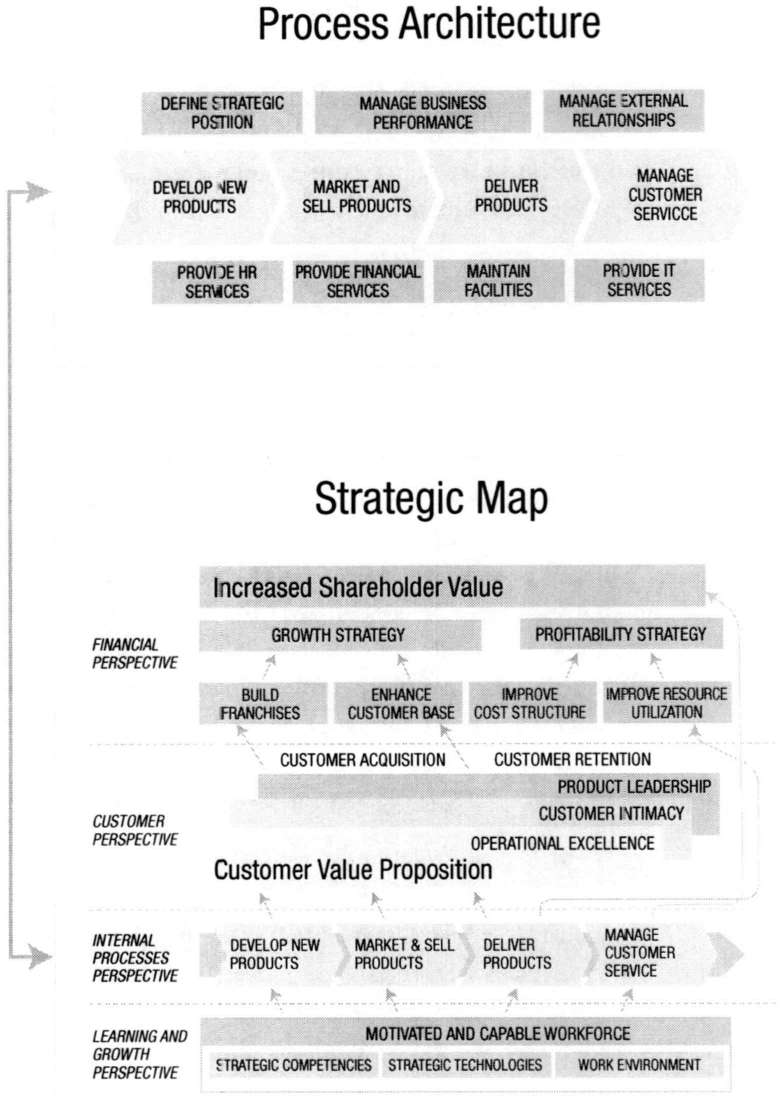

Figure 9: Connection between a process architecture and a strategic map

A good connection between a process architecture and a strategic map is, therefore, critical: it enables leadership to begin thinking in terms of processes, and treating them as a priority. By working on critical internal processes, leaders can increase the company's market share (customer perspective) and improve its financial results (financial perspective). In other words, by investing in processes, we can generate growth and profit. This is the simplest argument to demonstrate to leaders that working with BPM is something relevant!

Once process architecture and strategic planning techniques are well connected, leadership will naturally give priority to monitoring processes in greater detail, as they will be linked to strategy. Goals will be defined based on process architecture. This is the starting point for aligning process execution, in all business levels, to achieve the defined strategy.

GILLES MORIN
Founder, BPMPlus, Inc.

Helping decision-makers to harness the full business power of BPM as a new management discipline and strategy execution lever is part of my everyday life. I use a simple, five-step methodological framework to help them connect vision, strategy, execution, processes, and results. The methodology I use was designed by BPTrends. It integrates a mixture of industrial engineering, and Lean and Rummler's concepts and principles—and has been used over the past ten years. Interestingly enough, each time the management or executive team is exposed to the approach, they go through the same 'ah-ha!' moment.

First, the CxO look at me with circumspection when hearing the story about how BPM can help fully align and consolidate a management team on strategies and execution plans. At the first two workshops, sales VPs scratch their head and look at their cell phones, wondering, "What am I doing here?" The CEO is ready at the first workshop to aim and shoot at problems. Yet, they realize that they had hardly spent any quality time talking about business strategy, long-term targets, business models and execution of their strategies. They spent most of their team-time talking about operational and short-term issues, and managing their BU using past performance data—which is like driving your car using the rear mirror!

Progressing through the workshops, they discover that words mean different things to each other. Think about the words *customer*, *partner*, *strategy*, *goals*, *outcomes*, *cloud*, just to name a few. For those of us who facilitate workshops to document the existing operating model, or facilitate Kaizen, we know all about words meaning different things to different people—just think about your last workshop experience when the room was heating up with arguments between players committed to their different 'see' of the same problem. Agreeing on a common vocabulary is the first stepping-stone to a more effective working session.

Once they start talking about strategic intents, execution, targets or goals, the discomfort becomes noticeable. Some teams are simply not able to talk about real goals as measurable metrics. Sales metric … yes, easy! Strategy execution performance metrics … hum … not so! This is particularly true in a culture allergic to performance measurements or accountability. Anyhow, spending time over strategy-related discussions is seen as theoretical and, often, operational managers just want to get to the hard stuff—operational problems and solutions!

The code here is the word 'theoretical'. This is used whenever an executive has issues with business concepts and strategic thinking and framework. At this point, we are starting to get some good alignment on targets, purposes, outcomes, common business languages, and a common understanding of the full business context.

Then we get to define the 'organization value creation model' using processes, value streams, and value-chain perspectives, and agreeing on governance, core and support processes, definitions and outcomes for each key process. Again, a few workshops later, and not without constructive confrontations, the full management team comes to an agreement about how they operate and create value. We then start prioritizing processes based on their contributions to strategic intents and stakeholders' needs, and based on their existing pain level (how broken they are). This is the first real tipping point of the engagement strategy.

Interestingly enough, governance processes often are part of high-pain and high-gain processes. The CEO often goes into denial when hearing leaders indicating that they either have no clear understanding of strategies and strategic targets, or having no clue on how priorities were set. The CEO takes for granted that what's clear to him is 'automatically' clear to the leaders, yet wonders why strategies and results are not materializing as fast or as efficiently as he or she would have expected. The methodology we use makes them realize that they were missing a critical link, connector, and purpose driver— their process architecture!

At the end of the business architecture exercise—after agreeing on their process-driven value creation model, prioritizing high-pain and high-gain processes and capabilities, and sweating it out to define their heat map or road map (after 10 or 15 half-day workshops)—everyone around the table, including the executive sponsoring the exercise, openly states that this exercise was a clear and strong moment of truth. They would not do it differently— this was highly valuable to get everyone on the same page. They say it will stop internal competition to get IT dollars based on fuzzy prioritization criteria, or who speaks the loudest. Decision-making is accelerated. In some case, outcomes may be that while IT budget is reduced, value creation is increasing.

The right or valid business architecture leads to a valid strategy execution plan, and forces the clarification of long-term targets and short- and mid-term goals. It sets clear criteria to connect strategic intents, strategies, goals, processes and capabilities investment projects and results. Teams talk about performance dollars rather than IT dollars; tactical and operational governance mechanisms are realigned to support priorities. A purpose-driven organization is born!

The management team has full visibility and traceability over targets decisions and results. Is this not, in good part, what a management team is about?

BPM valued by management *is* a strategic tool. No, it does not replace strategy making, but it does focus top management attention on strategy validation and execution, and improves decision-making in major ways. People understand each other when they talk; words means the same thing; decisions are somewhat faster and often of better quality. But again, it does not replace, nor is it, the business strategy. It does not eliminate the needs to validate strategies; it is one means to doing it. It is, however, a very efficient way to execute on agreed strategies.

....

CHRIS POTTS

Corporate Strategist, Dominic Barrow

BPM is a strategic capability that emerged after many of the commonly used strategy models were created. As a result, while BPM's role in organizational strategy may be clearly recognized in some enterprises, in others it remains misunderstood and undervalued. In this respect, BPM is not alone. There are other strategic capabilities that are similarly missing from traditional strategy models—in particular, enterprise architecture,[1] investment in change, and sourcing.

A common approach in organizational strategy is to design the enterprise using an operations-oriented model, such as Porter's Value Chain.[2] Such models have proved durable because they offer managers a useful and valued framework. They also divide the organization into discrete spaces that managers find meaningful (e.g. marketing and sales, customer service, human resources). The overall architecture of Porter's model is its expression of an enterprise's activities using two macro-spaces, 'primary activities' and 'support activities', which also resonate with many managers.

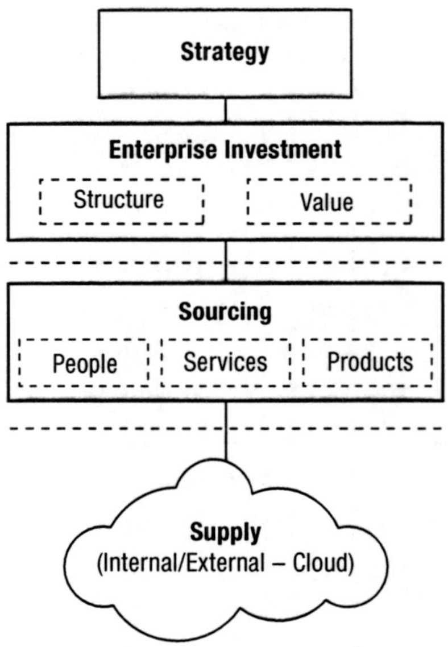

Figure 10: The Value Chain for Enterprise Investment

Whatever model an enterprise uses to design itself, a reasonable question to ask seems to be: where does BPM fit? In an operations-oriented model such as Porter's, the obvious answer would seem to be that BPM must be somewhere in the support activities, since it transcends all the primary activities. In truth, the question of where BPM fits in an operations-oriented model is not as reasonable as it may seem.

To explain the architecture of any entity, including an enterprise, differently oriented models are needed to answer different questions. For example, a vertical 'slice' through a building will not answer many questions about its floor plan. Similarly, to discover BPM's role and value (and how BPM inter-relates with other strategic capabilities), instead of an operations-oriented model, we need a strategy-oriented one.

The essential difference, characteristically, between an operations-oriented model and a strategy-oriented one is that the former is focused on activities and the latter is focused on investments. The following example of strategy-oriented model, from DefrICtion,[3] is called *The Value Chain for Enterprise Investment*, and is more fully described in my article of the same name.[4]

A strategy-oriented model, such as the one shown here, provides an entirely different frame of reference for the question "Where does BPM fit?" The answer is that BPM is a strategic capability that designs and guides investments in the enterprise's structure, and positively impacts the value that the structure delivers. By taking a process-based view of the enterprise's structure, BPM is a close companion to, while best considered different from, enterprise architecture. In practice, therefore, BPM collaborates with other strategic capabilities to:

- influence the organizational strategy
- design investments in change
- oversee the success of those investments

BPM is not an operational support activity. It is a core strategic capability. In organizations where BPM's true role and value has yet to be realized, the essential first step is to check the models being used to design the enterprise. If those models are operations-oriented and activity-focused, then the challenge for BPM (together with other strategic capabilities) is to socialize different and complementary models—ones that are strategy-oriented and investment-focused.

References:

[1] Author's note: the term 'enterprise architecture' here is shorthand for all forms of architecture relating to an enterprise.

[2] *Competitive Advantage*, Porter ME, Free Press 1985

[3] *DefrICtion*, Potts C, Technics Publications, 2012

[4] *The Value Chain for Enterprise Investment—Why Innovations and Investments Fail, and What Boards Can Do About It.* Potts C, www.dominicbarrow.com/writingarticles.html

PROFESSOR MICHAEL ROSEMANN

Head of Information Systems School, Queensland University of Technology

I believe BPM can play two essential roles in the execution of a corporate strategy: as a strategy enabler, and as a strategy accelerator.

First, outstanding process efficiency, or process agility, can *enable* competitive advantage. A highly streamlined value chain will fuel economies of scale and cost advantages that can help secure strategic opportunities. Typical examples are insurance companies who have consolidated claims handling across various lines of business, or low-cost retailers and airlines. These examples show how a strategy centered on cost effectiveness relies on BPM as an essential approach to execute the strategic objective. However, corporations focused on quality leadership will appreciate BPM approaches closer to quality improvements, such as Six Sigma.

Second, far less explored but increasingly important, is the role of BPM as an *accelerator* of the strategy-to-execution process. In this case, BPM is not used to manage transactional processes, but as an approach to manage a fundamental transformational process. Organizations that are able to model, analyze, improve and, where possible, automate, support, and monitor the strategy-to-execution process will have one essential advantage: their strategy latency will be reduced. Strategy latency describes the time from initial strategy design to its execution. With shorter strategy latency, organizations can react faster to environmental changes and have an overall higher corporate agility.

ANDREW SPANYI

Founder & Managing Partner, Spanyi International

BPM ENABLES EXECUTION

Business Process Management (BPM) has the potential to make a significant contribution to executing organizational strategy, mainly because customer focus and cross-departmental collaboration are needed for its execution. The scope of the potential depends largely on how BPM is viewed by the senior leadership team (SLT). The potential for BPM to contribute to strategy is significant whenever the SLT believes that customer value is created via workflows that cross over departmental boundaries, and views BPM at the enterprise level. On the other hand, if the SLT sees BPM as simply technology-enabled process automation, then the potential for BPM to enable organizational strategy is limited.

There is ample thought leadership on the role of process in strategy—including foundational work by Dr. Michael Porter, as well as the work of Michael Treacy and Fred Wiersema, and Robert Kaplan and David Norton.

Dr. Michael Porter is widely recognized as the father of modern views on strategy through his work on competitive advantage via three generic strategies. He advocated a view that embraced the central role of 'activities' in achieving a competitive edge. Porter wrote, "Activities, then are the basic units of competitive advantage. Overall advantage or disadvantage results from all of a company's activities, not only a few."[1] Further, he understood that the critical activities were cross-functional in nature, as evidenced by the following passage:

> *"Strategy is creating fit among a company's activities. The success of a strategy depends on doing many things well—not just a few—and integrating among them. If there is no fit among activities, there is no distinctive strategy and little sustainability. Management [then] reverts to the simpler task of overseeing independent functions…"*[2]

Porter only alluded to the importance of 'process' in organizational strategy, and while he provided some insight into the 'why'—his work did not sufficiently clarify the 'what' and the 'how'. In contrast, Treacy and Wiersema explicitly acknowledged the importance of process redesign for firms who seek to establish competitive advantage through the value discipline of 'operational excellence'.[3] They also implied that attention to core process performance is important in achieving competitive advantage via their other two market disciplines: 'product leadership' and 'customer intimacy'.

Following closely on the heels of Treacy and Wiersema's work, Kaplan and Norton built on the concept of value disciplines with their thinking of how a balanced scorecard in performance measurement can assist in translating strategy into action.[4] This explicitly recognized 'process' as one of four principal variables in performance measurement, but gave little guidance on 'how' process management can enable strategy execution.[5]

These thought leaders of the 1990s made reference to re-engineering and process redesign—but not to business process management (BPM), as that specific term was coined a few years later by the information technology community. Simply stated, organizations, in formulating strategy, typically want answers to at least the following questions:

- How will we grow our top line? Will we emphasize organic growth, or through mergers and acquisitions?
- How will we maintain or even improve margins?
- How will we attract the best people?

The implementation of whatever strategy an organization chooses in each of these areas relates to a specific end-to-end business process. In the case of organic growth, the operative construct is a product/market matrix, and success will depend on the performance of the new product/service process and the sales process—also known as the 'inquiry to order' process.

In the case of maintaining and improving margins, success will depend on controlling expenses in the order-fulfillment process and the set of supporting processes. Similarly, the implementation of the strategy to get the best talent will revolve around the recruiting and onboarding process.

Invariably, the implementation of strategy requires cross-departmental collaboration. In other words, no one executive typically has sufficient authority for implementation success, and influence is needed more than control. Yet, a company can only take full advantage of BPM to accelerate strategy implementation when the senior leadership team works together to achieve:

- a common language around end-to-end processes
- a set of shared beliefs
- a simple and effective method to prioritize process improvement and management

The SLT needs to have a common language around end-to-end process in order to make the tough choices that strategy implementation typically requires. What's needed in this respect is a one-page model, or text-based framework, that clearly defines each of the high-level end-to-end processes, their boundaries and outputs. Note that this is dramatically different to what is typically involved with enterprise architecture or business architecture initiatives—and even process architecture efforts where, all too often, the models are not connected to strategy, take a lot of time and effort, and are characterized by a failure to gain a shared understanding of the 'big picture'.

Similarly, it is important that the senior leadership team of the firm share a set of beliefs, such as the following:

- Customers don't care how a company is organized, or what information systems they operate; customers care mostly about value for money, and flawless delivery of products and services.
- Customer value is created via workflows that cross over departmental boundaries.
- Organizations are complex business and social systems wherein a change in any one component is likely to have an impact on other components.

Summarized below is a short five-statement instrument that can be used to test the extent to which the members of the SLT have shared values. As a leadership team:

- We regularly measure what matters to customers.
- We regularly refer to a one-page framework that depicts how value is created.
- We regularly discuss how work flows across traditional organizational boundaries.
- We frequently use cross-functional teams to improve performance.
- We recognize the contributions of people who have improved results for customers.

It is the combination of a common language around processes, and a set of shared beliefs, that form the foundation for success and enable the SLT to use a simple and effective method to prioritize process improvement and management. Such a method needs to be implemented in weeks, not months. The fundamental question that the process improvement prioritization method has to address is which end-to-end business processes need to be improved, and by how much, to achieve our strategic objectives? Note that there are three prerequisites needed for an organization to answer this question:

- Clarity on the company's strategic objectives.
- Clarity on the current performance of each end-to-end process (cost, quality, and timeliness), and the size of the gap to be bridged.

- An agreed upon method of prioritizing process improvement and management.

For BPM to enable strategy execution, the SLT needs to reach agreement on the extent of improvement needed for each end-to-end process in light of the strategic objectives. The typical categories are transformative, incremental improvement, and monitoring or management. The challenge is not just clarity on the scope of process change—but also clarity on the capacity of the organization to absorb the planned change.

BPM, when viewed broadly at the enterprise level, can make a significant contribution to strategy execution. It can validate—and sometimes even challenge—strategic direction. It can provide clarity and focus. It can reinforce that strategy begins with the customer. But it is not a substitute for strategy. Wisely deployed, BPM enables strategy execution.

References

[1] Porter, Michael, *What is Strategy?*, Harvard Business Review, Nov/Dec 1996.

[2] Ibid.

[3] Treacy, Michael & Fred Wiersema, *The Discipline of Market Leaders*, Addison-Wesley, 1995.

[4] Kaplan, Robert and David Norton, *The Balanced Scorecard: Translating Strategy into Action*, Harvard Business School Press, 1996.

[5] The work of Dr. Geary Rummler and Alan Brache actually pre-dated the work of Porter and Kaplan, and Norton provided clear guidance on the role of process in organizational strategy.

QUESTION 4

WHAT'S NEXT FOR BPMS?

The interest in business process, and especially in business process reengineering (BPR), was kicked off in 1991 in articles and books by Michael Hammer and James Champy (*Reengineering the Corporation*), by Thomas Davenport (*Process Innovation*), and others. Many would say that the current round of interest in BPM was kicked off in 2003 by the book by Howard Smith and Peter finger (*Business Process Management: The Third Wave*), and by the availability of a new generation of web-based workflow tools—usually called BPM Software (BPMS) tools.

Do you think this is an accurate characterization of the current market? In any case, what role do you think the various BPMS tools are playing in the evolution of the current business process market?

OVERVIEW

Ever since BPM started attracting attention in the early years of this millennium, there has been contention about whether it referred to a generic management approach to process improvement, or to a new class of software (which many prefer to term BPMS, or BPM software). Our authors present different perspectives. All recognize that any process work, today, must rely on a large IT component. They also recognize that senior management is very concerned with linking strategic concerns with specific business processes and having tools to organize and control strategically driven transformations.

Our authors hold out hope that the newer BPMS tools will increasingly support the various concerns that managers have for process management. For instance, the graphic interfaces in the tools are increasingly sophisticated, and offer senior managers with more of an overview and, at the same time, more detail than ever before. Whether one is interested in seeing how a strategic initiative is being implemented, or determining where a specific set of items is within one's worldwide supply chain, the latest BPMS tools make this possible. At the same time, good graphic interfaces can help remind middle managers of the way a major process integrates the work of several departments. It simultaneously integrates the work of specific groups of people with software applications and the activities of business partners. Finally, our authors emphasize the importance of being flexible and creating tools that can handle a specific and growing number of problems that organizations are trying to deal with.

....

AHMAD ALIBABAEI

Assistant Professor, Shahid Beheshti University of Medical Sciences

Business Process Re-engineering (BPR) was introduced in the early 1990s by Davenport and Short (1990), and Hammer and Champy (1993). This approach to process improvement attracted much attention because it promised significance improvements in business. These early writers of BPR emphasized the radical re-engineering of processes, and early attempts realized few benefits. Some classic cases—like Ford's re-engineering of its accounts payable section, or the processing of insurance applications at Mutual Benefit Life—were successful, but most ended in failure. This led to BPR being seen as risky.

Between 1997 and 2003, the emphasis shifted from BPR to other forms of process improvement, including:

- Tool Development—ARIS, Visio, First STEP toolset; Prime object

Tools; workflow modeling tools.

- Modeling Techniques—Dynamic process modeling; Agent relationship modeling (ARM); Two-phase cognitive modeling (TCM); Using IDEF-0 for enterprise modeling; notion of soft-goals in business process modeling; Modeling the regulative role of business processes.
- Methodologies—Stage and activity framework (Kettinger, Teng et al., 1997); agent relationship modeling analysis (ARMA) (Glykas and Valiris 1998); GRAI methodology (Cameron & Braiden, 2004); CIMOSA methodology (Wu, 2002).

In 2003, when a new field of study called Business Process Management emerged, a variety of software development tools was also introduced. These tools are usually termed Business Process Management Software (BPMS). BPMS can play different roles; it can be an enabler, facilitator, and implementer of BPM.

Based on my experience, the market success of BPMS was limited for two reasons. The first is related to the role of IS vendors in the market. They introduced ERP systems in early 2000, just before BPMS was introduced to the market. When BPMS was introduced to the world, ERP vendors were established and stronger than the newer BPMS vendors were, and they viewed the BPMS vendors as rivals. Recently, however, many of the BPMS vendors were acquired by strong IS vendors and, today, ERP systems and BPMS are considered as complimentary systems. To date, the benefits of using BPMS has not been described as well as enterprise systems, and most organizations do not have any idea about what BPMS applications could do for their businesses. Recently, some concepts—such as value-driven business process management—have been more clearly explained.

When BPM was introduced at early 2000, many organizations that wanted to implement BPM started by redesigning processes, and later added automation using ERP or BPMS software. Nowadays, organizations looking for improvement in their information systems often choose BPMS. This means that many BPM initiatives, today, are being driven by a desire to adopt new technology. As knowledge of the benefits of BPMS spreads, its use can be expected to grow.

••

ERIC HERNESS

CTO & Chief Architect (BPM), IBM

The state of BPM, and the market for BPM in general, are strongly influenced by the role that technology can play. That role is primarily one of enabling and accelerating the adoption of BPM. In describing this role for BPMS tools, it is reasonable to cover this by organizing the contribution of tools into a few key aspects:

- BPM tools and BPMN notation
- Tools as facilitators of collaboration
- BPM tools as automation accelerators
- BPM tools and business insights

By looking at each of these elements, we can find an interesting and relatively complete perspective on the influence and potential for BPMS tools as it relates to enabling true realization of the BPM approach.

BPM TOOLS AND BPMN NOTATION

The current BPM market is built on a many interesting foundations, each offering a contribution to the current business process market. In recent years, BPMN (Business Process and Modeling notation) as a way to capture business process, and the various BPMS tools that embrace and support BPMN, have been key transmitters and carriers of the overall business process cause.

BPMN 2.0 has brought a level of maturity and completeness to modeling business processes that allows usage by a number of stakeholders in the business process journey. Business process modelers, and other business roles with a vested interest in graphically capturing business process models, can leverage a subset of the notation to get started, to simplify communication, and to foster process improvement efforts.

Aided by business-created BPMN diagrams, or just starting from a blank canvas, IT developers are able to leverage BPMN for describing business processes that will run in a BPMS. This continuity—between the notation leveraged by the business stakeholders and those in IT responsible for executing processes—further blurs that line between business and IT. This is what the market needs, tools that are positive contributors to moving forward the promise of BPM. Reality is that there is usually change, to some degree, in the top-level BPMN in addition to the detail added during automation—but there is still something about having the same notation that adds some level of comfort and consistency for all involved.

In fact, while this explanation mostly looks like an endorsement for the BPMN notation, the notation itself would not have such widespread adoption if it were not for the tools that support it. It is a powerful notation, and one that is best served up via tools versus hand sketching or, even, just basic graphics. Tools enable the power of the notation and, thus, the benefits of the notation are unleashed.

Tools as facilitators of collaboration

With a consistent notation in place, BPM tools now not only play the role of capturing and organization the BPMN models, but also build around those models an approach for collaboration, and add support for capturing business stakeholder communications and interactions. It is often stated that the more aligned that the business stakeholders are on process definitions, the easier the path to proper and valuable automations will be.

IBM's Blueworks Live, combined with IBM Business Process Manager, offer an example of the role of BPMS tools and the current market evolution. Blueworks Live is built for non-IT roles, specifically to enable business stakeholders to capture, collaborate and refine process definitions and related artifacts. With over a million processes modeled, the value of such an approach is proven. Examples of process maps and process diagrams can be seen by trying Blueworks Live at https://www.blueworkslive.com/or attending regularly scheduled demos.

The collaborative and social features of IBM Blueworks Live allow you to:

- easily collaborate on daily tasks with co-workers across teams, departments, and the entire organization
- access communities focused on process improvement
- document your processes in a way that is structured and usable by anyone in your company
- keep your team connected, on the same page, and working effectively

Because Blueworks Live has a SaaS form factor, traditional barriers to entry from an infrastructure perspective are largely removed, and the business stakeholders can be quickly empowered and productive. BPMN, as a standard, means there is community and easy access to education and insight about proper modeling approaches. The downstream effects of tools like this are:

- Better specificity on processes chosen for IT-enabled automaton projects, thus reducing churn and IT development efforts.
- Stronger likelihood that processes chosen for automation deliver the most benefit to the business.

Increased business buy-in and sense of ownership of processes in general, and in those processes automated by a downstream BPMS.

BPM TOOLS AS AUTOMATION ACCELERATORS

Taking that BPMN notation from initial specification by the business stakeholders into the BPMS tool, such as IBM Business Process Manager provides a contract that is much stronger and more accurate than textual specifications, or a picture where the objects lack definition and subsequent serialization format.

IBM Business Process Manager is a platform to run business processes. These types of tools are accelerating process automation and, thus, the initiation of the continuous process improvement cycle. These kinds of tool allow developers to quickly create process automations, complete with customized user experiences, all on a scalable and resilient infrastructure.

These tools have been around for a number of years and remain key enablers of the BPM market. IBM BPM, for example, has a mature and proven set of collaboration capabilities, including strong support for 'playbacks', which further enhance the fidelity of stakeholder feedback.

Playbacks, combined with a fast turnaround time for making changes, mean a tool-supported discipline and rigor that greatly improved the quality and timeliness of the completed process automation. In recent years, we have seen further evolution of these tools in areas such as:

- *The ability to easily create mobile-ready user experiences.* These kinds of capabilities, and the general user features, make it easy to build appealing user experiences that business stakeholders make part of how they work, not an extra task they have to perform.
- *The support of SaaS and other cloud-based footprints.* This is another key accelerator on the path to delivering value. No longer is it necessary to wait for infrastructure teams to acquire, install, configure, and ready the hardware and software platform upon which process automations execute.

- *Enablement of team development in a scalable and consistent approach.* The ability to share assets across projects, the ability to govern process deployment, and the features managing inflight process instances all make it easier to transition from one project to a fully-fledged BPM automation program.

BPM TOOLS AND BUSINESS INSIGHTS

Once processes are modeled and automated, attention turns to visibility and the role played by BPM tools to facilitate visibility.

First, that BPMN continues to play a role. It can be used as a guide for all process participants to see where a specific process instance is at runtime, as well as be the canvas from which various forms of visibility are enabled. See www.bit.ly/visualisation-eric-herness for an example of the visualization of a specific BPMN process instance. This visualization is for the business process participant and other interested observers. There is value beyond just that enjoyed by those modeling for documentation and those modeling for execution.

Next on the visibility agenda comes dashboard and visualizations that focus on individual and team performance. These are complemented by dash-boarding capabilities for processes themselves.

BAM products, such as IBM Business Monitor, fit into the broader picture of BPM tools. These tools allow more comprehensive and powerful visualizations, not only looking at teams and processes, but also allowing creation and visualizations of KPIs built from real process executions that link to business objectives and higher-level business value chains.

Finally, we are in the era of big data and analytics. Many of the analytics tools that are accompanying this big data world can be used for enabling new visualizations over our process execution and task execution data. These offer the possibility to have more and different insights with a few clicks, versus the old world of waiting for custom reports to be constructed that were essentially rigid and single purposed.

FINAL WORD ON BPM TOOLS AND BPMN

BPM tools continue to play a key role in the BPM market. They are accelerators and enablers in every way. BPMN as a notation can really only reach it's full potential when supported by BPM tools in a first-class way. BPM tools build on that notational support, and add a level of support for collaboration and socialization to the mix. BPM tools further accelerate the path to process automation and the path to continuous process improvement. BPM process automation tools are increasingly easier to adopt and leverage, not only in terms of having personas that fit the various user constituencies, but also in that they are available now in various cloud footprints. SaaS offerings, in particular, for these tools make acquisition time nearly zero, and greatly improve the initial time to value.

Finally, we are in the beginning of a renaissance around visibility. BPM tools have traditionally offered visibility and, thus, provided a catalyst for insights and continuous process improvement. This is now assumed and necessary. A new era of visibility is upon us, fueled by the analytics capabilities that accompany the era of big data and analytics. Bringing these capabilities to bear on our process execution and task execution data holds great promise.

Tools will continue to be key drivers in the success of BPM and the overall BPM market.

....

PETER MATTHIJSSEN

Managing Consultant, BiZZdesign

In the world of BPM, there is a large, active group of tool vendors providing all kind of Business Process Management software. The functionality of these suites range from capturing and documenting processes (and analyzing and visualizing processes), to executing processes. When this last phase of execution is also included, the term BPMS is used. Depending on the type of processes and challenges at hand, different software suites will provide the best support.

Some practitioners and vendors might state that BPM is all about automating and executing processes. This is a very technical view of BPM, which is, in my opinion, too narrow. Simple and predictable processes might be a candidate for automation, and there is powerful BPMS software available that can transform BPM diagrams to working code. With all technical developments, more interesting developments can be expected in this field in coming years.

However, in my opinion, BPM is a broader discipline that is not just about technique, IT, and BPMS. It is also about people. It is about: 'thinking in processes'; how do people collaborate with each other (and IT) to deliver value to a customer?

Instead of thinking in tasks and departments (vertical view), BPM always has a broader horizontal view, connecting tasks and departments from customer to customer.

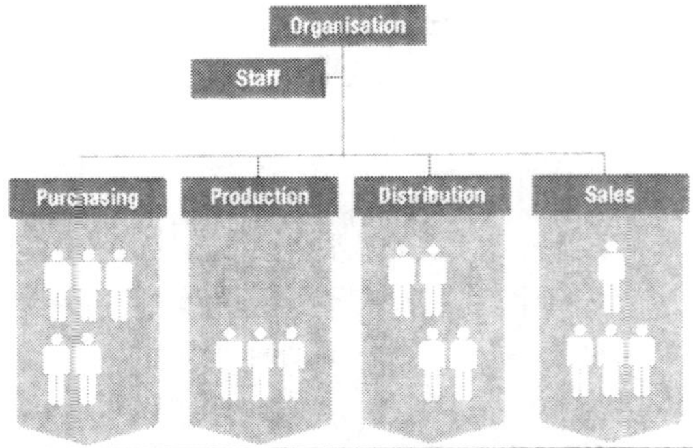

Figure 11: Thinking in departments—vertical view

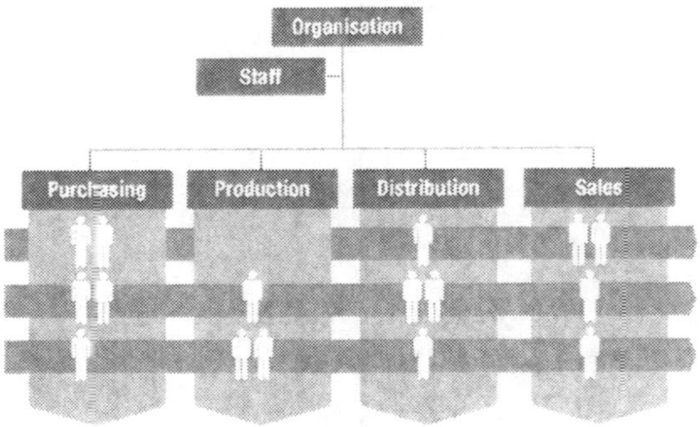

Figure 12: Thinking in processes—horizontal view

BPM tool functionality that supports 'thinking in processes' includes:

- process architecture to capture end-to-end processes
- process analysis to streamline end-to-end processes
- process visualization to communicate processes in an effective way and stimulate collaboration.

Regarding BPM tool functionality, also in the field of visualizing and analyzing processes, interesting developments take place—for example, with goal and target-group specific visualizations. BPM more and more plays a powerful role in supporting business with unambiguous, just-in-time, just-enough information to take the right decisions in a changing environment.

....

GILLES MORIN
Founder, BPMPlus, Inc.

There are visionaries out there who have written ground-breaking books about BPM. Future Strategies has published an excellent series of books around BPMS and BPM: *Social BPM*; *BPM Everywhere: Internet of Things*; *iBPMS*; *Empowering Knowledge Workers*, *Taming the Unpredictable*, to name a few.

Listening to these gurus talking about how the new generations of iBPMS made me realize that if BPM is a new management discipline, iBPMS is restructuring and transforming new business platforms that can change the game of delivering more value to customers. BPMS is mainstream—the real challenge is how you approach it, get the right capability in place, set the right architecture model, implement it and manage it.

BPMS technologies cover the full spectrum of process lifecycles, form discovery to monitoring and improvement. They now embed powerful analytics, decision management, and connectivity capabilities. We all know that technology will always be two to five years ahead of the market. Organizations can now access low-end to high-end tools, hybrid platforms supporting the work of knowledge workers (case management), and back-office workers (BPMS). The new generation of fast-learning curve tools clearly contribute in accelerating BPM maturity, given the right minimal capabilities are in place and that the right entry projects have been selected.

I strongly recommend reading *BPM Everywhere* by Future Strategies Inc/ Workflow Management Coalition (WfMC), or any of Peter Fingar's books describing the next wave and the third wave of BPM. They simply reframe our common views about BPMS.

One very common mistake I see is clients acquiring BPM tools that are built for high maturity BPM organization. If you are low BPM maturity, or low process culture maturity, you can now find tools adapted for this situation. Too often, I see an architecture team having been seduced by vendors to buy fancy and complex architecture tools, complex BPMS platforms, and trying to fit them back into their own 'complex' solution delivery world. This leads, all the time, to huge waste and kills BPM initiatives. It does not need to be that way anymore.

In today's context, BPM technologies must be part of BPM and a wider agility and customer experience corporate program. This is, however, one lever to transformation. Burlton's Hexagon gives a useful view of critical capabilities to be aligned to fully leverage a corporate BPM investment program.

CULTURE

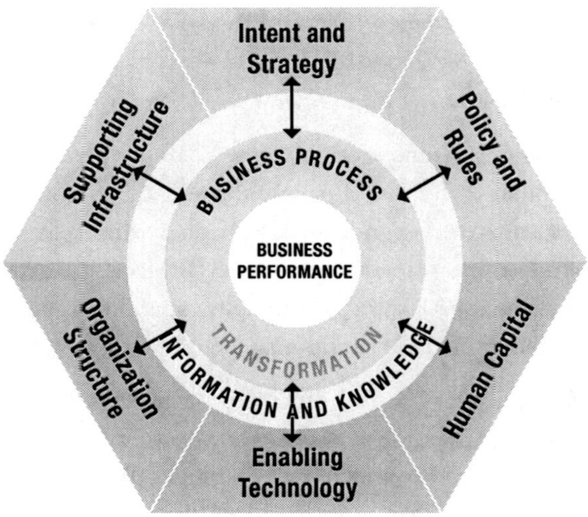

Figure 13: The Burlton Hexagon

For 'Enabling Technology', read BPM technologies, methodologies, and tools. This is only one of the ten critical capabilities that must be aligned to maximize BPM program benefits realization.

This view helps to reframe another common mistake, that BPM and BPMS are the same. They are not! Thinking that BPM or BPMS is the same is a costly mistake, as BPMS alone, like any other business technology, does not lead to business benefits.

PROFESSOR MICHAEL ROSEMANN

Head of Information Systems School, Queensland University of Technology

The future evolution of BPMS will see a stronger focus on predictive and advisory capabilities. Rather than the current strengths of these systems, which are characterized by high modeling, analytical, execution and monitoring capabilities, I believe the next evolution of BPMS will see much enhanced capabilities in three areas.

First, future BPMS will have higher levels of context-awareness. Current BPMS are largely disconnected from their environment, and support an isolated process design and execution. Most processes, however, do not occur in isolation. The required resource allocation is a function of the demand for the process. Seasonal influences might require alternative processes (summer sales, start of the semester, end of the financial year), and disruption in the environment might fundamentally change process priorities (e.g. in case of disasters). Context-aware BPMS will be characterized by a correlation of relevant external variables with process-internal variables. For example, a process such as production or sales might be highly dependent on weather forecasts. Such systems will allow the process designer to specify relevant contextual variables and link these to relevant internal process elements.

Second, future BPMS will have enhanced process-mining capabilities to the point that the model-to-execution paradigm will be reversed. The more system capabilities move towards real time process mining capabilities, the more process models will always be updated based on actual process executions. In these systems, log files will be analyzed and deviations will be used for process model adjustments supporting accurate decision-making and converting process models, a central BPM artifact, into living documents. Further down, it can also be envisaged that process mining itself will have a stronger forecasting component. While current process mining is largely based on historical data, it will not be too challenging to embed typical forecasting capabilities into process mining solutions. Based on identifiable trends, such enhanced BPMS could predict factors like process demand, preferred resources, or future probabilities at splitting points along a business process.

Third, and perhaps most important, future BPMS will have stronger advisory capabilities. Process improvement or innovation services will be integrated into BPMS, and proactively suggest alternative process designs to the system user. Such design proposals could be generated in various ways. First, they might be based on pre-defined process improvement patterns that, in combination with artificial intelligence / machine learning solutions, would propose relevant process designs. An example would be to make a step optional, or to conduct activities in parallel if process time is an issue. Second, future process improvement systems might be based on a subscription model. Such systems would rely on a repository of typical process templates (e.g. usage-based pricing) and would automatically propose alternative process designs when a process template is deemed as being relevant. For example, innovative payment solutions, such as credit card details as part of a customer record (Apple, Uber), or voice controlled payment solutions (e.g. Google Handsfree) could be automatically proposed if a current process includes a payment activity. In these scenarios, the process solution comes to the process, as opposed to the current form where a 'broken process' searches for a solution. Such process-recommender systems will accelerate the organizational process improvement capabilities and create more reliable—that is, less people-dependent—process designs.

....

DR. WIL VAN DER AALST

Professor, Eindhoven University of Technology

To understand the current business process market, it is good consider the roots of today's Business Process Management (BPM) systems. In the seventies, people like Skip Ellis, Anatol Holt, and Michael Zisman already worked on so-called Office Information (OI) systems, which were driven by explicit process models. Ellis et al. developed OI prototype systems such as Officetalk-Zero and Of-ficetalk-D at Xerox PARC in the late 1970s. These systems used variants of Petri nets to model processes. Another example from the same period is SCOOP (System for Computerizing of Office Processes), developed by Michael Zisman. SCOOP also used Petri nets to represent business processes. Officetalk, SCOOP and other OI systems were created in a time where workers were typically not connected to a network. Consequently, these systems were not widely adopted. Nevertheless, it is good to realize that the vision still driving today's BPM systems was already present in the late 1970s.

A second wave of BPM-like systems emerged in the mid-nineties. Numerous vendors started to offer generic Workflow Management (WFM) systems. There was the expectation that WFM systems would get a role comparable to Database Management (DBM) systems, i.e., data would be subcontracted to DBM systems and processes would be subcontracted to WFM systems. DBM systems managed to become an integral part of almost all information systems since the 1970s. However, WFM systems were not widely adopted and (unlike DBM systems) did not manage to become an integral part of the typical information system of an organization. The early WFM systems were focusing too much on automation, not acknowledging the management aspects and the need for flexibility. Processes can also be captured using conventional programming languages. Indeed, most workflows are hard-coded and hidden in application programs.

As mentioned, one of the pitfalls of the classical WFM sys-tems was the lack of management support. The focus was on automation rather than the ability to analyze, manage, and control systems. At the turn of the century, a third wave of BPM-like systems emerged. These systems had a broader scope than WFM-technology: From process automation and process analysis to operations management and the organization of work. The trend to provide better management support is still ongoing in current systems. Also there have been various attempts to make these systems more flexible than WFM systems. Declarative BPM/WFM systems and case management approaches signify this trend towards more flexibility.

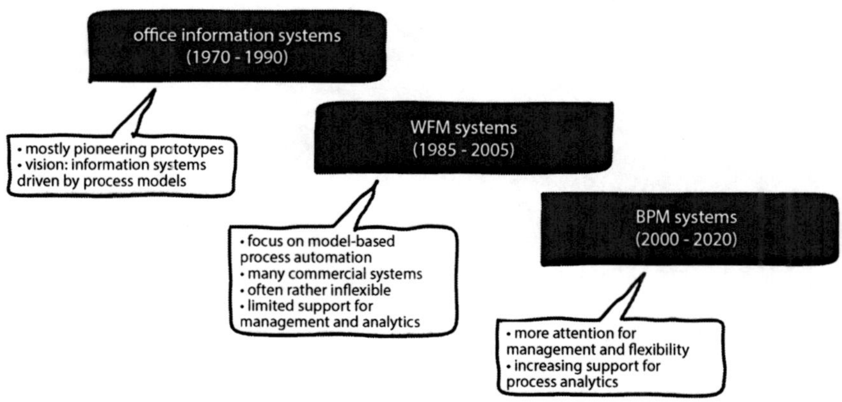

Figure 14: Three "waves" of process-aware information systems

BPM should aim at improving operational business processes, with or without BPM systems. For example, by modeling a business process and analyzing it using simulation, management may get ideas on how to reduce costs while improving service levels. It is often not necessary to introduce a full-fledged BPM system. More important, BPM approaches should exploit the event data widely available in today's organizations. Many BPM authors (including Smith and Fingar in their 2003 book) fail(ed) to see the importance of business process intelligence and process mining. Discussions on the definition of

BPM and the references to the pi calculus now seem silly. Most process improvements and innovations are driven by data. Unfortunately, processes are not at the forefront in most data science and Big data initiatives. The BPM community should take on the challenge to make these initiatives more process-centric.

QUESTION 5

IS THE MATRIX WORTH THE EFFORT?

Taking a cross-functional process view of an organization cuts across all of the authorities and conventions defined by a traditional organization chart. Thus, a process view requires a very different way of looking at an organization, its people, and their teams. It places more emphasis on building a culture of collaboration rather than on siloed working, reporting, and management. The shift to a dual functional and process view can be difficult.

Is it worth the considerable effort required? What benefits do you see that justify the efforts required, over the long term, for such a cultural and operational change? Have you seen this work?

OVERVIEW

Answers to this question generally support the view that, if you accept the importance of cross-functional process performance management and, therefore, BPM, some form of matrix management is not a choice, but a necessity. If that brings complexities with it, they must be dealt with and not avoided. There is general support for the idea that the effort is worthwhile.

Given that the organization chart is silent on the issue of cross-functional process management, something additional is required. BPM disrupts the traditional management model replacing siloed line management control with collaborative working. The many difficulties of matrix management are noted, and different models are canvassed.

Several authors note that in looking for cost benefits, we should not focus only on the costs and effort. Where are the benefits? Are there many organizations operating with depth and breadth at the highest levels of BPM maturity? Anecdotally, it is said that BPM maturity is improving, but there is no data. Indeed, such hard data would be difficult, perhaps impossible, to collect. At the level of an individual organization, it is vital that benefits be delivered, measured and tracked—else, the most sophisticated management structure is irrelevant.

....

ROGER ADDISON

Performance Architect, Addison Consulting

CAROL HAIG

Principal, Carol Haig & Associates

Born out of the aerospace race, matrix management is a 'mixed' organizational form in which normal hierarchy is 'overlaid' by some form of lateral authority, influence, or communication. In a matrix, there are usually two chains of command: one along functional lines, and the other along project lines.[1]

This is a formal definition for a 'Matrix Organization'. In our experience, consulting with a range of organizations, we have not yet seen a wholly successful Matrix Organization. That said, we have observed effective cross-functional teams established to bridge traditional vertical business units. We are inclined to agree that, today, matrix structures are more common and are likely to exist in some form in most larger, more complex organizations.[2]

THE PERFORMANCE ARCHITECT'S VIEW OF MATRIX ORGANIZATIONS

It is these other forms of matrix organization that interest us as performance architects. Performance architects focus on analyzing work situations and then using models and tools to develop and simplify how work can be done to produce desired results.[3] In most companies, achieving targeted results is a responsibility shared among all employees regardless of role, so assembling a group from multiple functions to meet those targets is logical.

Organizations regularly pull together skilled specialists from different functions to develop a project to completion, at which point the team is disbanded. Such a project might be a merger or acquisition. During the life of the project, team members report both to their regular manager and to the project manager or team lead, creating a short-term Matrix Organization. They may work exclusively on the matrix team for the duration of the project, or they may divide their time between their regular responsibilities and their role on the matrix team.

In some workplaces, cross-functional teams are permanently assembled to address needs that are known to reoccur, but not at known times. An example might be a safety committee at a manufacturing site. Such a team may have permanent safety professionals as members and add other stakeholder representatives or technical experts when required. When the safety need is met, members return to their regular assignments. These team members, too, will have dual reporting relationships while working on their safety assignment.

MATRIX ORGANIZATION BENEFITS AND CHALLENGES

A Matrix Organization can address a number of organizational issues while contributing to desired results. These apply as well to a large multi-national organization as they do to the project and team-driven examples we have been discussing. Benefits include increased:

- Focus on multiple business goals
- Exchange of information among individual workers and functional areas
- Economies of scale
- Speed of response to local commercial or functional needs
- Cross-functional problem solving
- Innovation
- Accelerated delivery of products and services.[4]
- The characteristics of a Matrix Organization are comprised of challenges that must be carefully evaluated and managed for the matrix to produce results efficiently. These include:

- Unclear roles and responsibilities
- Ambiguous authority in decision-making and problem-solving
- Mixed signals from different reporting relationships
- Misaligned goals
- Internal conflict and politics
- Reduced accountability
- Lack of a monitoring process to detect and identify matrix performance problems.[5]

With the parameters of a Matrix Organization established, and assuming the challenges like those above are managed successfully, we can take a brief look at how business processes are developed, implemented, and managed in a matrix format.

BUSINESS PROCESSES IN THE MATRIX ORGANIZATION

Regardless of how business processes are established, and in what sort of organizational structures they are situated, all processes require a building method and a maintenance protocol. In addition, every process in every organization needs an owner. That owner is responsible for managing the process for as long as it is in use, or for ensuring that an appropriately skilled employee manages it.[6]

Teams composed of experts from various functional groups often develop and maintain processes. The resulting processes likely benefit from the different abilities of the development team's members. Such teams are Matrix Organizations created to work on specific process-development needs. These teams stand to succeed or struggle based on how well the challenges of the Matrix Organization are managed.

Notes and References

[1] Addison, R. and Haig, C. Performance architecture: A process management framework. December 2014. Retrieved from: http://www.bptrends.com/performance-architecture-a-process-management-framework/

[2] Addison, R. and Haig, C. Performance architecture: Performance improvement—The case for horizontal oversight.April 2010. Retrieved July 2015 from: http://www.bptrends.com/performance-architecture-performance-improvement-the-case-for-horizontal-oversight/

[3] Cassidy, C. The new matrix management. Retrieved July 2015 from: https://www.matrixmanagementinstitute.com/resources/articles/new-matrix-management

[4] Larson, E. and Gobeli, D. Matrix management: Contradictions and insights. California Management Review, Volume XXIX, Number 4, Summer 1987. Retrieved July 2015 from: https://d31owemgwclw9w.cloudfront.net/content/CEPL/CEPL551/cepl551_234_matrxprint_en-us.pdf

[5] Matrix Management. Retrieved July 2015 from: https://en.wikipedia.org/wiki/Matrix_management

[6] Toto, J. Leadership in matrix organizations—Issues and success factors. December 2014. Retrieved July 2015 from: http://www.the-leaders-edge.com/files/hip_in_Matrix_Organizations_-_J_Toto_12-2014.pdf

[7] What is a matrix organization structure? (March 2014). Retrieved July 2015 from: http://www.global-integration.com/matrix-management/matrix-structure/matrix-organization-structure/

JIM BOOTS

Owner, Global Process Innovation

The benefits of creating a culture of collaboration—with processes at the center of many collaborative discussions—probably depend on the type of organization in question. If the organization is not very large and/or if the operational complexity is low—meaning that most workers are low-skill or unskilled—then the investment in changing the culture is probably unprofitable. However, for large organizations with complex processes, the benefits from a BPM-driven cultural change should deliver many times the required investment. Benefits to a large, complex organization that fosters a collaborative culture based on process management should include:

- Faster on-boarding of personnel due to clear representations of process responsibilities. Organizations with well-articulated processes have reported 50% or greater reduction in on-boarding time.
- Greatly reduced time searching for forms, templates, policies, and

other documentation needed by personnel to perform their tasks. Many studies have reported industry averages as high as 20% or more of staff time spent looking for information needed to perform responsibilities. With some BPM software now available, all relevant information is linked into process representations, so they are one click away. Of course, to keep all process-enabling artifacts up-to-date requires stewardship. But the time savings for personnel can be so great that the entire BPM initiative is paid for through higher workforce productivity (not to mention less frustration).

- Much more efficient and effective improvement efforts due to the high quality of collaboration that comes from using up-to-date process representations. Incident investigations, Lean Six Sigma improvement efforts, and performance discussions will all be done better.
- Improved understanding of workflow hand-offs with vendors, and implementation of outsourcing and merger arrangements. One energy company used process diagrams to discuss complex sub-sea installation processes involving several vendors. All came away with a clear understanding of their deliverables and how they would help achieve the overall project objectives.
- In general, greater pride, knowledge, satisfaction, and confidence among workforce personnel. This leads to reduced workforce turnover and greater discretionary efforts.

So, how hard is it to create the organization necessary to derive these benefits? Perhaps less so than many would expect; yet, it is not a trivial exercise to identify and nurture the roles that will be needed. Key roles that will be needed in a BPM-mature organization include:

- *Management Sponsor.* Ideally, this will be the highest-level position in the organization, and the person will be an effective advocate and adopter of the BPM approach.
- *BPM Manager or Program Coordinator.* This person will oversee the placement of personnel in other BPM roles, the selection of technologies, the establishment of standards and methods, and, ultimately, will be accountable to the Management Sponsor for the success of the initiative. This role may be the only full-time role required for the organization to get the most from its BPM efforts.
- *Process Sponsors.* Typically, these will be existing managers who will take on the additional role of overseeing the performance of processes under their control. Their two key responsibilities are: (a) using

process representations as a key part of discussions about changes that may be needed; and (b) ensuring that capable Process Advisors are in place.

- *Process Advisors.* These are people working in a specific process area—typically, with deep experience and trusted by others in the organization—who ensure process content is kept up-to-date, accessible, and as useful as possible to all personnel working within the assigned process scope. A given Process Sponsor may have multiple Process Advisors reporting to him or her, covering multiple process areas and/or multiple locations performing a similar process. Process Advisors are the 'engine' of strategic BPM. A large organization of 2000 people might have as many as 100 or more Process Advisors. This structural approach democratizes BPM, putting process representation in the hands of people who are close to the work. Process Advisors ensure the organization maximizes its return on its BPM investment by enabling higher productivity across the organization. In most cases, this role of Process Advisor would consume a small fraction of an employee's time; but, for some processes of particular importance or complexity, full-time attention may be justified.
- *Process mappers/modelers.* These are people who know how to use selected BPM technologies to create process representations. Typically, a person creating intuitive 'process maps' intended for collaborative use by personnel will be different than a person creating 'process models' that are intended to automate all or part of a workflow. The first type is critical for enabling strategic BPM, whereas the need for automation modelers will depend on whether automation is part of the BPM initiative.
- *Various technical and support personnel (as needed).* If BPM technologies are implemented, then probably someone in the IT department will be assigned to manage technical aspects of the software. Also, depending on the size and complexity of the organization, the BPM Manager/Program Coordinator may need, for example, other staff members to help with documentation of BPM standards.

Have I seen this approach work? Yes, more than once, but only up through the early stages of maturity. Unfortunately, management changes and marketplace events have intervened prior to the needed vision, roles, and organizational knowledge becoming embedded in the organization's culture. Nevertheless, the roles and interacting responsibilities of a process-oriented collaborative system have been tested and shown to work.

The mindset that management needs in order to nurture a BPM orientation is one of broad-based process engagement, wherein employees have routine interaction with a compelling electronic interface displaying personalized, role-specific content. It will be rich content because it will have been built and maintained by process subject matter experts throughout the organization. (These internal experts exist now in almost every organization, but are probably not having their knowledge and wisdom tapped into.) Their collective contributions, if properly governed, will create a comprehensive and integrated representation of the organization's process architecture.

In other words, strategic BPM is social BPM. It is useful to compare social engagement with an organization's graphical process architecture to other social technologies, such as Facebook, Twitter, and other social websites. Those sites work well because their founders have created a compelling platform upon which a more or less democratic forum can operate. The users then create content and even take ownership—for example, within the app's social framework for group sites. The intention of an ideal process engagement app also must be to make it easy to democratize content access, creation and change. In a mature BPM organization, think of Process Advisors as leaders of groups interested in the important work that they and their colleagues do. The process architecture should be a receptacle into which employees showcase the pride they have in their jobs.

W. Edwards Deming's *14th Key Principle* reads "Put everybody in the company to work to accomplish the transformation. The transformation is everybody's job." A compelling process engagement platform has the potential to enable this principle. Experience shows that younger employees, perhaps due to having grown up electronically enabled, readily engage with a compelling process interface and begin collaborating with colleagues without prompting. Evolving representations of processes that assist performers with tasks will be part of the future workplace.

In many ways, strategic BPM can be thought of as a technology-enabled next phase for TQM, and, because it includes process engagement by the entire workforce, its impact should be greater than Lean Six Sigma. The world awaits a paragon organization to show the way. Leaders and experts involved in a truly successful strategic BPM implementation are likely to become moderately famous as they extend Dr. Deming's legacy.

•••

ROGER BURLTON

President, Process Renewal Group

I do not think that this is even a question if an organization wishes to become process centric and customer driven. There is no choice but to take on these softer changes. The famous quote from Peter Drucker says, "Organizational culture eats strategy for breakfast." It is still true. Major programs that fail are primarily due to this. Most acquisitions and mergers that work do so because cultural considerations are handled well. The integration of Mars, Inc. and Wrigley was a major success because the two family-owned and operated ventures exhibited very similar cultural attributes—this was known as a critical requirement when agreeing to merge.

There are the 'hard stuff' parts, such as organizational structure, KPIs, targets and individual MBOs as incentives. All of these are based on business outcomes and stakeholder needs and expectations of the core processes. That means that every process will need to have a clear set of goals, performance indicators, and performance targets. Without these, the process cannot be evaluated and optimized. Also, without these, the association of business outcomes cannot be translated into shared group and personal outcomes and accountabilities, without which the incumbent culture will remain and drive sub-optimal performance. Individual managers are not stupid, and will work towards their own, albeit conflicting, incentives driven by a dysfunctional organizational structure. Changing the structure of the measurement of people is an absolutely necessary condition for success, but by no means sufficient. Culture, which I would define as 'the behaviors of a group in response to business situations and conditions', will not create itself, even if formal incentives are aligned. There is more to be done.

The culture change journey can be described by Sasha Aganova's extension of the Johari Window model. Navigating the journey from 1 to 2 is the formal training to develop base competency; from 2 to 3 requires observation and coaching from above; from 3 to 4 is peer collaboration and natural reinforcement in the group towards the behaviors needed. To define the required behaviors, a formal specification of the structural and cultural attributes is needed. Typically, the latter is missed. We must describe clearly the current behaviors that must change, and the target behaviors that must be established. This is not an accident, but a missing aspect of process change in most efforts. Based on this, the mechanisms for measurement, accountability, observation and coaching can be defined and the capabilities developed as part of the change initiative and the initial period of operation.

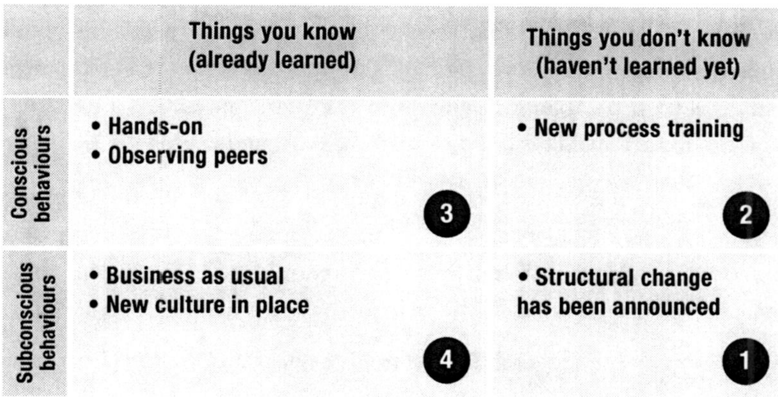

Figure 15: Johari Window model

....

FRED CUMMINS

Business Systems Architect, Agile Enterprise Design, LLC

A MATRIX IS A COMPETITIVE NECESSITY

In today's world, a matrix organization is not a choice, but a necessity. At the same time, the matrix that is needed may be somewhat different from the traditional interpretation. Here we consider matrix dimensions as the lines-of-business hierarchy versus a shared capabilities hierarchy.

Most businesses already have a matrix organization, though they may not acknowledge it. The silos of the traditional line-of-business organizations are not isolated. Of course, there are shared services, such as accounting, purchasing, and human resource management. Usually, IT is a shared service. These may not be considered to represent a matrix organization because they are not in-line with the production of the end product or service.

However, there are other collaborations that engage participants from multiple silos. These may include collaborations for method sharing among knowledge workers, and activities based on risk management, regulatory compliance, or security. These may still be considered ancillary support services, and they may not be formally managed by a distinct management hierarchy.

The modern enterprise executive realizes that there are capabilities required in multiple silos that should be consolidated for economies of scale, flexibility, security or control. The consolidation of such operations results in organizations that must serve the needs of multiple silos. If an organization providing a shared capability reports to the management of one silo, then their performance will be biased toward that managing silo.

In fact, in most enterprises, there are many capabilities that should be consolidated across lines of business (silos). The management of these consolidated capabilities is not just different because it should be independent, but also because these capabilities must be managed as providing shared services.

Consolidation and management of shared services requires a robust business modeling capability. VDML (Value Delivery Modeling Language) has recently been adopted by OMG for modeling business from a management perspective. This includes modeling capabilities and their relationships to organizations, processes and shared services.

VDML promotes the alignment of business processes with capabilities to describe business operations. A *capability* describes the availability of the personnel, skills, resources, methods, facilities, and intellectual property to perform a particular type of work. Capabilities are identified at a fairly fine level of detail so that they can be engaged in different contexts, such as multiple lines of business. In VDML, these sharable capabilities are called 'capability methods', and they describe the activities and flows of deliverables to apply a capability and deliver a result. These capabilities are intended to be available as services, and the scope of the capability method is the scope of the process that applies the capability.

The leadership of shared services must manage services to optimize the value to the enterprise, not a line-of-business. At the same time, a shared service must be responsive to the needs of its consumers. Shared services must have well-defined interfaces and level-of-service specifications. Consumers of a service should all use the same interface so that the capability method implementation is independent of the contexts in which it is used. This enables capability methods to be improved without impacting the consumers. A capability method may engage other shared methods to accomplish its purposes. The service provider must understand the impact of disruptions of service on possible requesters, and reflect this in service agreements.

The scope of each capability should be sufficiently granular to enable it to be relatively generic in functionality, and useful in different contexts. A consolidated capability should be able to make some changes to the implementation to improve the service without the knowledge or approval of the consumers of the services, as long as the interface and level of service are maintained. This opens the door to more local initiatives and innovation by people who best understand the nature and evolution of the capability, as well as opportunities created by new technology.

The matrix should consist of the line of business management hierarchy and the shared services management hierarchy. The shared services hierarchy should bring together similar capabilities under shared leadership. These aggregations of similar capabilities enable economies of scale in workload balancing, expertise, policy compliance, improvements and, probably, culture. With consolidated capabilities, there are fewer places to implement business changes or controls.

The shared services hierarchy must optimize performance from an enterprise perspective since it participants in the operation of all lines of business. When considering investments in improvement, the analysis must consider the impact on the affected capabilities and the lines of business that consume their services. Some lines of business may consider some improvements more important than others, and such differences must be resolved for an enterprise optimum.

VDML supports identification of dependencies between services and consumers, and it supports tracing contributions of value-to-value propositions for customers and other stakeholders. This evaluation of the impact of changes can improve objectivity for consideration of investments and priorities for change. It also supports similar analysis of a configuration for new business using shared capabilities, for analysis of merger compatibility, and opportunities for economies of scale.

....

GABY DOEBELI

Enterprise Architect, Brisbane City Council

The way an organization delivers its products and services is via its business processes; therefore, it is my belief that process-based management is a key to managing an organization, and one of the essential attributes is a culture with a focus on business process management and improvement. The infrastructure required to build a matrix organization and culture does require considerable effort and, possibly, years to implement and embed into an organization. Business design and operating principles across the different functions and practices require integration and alignment to support this goal. The values, behaviors, and capabilities required to succeed in a matrix management structure differs from those set up on a divisional or line management structure. The matrix organization is a design that combines functional and divisional structure, and drives a non-silo approach where strong cross-functional teamwork is performed to achieve business objectives. A matrix organization and culture is a top-down approach and spans across the enterprise.

There are benefits and limitations to the different categories of organizational management structures like a project, hybrid, matrix, line and divisional structures. For the purpose of this article, I have focused only on the advantages and disadvantages of the matrix organization and the pure divisional management structure.

The BPM practice is associated with a matrix management structure. The cultural values and behaviors in a matrix organization are of continuous problem finding and solution creating, with a strong focus on customer needs. It encourages continuous learning, applying common sense, and efficient exchange of information across teams and employees that are empowered to recommend solutions and take part in the running of the organization. A matrix-structured organization treats BPM as a management practice. It sees its processes as a business asset and, therefore, sets the strategies and performance objectives through the process lifecycle. Often, a team of professional BPM staff is assigned to support and build the capability in an organization to apply BPM. In summary, the benefits that might be achieved overall are a more responsive workforce to change, flexibility of resource allocation, and a more efficient delivery of products and services to the customers.

A disadvantage could be a more complex internal business management structure, as a matrix organization requires dual authority and decision-making, which includes additional roles and responsibilities that might create some tension and confusion among employees. This risk has to be managed to limit miscommunication that might lead to dissatisfaction among employees. The cost of running a matrix-managed organization might also increase, as there are additional roles required.

An advantage for a pure divisionally structured organization is that these are mostly simple structures where responsibility and accountability relationships are hierarchical; this promotes fast decision-making and is easy to understand. These structures allow great flexibility and are easily understood by employees.

The disadvantages can be limitations in specialists in planning, the overload of key employees, and that some staff might resent their lack of authority and this might create conflict. This structure is most effective in small organizations and might become ineffective if a business grows into a large enterprise.

Personally, I have experienced organizations that have embarked on the BPM journey applying the practice as a management tool and that have succeeded to various degrees. Organizations that are able to track and show the benefits of the BPM seem to sustain it, even through senior management changes—those not able to clearly state and show the value, seem to have no future.

In summary, the BPM practice in a matrix organization requires the infrastructure, and can only be sustained when integrated and aligned with other management disciplines. The practice requires management and monitoring to show benefits and value to the organization; only then does it have a future.

....

LEANDRO JESUS

Co-founder & Director, EloGroup

An organization creates value to its customers through processes that produce and deliver products and services. However, management systems are usually based on well-defined job functions and organizational charts.

We all understand traditional functional management, because it lacks process orientation, does not always ensure the best products or services will be delivered to customers. On the other hand, building a matrix organization—assigning managers (owners) to organizational processes—may sound challenging in the sense it promotes a significant cultural change. How to face this question?

We do not believe in promoting the shift from a functional view to a matrix organization by naming a manager for each of the existing organizational processes; we have seen lot of confusion and little effectiveness in the market in this direction!

We understand an adequate management system should assure work is well performed in order to meet customer needs. Process orientation should be used to complement, rather than substitute, traditional management. In this sense, before indiscriminately creating a process manager position, we must analyze what are the real limitations of our existing functional practices.

Certainly, every process needs to be managed and, in fact, many already are by our usual managers—and that management may be enough. Thus, what we need to determine is in which cases functional management is enough, and in which cases establishing an additional governance mechanism is important to take care of the end-to-end process. Let's look at a hypothetical example in the figure below:

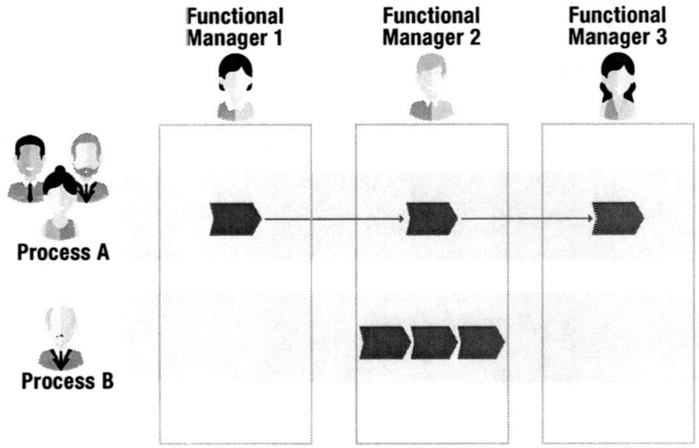

Figure 16: Functional vs Process Management

Process A is decomposed into activities that involve three distinct business functions. It's typically cross-functional, and requires a lateral coordination mechanism. Consider, for example, a product development process (from idea to launch). The process requires the involvement of many different areas, such as marketing, R&D, finance, and operations to effectively launch a new product and analyze its impact on current operations. It is, therefore, quite cross-functional. Letting this process happen under the sole coordination of one area might negatively impact its performance.

Process B, on the other hand, is decomposed into activities that are totally, or predominantly, in the scope of a single functional unit. Managing this process is possibly something that already properly occurs in the current structure—that is, a functional manager already handles it. This is the typical case in which managing the process is an assignment to the existing functional role, and thinking about any additional governance structure just makes something complex that already works. For example, a product manufacturing process (from raw-material processing to finished goods inventory) is usually handled largely by an operations area.

Even for cross-functional processes, day-by-day management is not always better activated by the assignment of a process manager. We have seen many success cases based on the creation of committees with existing managers, or simply based on establishing shared goals that should be tracked by them in regular meetings. What is common, in both cases, is that the process manager's role, in practice, is not being implemented by a new position. It's primarily not about *who* manages the process, but about *how* it's better managed to effectively reach its targets.

We suggest that, before moving into a more complex discussion on governance, the company start with a simpler, more pragmatic view of activating management meetings for each typical cross-functional process. These day-by-day management forums should concentrate efforts on solving integration problems, which are unlikely to be solved by continuous improvement cycles within functional units. Thus, process orientation complements and reinforces functional management in an organic manner.

MATTHEW J. MORGAN

Head of Process & Metrics Excellence, Bridgewater Assoc.

The journey is a long one and, unfortunately, I cannot yet report a total success from an enterprise that has achieved the highest maturity levels implied by the full cultural embrace of process-oriented management. However, I have experienced several organizations that have made material progress in this direction, reaping benefits along the way.

At the lowest levels of maturity, organizations seem to unwittingly accomplish the biblical guidance of the alms-giver (let not thy left hand know what thy right hand doeth). Without coordination among different parts of the organization, there are often redundant initiatives whose costs add up over time and whose work can, at times, be at cross-purposes.

While movement towards a more collaborative culture can be both painful and intensive, the cost savings alone in rationalizing redundant initiatives and organizations can make it worth taking the initial steps. As organizations can start to identify and then eliminate such non-value-added redundancies, they position themselves for even greater gains through better coordination and accomplishing their goals.

I will address these benefits further in Question 7 on the return on investment of BPM. However, before concluding this discussion, I want to address the cultural dimension more specifically. Aside from financial implications, a culture of collaboration has benefits from a human-relations perspective. Employee engagement and 'net happiness' will be greater as people are aligned to a common purpose and work with one another rather than at cross-purposes. The enhanced cultural atmosphere alone could be considered justification for the effort.

At the business unit level, I led a turnaround operation in the hospitality industry in which the hotel's operational delivery was poor, and departments were extremely siloed. One of the key performance indicators I began tracking was the average response (across the organization and in departments) to the employee survey question: *do employees from different departments work well together?* I even included improvement of this metric as a performance objective for each of my direct reports (the department heads). In addition, I established programs, such as cross-training and cross-utilization, 'internships' in other departments, and similar initiatives.

One of the (many) underperforming operational metrics of the hotel was the cleanliness of rooms (based on both guest satisfaction surveys, guest complaints to the corporate customer services office, and my own audits). The housekeepers' performance levels and motivation were low, so I brought in more supplies for them to better accomplish their work, and established incentives, training, and inspections. A hotel's housekeeping department is dependent on the engineering department to repair maintenance defects identified by housekeepers (and engineering depended on housekeeping to identify problems that must be fixed). I asked those two departments to merge their daily stand-up meetings once each week. This provided an opportunity to improve communication and mutual understanding between departments in which mistrust had grown over time. I also sent other associates from departments throughout the hotel (including myself) to spend shifts cleaning rooms with housekeepers to improve cross-departmental understanding and engagement.

A signature program in this approach was the 'Adopt a Housekeeping Section', in which managers from all departments sponsored a section of the hotel and its assigned housekeeper. (There were five sections of about a dozen rooms per floor, which was almost fifty sections in the hotel.) The managers partnered with housekeepers on improving the cleanliness of their assigned areas, helping occasionally during busy checkout days, checking rooms, and providing another channel of communication for reporting maintenance shortcomings.

This case study shows the benefits across a range of indicators as the employee survey question on working well together improved, as well as overall morale and front-line ratings of managerial effectiveness. In addition, the operational metrics on cleanliness improved. Availability of rooms (and thus the ability to sell the rooms) improved. All of this led to better financial performance and market share among the hotel's competitive set.

GILLES MORIN

Founder, BPMPlus Inc.

One of the first reactions we get from management teams that have seriously taken the BPM journey and started working at their processes transversally from end-to-end is that BPM is breaking down silos. People have to work together as part of one single value chain focused on delivering more value to customers and other stakeholders.

There are two schools of thoughts here. Some believe that BPM should start tactically, almost bottom-up, delivering process improvement projects here and there. They mention that organizations must mature on at least two levels (CMMI) before thinking about doing end-to-end process work, implementing strong process governance and completing a process-driven business architecture. Other practitioners believe that process governance and process architecture ought to be in place at the beginning, but in a way that it fits the existing culture and maturity. My view is more the 'meet in the middle' one. I believe that with the right mix of lean culture changing ingredient, architecture plots, process improvement projects and process automation sprints you have more chance to get where you need to go faster and with more success. It's a matter of adopting the right execution strategy, and there are no ideal or unique ones.

Obviously, matrix-driven organizations do not go through the same hurdles in implementing matrix management where you have functional managers also accountable for a cross-organizational value stream. They have already adapted key capabilities, such as roles, performance management systems, communication processes, reporting systems, rules, etc.

Most often than not, organizations have not developed such matrix organizations and a process/systemic thinking culture. In these situations, we often use process project governance as a first step toward a more robust matrix organization. Then, after few projects, after bigger process projects cutting across multiple departments or teams, matrix roles and behaviors seep in. The implementation of a matrix organization with decision-makers playing dual roles, and with vertical and horizontal accountabilities, cannot be done in a flip-flop manner, unless this shift is imposed top-down with strong managerial courage and the will to change key HR management levers.

One barrier is that some leaders cannot make that change. We see similar issues trying to embed Lean thinking as a transformational and strategic program in large organization—this is why a Lean program includes a strong and non-negotiable 'Lean leader' training and coaching module. Often, operational managers have been promoted because they were the most senior and expert in their functional area. They may show strong vertical leadership; but showing horizontal leadership has a very different twist—it requires different leadership attributes, and not all vertical leaders can make that switch.

Is it worth the effort? Yes, if you are in a long-term path to build a change-driven organization and if you want an enduring competitive advantage. No, if you are in a turnaround situation or caught in an everlasting cost-cutting spiral. Building a process culture and matrix organization requires that you align at least four key levers: "T" leadership combining lateral and value stream thinking, and capacity to act or execute is highly sought for in many organizations.

PHIL SHORT

IT Director, Mars Canada

Business Process Management is the strategic approach to using the definition, understanding, and improvement of processes to manage the organization; and process governance defines the rules by which the strategy is deployed.

There are many interpretations of both process governance and process management. For me, process management is a strategic choice to use the understanding and management of business processes to achieve its strategic and operational objectives. An agreed-upon business process architecture is required as a first step in business process management, because without some representation of the business processes within the organization, you have none to manage. Once this process architecture is in place, the organization needs a way to use, maintain and evolve it. Process governance is put in place to perform this role and to ensure consistency across and collaboration between all processes. So, in essence, process management is the strategic approach to using processes to manage the organization, and process governance defines the rules by which this strategy is deployed.

If the organization is embarking on a BPM strategy, then process governance must start at the very top of the organization, and the most senior leader of the organization has to be committed to the process management approach. Most organizations operate using functional management; so, when a BPM approach is adopted, leaders have to have process, as well as functional accountability and responsibility. This results in a matrix organization where, operationally, leaders have to manage their function on a day-to-day basis—but, in addition, they have end-to-end process responsibilities to ensure that the core business processes are delivering the required value to customers.

Senior executives must take on these new process stewardship roles for core business processes. Let's consider a simple process architecture for a manufacturing company. This would typically have 'plan', 'make', 'sell' and 'deliver' core processes. It would make sense for the VP of finance to be the process steward for 'plan', the VP of manufacturing to be the process steward for 'make', and so on. They retain their functional responsibilities for all aspects of finance or manufacturing, but they take on the additional responsibility for the end-to-end health of the process they are assigned.

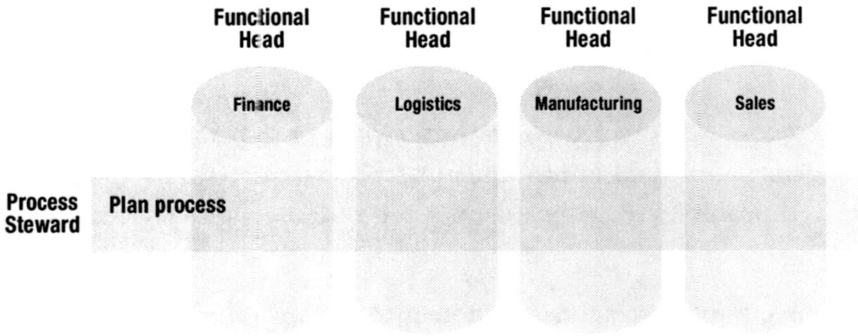

Figure 17: Function/Process Responsibility Matrix

This stewardship role has to be endorsed from the most senior leaders if it is to have real value The process stewards work with all functional leaders within their allocated process to resolve issues and make changes to improve performance. They are responsible for making sure that the process is understood and documented, that performance is monitored and improved, and they also become the project champion for any changes that have to be made to the process.

Let's consider the 'plan' process. In its simplest form, it would start with the input of a sales forecast and would end with a series of plans for manufacturing, inventory and financials. The process would be performed by some finance roles, but would also require involvement from sales, logistics and manufacturing roles. The responsibility of the process steward is to ensure that the end-to-end process is understood by all functions, and that it is documented and delivers the required outputs and outcomes. The process steward has to, therefore, take off his/her functional hat and consider the cross-functional nature of the process. Without a process-governance structure, changing or improving processes that cross functions is very difficult since there would be no one responsible for the health of the end-to-end process—only the individual functional components leading to sub-optimal compromised solutions.

In a complete process-governance organization there would be a level below the process steward that would have similar responsibilities to the process steward, but for the sub-processes. These process managers, or functional experts, would likely be department managers or team leaders keeping operational responsibilities along with added responsibility for the analysis and documentation of their process. They would likely have some IT systems knowledge and how these systems enable their process. It is also likely that these process managers would be key members of project teams when changes to processes or enabling systems are undertaken. The process-governance organization is completed with the lowest level that represents key users of the IT systems. They are experts in the use of the IT systems, and would be responsible for establishing work instructions for how these are used within the process, and for training other users in effective system operation.

Another aspect of process governance is establishing standards and the provision of tools, techniques, and expertise to facilitate good process management. This can be anything from some simple documented guidelines to a fully funded and functioning process center of excellence. It is my view that process governance should probably evolve from the former to the latter. I have worked in an environment where process management has evolved from basic concepts to assist in IT ROI, to one where a true function/process matrix organization is in place and is now an integral part of the culture. This was accomplished using some process pioneers working on peer-to-peer training and informal standards. It created a track record of successful project delivery and business performance advancement through process improvement. In truth, the cost of this has been minimal and, because of the evolutionary nature, process is now embedded in the culture—now there is an informal center of excellence that ensures that the standards continue to evolve. The challenge of implementing a formal process center of excellence is the constant need to justify its existence and funding. The need for governance to provide standards within a BPM approach is without question; however, the method of delivering does not have carry a large price tag.

In summary, I do not believe that you can truly embrace business process management without some form of governance to promote process knowledge and performance, and to foster standards in tools, techniques, and documentation. It is possible, and maybe even essential, to introduce the levels of governance over time as the organization reaches higher levels of process maturity—but it is not possible to successfully implement a BPM approach without process governance.

....

PROFESSOR JAN VOM BROCKE

Hilti Chair of Business Process Management, University of Liechtenstein

BPM research and practice have long focused on technological and methodological issues. However, many practitioners and academics increasingly understand that cultural resistance is a key factor to the failure of BPM initiatives. This is one of the reasons why people have started to view BPM more holistically, which includes the consideration of social phenomena such as culture.

While culture is increasingly considered as an essential success factor for BPM projects, the underlying mechanisms of how culture interacts with BPM have long remained unclear and under-researched. However, more recent studies have started to explore the relationships of various cultural groups and concepts in the context of BPM (Schmiedel et al., 2015).

For example, the model of BPM culture by vom Brocke and Sinnl (2011) provides a more holistic understanding of the various notions of culture in BPM and their interrelations. The model consists of three main elements: i) BPM culture; ii) cultural context; and ii) cultural fit (see the figure below).

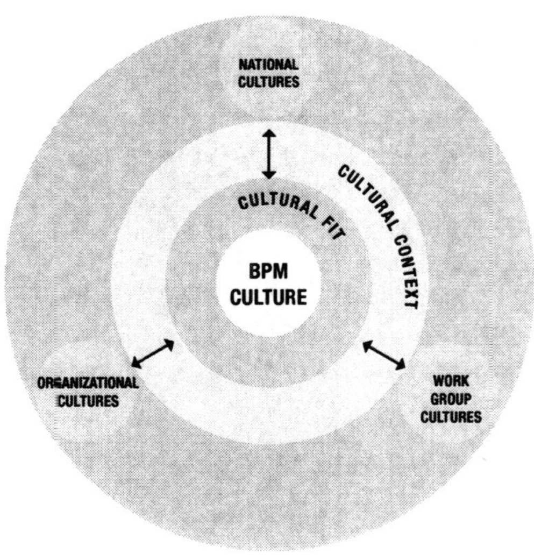

Figure 18: BPM culture model (vom Brocke, Sinnl 2011)

- BPM culture is understood as an organizational culture that supports reaching BPM objectives. As values are the core elements of culture, BPM culture consists of values that support the success of BPM projects and that are inherent in BPM as a management approach. In other words, BPM culture represents values that an organization has to embrace in order to do effective BPM.

- The cultural context comprises all kinds of group cultures that are present when starting a BPM initiative, such as organizational, national, and work-group cultures. These often share strong relationships, and form a complex cultural environment that a BPM project faces in the beginning.
- The cultural fit refers to a basic congruence between BPM culture as a requirement for successful BPM (to-be culture) and a given cultural context (as-is culture). According to the model, the phenomenon of cultural resistance in BPM projects occurs due to a lack of cultural fit between BPM culture and cultural context.

Internal and external customer orientation, continuous improvement and innovation, accountability and responsibility, and formal and informal cross-functional teamwork are key cultural values that determine BPM success (Schmiedel et al., 2013). To actively manage culture in BPM, it is essential to understand the critical cultural elements for effective BPM, and be able to measure the extent to which these elements are present in a given organizational culture (Schmiedel et al., 2014).

References

Schmiedel, T., vom Brocke, J., & Recker, J. (2014). Development and Validation of an Instrument to Measure Organizational Cultures' Support of Business Process Management. *Information & Management, 51*(1), 43–56.

Schmiedel, T., vom Brocke, J., & Recker, J. (2015). Culture in Business Process Management: How Cultural Values Determine BPM Success. In J. vom Brocke & M. Rosemann (Eds.), *Handbook on Business Process Management: Strategic Alignment, Governance, People and Culture (International Handbooks on Information Systems)* (2 ed., Vol. 2, pp. 649–664). Berlin et al.: Springer.

Schmiedel, T., vom Brocke, J., & Recker, J. (2013). Which cultural values matter to business process management? Results from a global Delphi study. *Business Process Management Journal (BPMJ), 19*(2), 292–317.

vom Brocke, J., & Sinnl, T. (2011). Culture in business process management. A literature review. *Business Process Management Journal (BPMJ), 17*(2), 357–377.

QUESTION 6

WHY A PROCESS ARCHITECTURE?

Architecture is an important concept in contemporary management. There are many forms and definitions of architectural constructs: enterprise, business systems, process, capabilities, information, application rules, services, organization, and resources, to name a few. Various architectural models give different prominence to process architecture—from low levels of importance to primacy.

How do you see the position of process architecture in the overall architecture of architectures? In what way do you suggest that a process architecture be best used?

OVERVIEW

There is no disagreement among our authors that a process architecture is a fundamental component of BPM. It is the touchstone for all BPM-related activity. The many pitfalls of building and using a process architecture are noted, but its considerable practical value as both a strategic and tactical tool is strongly endorsed.

In contrast to shared aspiration among the authors for a process architecture to provide a shared vocabulary, a *lingua franca* of business management, is their differing descriptions of what a process architecture actually is, and of the details of its content and context. Business approaches divided by a common language?

The place of process architecture in a larger context of business or enterprise architecture is thoroughly canvassed. While most authors support the idea of the primacy of process, it is noted that the most successful 'architectures' are related to IT assets. Process architecture is the odd one out in this context, as it demands strong and sustained business involvement, an involvement for which additional IT effort is no substitute. Process architecture is only useful if the business says it is, and it can only become useful if the business builds and sustains it.

....

TALAL A. ALSUBAIE

Managing Director, Modprex

For many reasons, organizations build a process architecture and integrate it to other architectures, such as those for strategy, in-formation, rules, and others. Here, my aim is to focus on how process architecture helps organizations in the area of process modeling and improvement.

Process modeling is a time-intensive task, and most organiza-tions do not gain significant benefit from this effort—often be-cause they lack a process architecture.

The first problem caused by the absence of such an architecture is that the organization lacks a connection between the strategy view and the processes that execute it. For employees, it is im-portant to be able to trace how the processes in which they are involved realize organizational objectives. This helps them to bet-ter understand the role they play in achieving the organization's strategy, and how can they contribute to this achievement. On the other hand, having such a link helps the organization to prioritize process improvement and modeling initiatives based on the stra-tegic impact of those processes. In addition, this link between strategy and the process architecture helps to clarify the impact of the strategy on the organization's processes, and how process per-formance impacts the strategy.

The second challenge of not having a process architecture is that this directly effects the use of process models. In my work as a consultant, I have seen organizations without a process architec-ture end up having hundreds, or sometimes thousands, of pro-cesses on a single level. This creates several challenges and prob-lems as summarized below.

1. Scope: Documenting the processes on a single level without having a process architecture ends up over-lapping the scope of several processes. Without an ar-chitecture, there is no clear view of where the first process ends and when the second process starts. A process architecture clearly shows process modelers the previous process and the process that follows, permitting more precise modeling and preventing the scrambling of multiple processes.

2. Level of detail: Having a consistent level of detail across the organization's process models is not easy without a process architecture as a guide. In a single organiza-tion, we see process models with as few as three tasks, and others with as many as thirty. Neither of these is necessarily right nor wrong, but consistency across process models is important to maintain readability and usability. A process architecture defines consistent levels, and this allows smaller, more manageable mod-els with a reasonable and consistent number of activi-ties—this makes them easier to read, understand, and follow.

3. Accessibility: Finding information about a certain pro-cess can be a challenge. It may be necessary to search through hundreds of process models; however, with a process architecture, finding a particular model will be much easier—since there will be a logical path from the value chain level to the target process.

4. Alignment: One of the main objectives of a process ar-chitecture is to facilitate alignment of processes. Mod-eling processes within a process architecture will show the upstream and downstream processes. This helps process modeling, showing the context in which the process executes, and documenting its impact on other processes.

5. Root cause analysis: When trying to improve the perfor-mance a process, we should focus on removing the root cause of the problem rather than just dealing with the symptoms. A performance problem may be seen in one process, but the cause of that problem can be in a different process that seems far away from the process in focus. Diagnosing that problem

without access to a well-aligned process architecture is difficult.

6. Priorities: Organizations lack sufficient time and re-sources to document and improve all of their process-es, and there is little purpose in doing so. However, focusing on certain areas of the process architecture—and using evidence-based analysis (e.g. pain-gain analy-sis)—allows better decisions about where to focus the analysis and improvement efforts. Using a process ar-chitecture will significantly help to: determine those areas of focus; communicate them to others; and un-derstand the complete end-to-end process and its rela-tionships with others.

This answer focuses only on how a process architecture helps or-ganizations with process modeling and improvement initiatives. Having a process architecture also delivers additional benefits: en-hanced process governance; an architecture of performance meas-urement; a better understanding of cross-functional value creation, accumulation, and delivery; and improved understanding of how strategy is executed.

....

JIM BOOTS
Owner, Global Process Innovation

Process architecture is a fundamental conceptual component of organizations which, when included with other architectural components, comprise the enterprise architecture—aka, the architecture of architectures. The enterprise architecture is the descriptive representation of all aspects of the enterprise *at varying levels of detail.* The italicized portion of that statement is important to understand. Each architectural component can be thought of as consisting of a hierarchy of elements, gradually decomposed to greater and greater detail. Additionally, some elements throughout the hierarchy—perhaps even all of the elements in a sophisticated organization—will have metadata associated with them; thus aiding further analysis. The ultimate purpose of addressing organizational needs with an enterprise architecture perspective is to reveal both high-leverage optimization opportunities (such as outsourcing entire functions or lines of business) and continuous waste identification and elimination.

Process architecture—managed as part of a mature BPM capability—can be a big contributor to the overall value proposition of enterprise architecture. Unfortunately, most organizations' enterprise architecture functions have not distilled much value from process architecture. This is partly due to the need for the process architecture to strongly involve business people rather than just IT people. When process management is reduced to an 'IT thing', its contribution to the organization is likely to be tactical at best, and possibly marginal and fleeting.

The figure below provides a representation of the major components of every organization's enterprise architecture (although, in the simplest organizations, some of the architectural components may have minimal practical content).

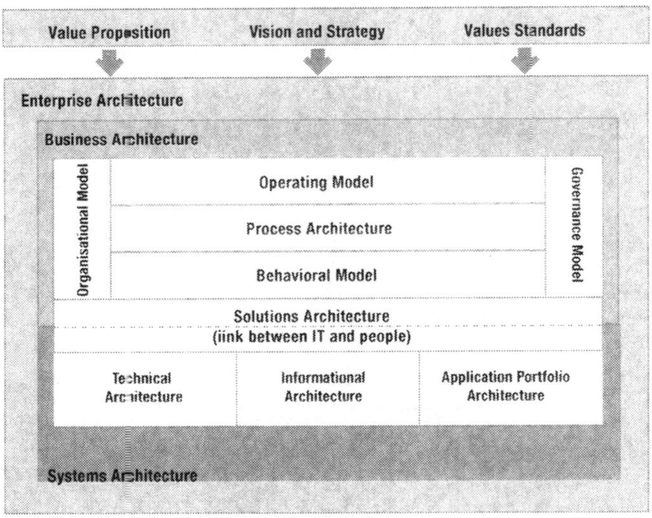

Figure 19: Conceptual representation of Enterprise Architecture

Note that this diagram is not a widely accepted representation of enterprise architecture, much less a universally accepted one. It is my representation, developed with insights from having been an enterprise architect at a large company for a couple of years. People who have seen the graphic have liked it because they thought it hit the mark. Readers can judge for themselves whether it is helpful.

Each of the components depicted in this enterprise architecture model has had books written about them. We do not have the space here to address each component with justice, so let's just skim the surface on a few components from the EA Model.

The Operating Model includes components such as legal entity type, markets served and customer types, employee base, supply chain model, public interface, financial model, functional capabilities, and operating locations. In simple terms, the Operating Model consists of facts that might be used to describe the company's business activities in an annual report.

The Information Architecture includes information types and data types. Some of these types will be further decomposed to sub-types, eventually decomposing to specific information/data elements, such as a specific annual plan, or a single pressure reading on an industrial pump.

The Application Portfolio Architecture typically divides the organization's applications into somewhere between ten and thirty application types, within which sub-types and, ultimately, specific applications themselves are detailed. The needs of the end-user base, and the functions of applications and their relationships to other applications, are key concerns when managing an application portfolio over time, as technologies and processes change.

Now let's address the Process Architecture. Components within this include roles, activities, inputs and outputs. The key purpose the process architecture plays is to represent activities and their relationships, and to show how they produce the organization's desired outputs. As with other architectures, it is organized in a hierarchical fashion for the sake of people who, at times, want to see the big picture and, at other times, want to see more detail. So, at the highest level of an organization's process architecture, we might expect to see some version of a value chain process with steps such as 'procure', 'make', 'sell', 'ship', and 'invoice'. In addition to such value chain steps, the top-level diagram may show some overall management processes and support processes. Once all the organization's highest-level processes have been represented on the top level of the process architecture, each high-level process can be decomposed—as many levels as necessary—until underlying activities are described at the task level.

Now that we understand what process architecture is and how it fits into the enterprise architecture, let's turn to how it best can be used.

There is a big gap in the way that a BPM-mature organization will use its process architecture versus a less mature organization (which may not possess anything even resembling a representation of a process architecture). Although there are relatively few organizations that have achieved high maturity, let's focus on one so we can paint a vision of what is possible.

In an organization with high BPM maturity, the process architecture becomes the primary platform around which conversations about the organization's performance revolves. This is true at the strategic level, where, for example, management may need to consider disruptive changes to its supply chain; and it is true at the lowest operational level where supervisors train, motivate, and reinforce employees in the performance of their assigned tasks. In all cases, a well-articulated process architecture enables a robust conversation in which terms and intentions are understood by all participants.

Here's an example. There is a serious safety incident at a manufacturing company where an employee is injured and off work for six months. In the least process-oriented organizations, there often would be a tendency to blame the injured person for not properly following procedures. However, in a mature organization with a well-articulated process architecture, management will have the means for an improvement-oriented discussion about the adequacy of processes:

- Select and train new employees—Did the new employee fit the specified profile? Was she/he properly trained and mentored?
- Follow appropriate procedures—Were the procedures used up-to-date, understandable, and appropriate? Was the right protective equipment available and used?
- Procure materials—Were materials and equipment as specified? Did anything change?

Because the process architecture is kept up-to-date and generally accessible, managers, supervisors, and employees have a shared platform for collaboration where all ideas for improvement can be judged with a common perspective on workflow-related activities and desired outcomes.

In addition to being a boon for incident and performance analysis, a well-articulated process architecture can serve as the primary training platform for employees new to a role. Organizations with carefully described processes have reported on-boarding time for new personnel to be reduced by more than 50%. Needless to say, in organizations with significant turnover, this can be a big time savings. More importantly, the confidence gained by new employees when they have a clear understanding of their roles and objectives—and how they relate to the bigger picture of the organization—is nearly invaluable.

A dynamic process architecture also can be a lever to improvement programs, such as Lean Six Sigma, because: (a) bigger improvement opportunities are easier to pinpoint; (b) improvement teams are more efficient because an 'as-is' representation of the target process already exists; and (c) changes needed for improvement are much more easily deployed and adhered to because personnel are fluent in understanding how changes in diagrams translate to changes in the actions that they take.

Perhaps the biggest benefit of a dynamically updated process architecture is the message of 'pride of work' that is conveyed when employees see that management considers the work of every employee important enough to be thoughtfully represented. Furthermore, by involving employees in the creation and vetting of the process architecture, everyone comes away with a deeper understanding of their roles and how they contribute to the organization's mission.

That is the vision for process architecture. Most organizations are not even close to that state. Conversations about processes, if they happen at all, tend to float off into the ether with little common understanding of what needs to change at a detailed level. Changes may be agreed (e.g. to please some vocal manager), but often they are insufficient to address root causes of inadequate performance. If process representations exist at all, they are typically contained in some non-managed artifact such as a flipchart or a Visio diagram, and such diagrams almost always lack the context of processes around them that feed inputs and receive outputs. Most importantly, employees have a very partial understanding of how the work of the organization fits together and why their roles are important for organizational success.

An organization's representation of its process architecture is the most important ingredient that distinguishes strategic BPM from tactical process improvement or automation efforts. By introducing a common platform for communication about the work of the organization, strategic BPM changes the behaviors of every employee. Strategic BPM empowers every employee with confidence, proper support and materials, motivation that comes from being part of a well-understood mission, and accountability for doing one's best.

It is time for management in every organization of significant size and complexity to commit to the rigor of maintaining a dynamic process architecture. The pay-off in terms of productivity, profitability, and employee satisfaction will be large.

ROGER BURLTON
President, Process Renewal Group

These days, there is a big emphasis on architecture as an enterprise management enabler. It was originally founded as an IT concept to define and glue together various IT assets and priorities (application, data, SOA, IT capability architecture). These perspectives are reflected in frameworks such as TOGAF.

Figure 20: Business Model Canvas

A broader view of architecture, as more of an enterprise concept, is reflected in BIZBOK and, especially, Zachman, which cover multiple concepts that must be associated to support a whole business point of view. The strategic side of the business model is gaining more attention, as seen in the growth in usage of the Business Model Canvas. There are many concepts that could be considered as shown in the diagram below. No framework or methodology covers all of these, but if one area is important to you, it should be included and connected.

Each of the published frameworks has some aspect of process in it, but some—such as BIZBOK and TOGAF—treat it lightly, preferring instead to focus on capabilities and treating processes as a tactical support for capabilities rather than a concept of the first order.

I believe strongly, and I have heard John Zachman say the same on many occasions, that there should be no hierarchies *among* concepts (e.g. process is *not* a subset of capability or vice-versa), only hierarchy within a subject of interest (e.g. a conceptual value chain can have multiple level 1, 2, 3 processes, and so on). Each concept, such as processes and data, should be separate and define its components hierarchically. Different concepts can be associated; however, in a many-to-many relationship (e.g. a process needs multiple capabilities, and a capability may require more than one effective process). This 'separate but associate' principle is at the heart of an agile architecture and a flexible business.

The glue that holds them together in the most effective way is the process architecture, since more enabling concepts and guiding factors can be directly connected to and from processes. Without processes, there is no architectural connectivity—and there is no traceability to business performance and the strategy of the value chain. There are methods that put process at the center, such as the BPTA approach, and many process frameworks that are predominantly about processes, such as SCOR and APQC Process Classification Framework. These are highly utilized to solve problems of defining the work and associating the resources required to it.

The process architecture is essential to defining the business. It is what we do, and how we do it. It informs and connects all the other aspects of business capability.

....

ANDREAS HAVLIZA

Consulting Principal, Team Leader, Leonardo Consulting

INDRAJIT DATTA CHAUDHURI

Senior Consultant, Leonardo Consulting

CLEMENT HURPIN

Consultant, Leonardo Consulting

A business process architecture (BPA) is the key element in a Business Process Management (BPM) framework! It should be the starting point of every BPM program or project, as it clearly defines the organization's process landscape. The aim of a process architecture should be to represent the organization's main processes and decompose them into sub-processes where required. If no process architecture is in place, BPM efforts are doomed to be localized and, most likely, difficult to be reproduced in other areas of the organization. The value of process architecture is manifold.

- *First and foremost, strategic oversight.* A process architecture provides a picture of how strategic intent is fulfilled. An organization's goal is to accomplish certain things, these things usually being described in the vision/mission statement. A BPA allows us to visualize this business, and literally see the flow of high-level steps that need to be accomplished in order to deliver the product or services to customers.
- *A holistic view.* A BPA is holistic; it can (and should!) represent the business as a whole. This is not to say that everything the company has ever done should be represented on one or multiple diagrams, but everything a company does should be represented at some level in the process architecture. This holistic picture gives us a platform that other artefacts can be related to: connecting programs and projects, re-engineering efforts, other architectures, etc.
- *A basis for improvement.* With the help of metrics assigned to processes, process evaluations can take place. From there, targets for improvement can be set and monitored. It can be identified where the problems occur, and countermeasures can be implemented.
- *Interdependencies.* A process architecture highlights process interdependencies and process interfaces that BPM projects need to be aware of, and helps, therefore, with the scoping of BPM projects.
- *Governance.* A process architecture also allows the assignments of

accountabilities—that is, process guardians with the responsibility to react to process anomalies—of those processes for which they are accountable. Ideally, the process architecture is set up in a top-down approach. Starting with a very high-level process map of an organization, and offering more detailed processes in those areas where required.

- *Replication.* A successful process architecture can make a strong basis to replicate a business model. Organization based on a franchising model can, for example, replicate their process architecture to represent the same business elsewhere—a strong head start.
- *Communication.* An actively maintained process architecture defines a common language and offers an organization wide reference to process areas and related artefacts. The key is to communicate the defined process architecture and to make it available to all stakeholders—ideally to all employees of an organization.

MATTHEW J. MORGAN

Head of Process & Metrics Excellence, Bridgewater Assoc.

In my approach to process excellence and operations strategy, I consider the process architecture as the key managerial artifact. I begin by understanding the value chain of the business. How does the enterprise provide value to customers? What is the high-level process? After understanding the conceptual sequence of the value chain, decomposing into sub-processes (and continuing to do this successively) helps managers and stakeholders have a view of the organization.

To provide context on terms of reference, regarding the different architecture disciplines, I consider that the business / process / capabilities architecture as the framework or anchor for other associated architectures (data, applications, technology infrastructure, etc.). For context, I consider the term *enterprise architecture* as the aggregation and alignment of these various architectures, and *business architecture* as the sub-discipline that is focused on business value (and, therefore, in this usage, generally synonymous with process and capabilities architecture). I have heard of controversy about the difference between a capabilities and process architecture. If capabilities are organized into value chains, then I don't see much practical difference between the two.

Business architecture provides a top-down model; a 'lens' through which the enterprise can be viewed. I would like to acknowledge Don Harder of Arc Partners with thought partnership on some of the foregoing ideas about business architecture. The model fosters alignment of business objectives, tactical demands, and investment priorities, and presents a cross-department, enterprise view of capabilities and how the business operates. The architecture provides a common understanding of capabilities (r high-level processes) that enables identification of process and technology gaps, overlaps, hot spots, and process improvement and consolidation opportunities. The business architecture can be integral in a wide array of use cases as shown in the table below:

Table 3: Business architecture use cases

POTENTIAL USE	DESCRIPTION
Business/IT alignment	Map IT applications, data, and infrastructure to business capabilities to understand and address gaps and overlaps.
Strategic differentiation	Identify capabilities that are differentiating versus commodity and determine improvement or transformation targets.
Benchmarking	Identify 'hot spots' for management attention by attaching metrics to capabilities and measuring performance against competitor or best practice benchmarks.
Business planning and reporting	Plan investments and anticipated benefits using capabilities to ensure continuity over time and impacts across departments.
Business continuity and disaster recovery	Use the business architecture as a framework for business continuity management.

Process architecture is generally built on a consistent hierarchy with defined and normalized levels and a consistent taxonomy. Third-party reference architectures can be helpful in providing a baseline taxonomy to ensure coverage of all related capabilities or processes, and to organize them into logical parent-child hierarchies and conceptually logical sequences. One of my favorite third-party reference architectures is the Process Classification Framework (PCF) of the American Productivity & Quality Center. The PCF also has the benefit of allowing organizations to acquire benchmarking data on various key performance indicators, organized according to the categories decomposed in the reference architecture.

Business capabilities describe the unique collection of business processes, IT resources, and services that departments employ to achieve their business goals and deliver value. Business capabilities are not specific functions or detailed processes. They describe what the business does, not how it does it.

Capability dependencies identify the specific processes and technology required to support a capability. These dependencies are managed by the other architecture disciplines, and include business process, technology, and service provider dependencies. See below for a simple object model depicting these relationships.

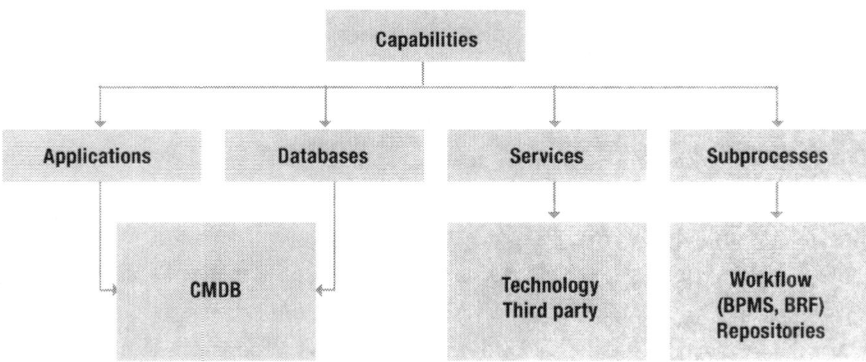

Figure 21 Business capabilities and dependencies

....

GILLES MORIN

Founder, BPMPlus Inc.

A VALID process architecture has high value at both strategic and tactical project levels. The process architecture is one of the two key blueprints composing the business architecture, with the capability map. The process architecture allows us to anchor the service and data architectures, whereas the capability map allows us to anchor the business application architecture. BIZBOK 4.5 has just been released, and is an excellent reference that helps to connect the dots between the different architectures or enterprise blueprints.

Strategically, we use process-driven business architecture to force alignment between the following: strategic intents and stakeholders needs (the strategic outcomes); the core capabilities of an organization (including its processes, technologies, data, rules, organizations, human capital, culture, etc.); the investment project portfolio (which includes all IT, process and capability dollar projects); and results. The process architecture is the only way to ensure full traceability between targets, decisions and results. We also use process architecture to force common language and shared meaning development amongst decision-makers. This may seems a bit theoretical, but it is the first stepping-stone to foster alignment. Finally, process architecture is a key lever to break siloed thinking and instill process driven culture. In that sense, a VALID process architecture, done at strategic level, is a transformational lever.

Sitting in between strategic and tactical levels, is the process architecture done prior to implementing a mission critical system, ERP, CRM or vertical business system-like policy management, or claim management system. A VALID process architecture provides the program team and decision-makers with a way to understand the full landscape impacted by a major IT change program. In this case, the process architecture is a strong decision support tool, helping to accelerate decisions and improve the overall quality of the decision process. It is also a key tool for clearly identifying what needs to be done to protect competitiveness or enhance differentiating business capabilities. This cannot be done without a VALID process architecture.

Lastly, at a more tactical level, doing a quick process architecture at the scoping phase is a good way to ensure that the project has the right scope to maximize results. A VALID process architecture can be seen as an insurance policy that reduce the risks of bad scopes and a tunnel-view project management approach.

I did mention VALID quite a few times. There are process architectures that are not valid and can cause more arms than good. BPTrends process-driven methodology is one way to build valid architecture. It sets the right context, anchoring the architecture on clear strategic outcomes, connecting outcomes, value delivery model, KPIs, and capabilities with a comprehensive multi-year roadmap. It forces socialization, embedding an engagement strategy and establishing a common language and meaning for all managers and executives. Best practices and standards do exist to design a valid process architecture.

When you see your CEO running around with the process architecture under his arm, or when you see investment committees referring to the business architecture as a key decision support tool, then you know that the process architecture is a valid business architecture piece!

....

CHRIS POTTS

Corporate Strategist, Dominic Barrow

That each business process has an architecture can come as a surprise to many people in mainstream management roles. Add in the observation that their enterprise also has an architecture, and we are obliged to demonstrate—in ways that managers can recognize—how the two architectures are different, are inter-related, and impact the enterprise's success.

Architecture originally meant the art and science of designing buildings, and a style of building (e.g. Gothic).[1] It is now applied to a wide range of entities—such as airplanes, ships, landscapes, and computers. The essential characteristics of an entity that constitute its architecture were documented by Marcus Vitruvius Pollio in the first century BC.[2] They are known as the Vitruvian Triad, and are *firmitas, utilitas* and *venustas*. The approximate English translations of these Latin terms are durability, usefulness, and beauty.

Unlike buildings, and the other examples mentioned above, processes and enterprises are not physical entities. Nevertheless, they manifest themselves in physical ways, such as human interactions, products, and documents. Designing processes and enterprises requires both artistry and science (most notably, psychology); we can observe the Vitruvian Triad in the results, and we can continually learn how to design them better.

Therefore, processes and enterprises, while not physical entities, have architectures and can be designed by architects.[3] By way of illustration, the 'architecture of a peace process'[4] is regarded as a meaningful and valuable concept, and being the architect of such a process a highly-valued role.

A 'process' and an 'enterprise' are different entities. Each has its own architecture, which overlap when an enterprise appears in a process. In reality, these overlaps are many-to-many—for example, in the process of building a house, many enterprises can appear, and each of those enterprises can appear in many such processes. The simplest picture of this overlapping relationship, between a process and an enterprise, looks like figure 22 below.

In the diagram above, a process is a flow of events towards an outcome (e.g. building a house, taking a vacation); an enterprise is a venture (e.g. a brick-laying company, an airline) that is structured to appear in particular types of process. This characterization of processes as flows and enterprises as structures helps people to differentiate between the two and explore how they interrelate.[4]

In the language of enterprise design, each intersection of process and enterprise is often referred to as a 'touchpoint'. A coherently designed enterprise, from a process perspective, is one that engenders a consistency of experience across touchpoints. Success in designing an enterprise, therefore, depends on recognizing that it appears in processes, via touchpoints, rather than has standalone processes of its own.

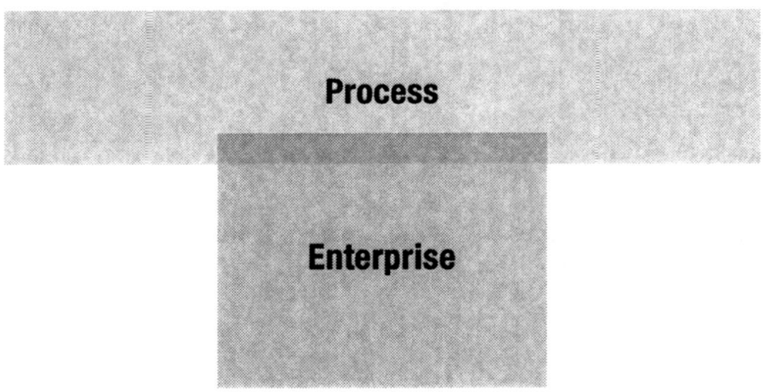

Figure 22: Relationship between Process and Enterprise (note the degree of overlap varies)

Most of an enterprise's 'internal processes' are fragments of external processes. Those external processes would probably happen whether the enterprise existed or not, and are largely beyond the enterprise's control. Each touchpoint is when an internal process impacts the enterprise's value to a stakeholder. It is, therefore, better to design internal processes from touchpoints-inwards, rather than let the internal process drive the design of the touchpoints. There are some exceptions, where the enterprise's internal processes are essentially its own, most especially in respect of:[5]

- Strategy formulation and execution
- Enterprise architecture and design
- Investment in both stability and change
- Sourcing people, products and services.

So, process architectures provide essential context for formulating strategy, designing the enterprise, and investing in change. An enterprise that understands process architectures has a clear advantage over one that does not. Also, by knowing the characteristics and constraints inherent in its own architecture, an enterprise can better seek to influence the evolution of the processes in which it appears.

Or to put it another way, in the language of architecture, the more an enterprise understands the durability, usefulness and beauty of each process in which it appears, the more durable, useful and beautiful the enterprise can keep designing itself to be.

References

[1] Oxford Reference Dictionary

[2] See the Wikipedia entry for Vitruvius

[3] Author's note: the term 'architect' is used here to identify someone who designs an entity that has architecture. It is recognized that 'architect' is a legally defined term in numerous jurisdictions, referring to a person who is qualified to design buildings.

[4] http://escolapau.uab.cat/img/programas/procesos/NOREFin.pdf

[5] The Consumer Has the Technology, The Market Has The Process. Potts, C, BPTrends, September 2011

[6] See my answer to Question #3 for a model of how these fit together, and the role of BPM

....

ALAN RAMIAS

Partner, Performance Design Lab

At the outset of any effort to define a given organization's process architecture, somebody always asks whether it is really necessary to spend time defining 'what everybody already knows'. But, of course, it always turns out that people differ greatly in what labels they apply to various processes, where they see boundaries between processes, how they define a process versus a sub-process or a process area. Even if the initial focus is on improving a single process, it becomes obvious at some point that other processes may need the same attention, and that processes affect each other and affect business performance. So, no matter how it gets there, once an organization wades into the realm of processes, eventually it confronts a question about whether to define its process architecture.

I have little doubt about the practical value of establishing a process architecture for any organization that wishes to understand its own complexities. A BPA can enable an organization to identify deficiencies, assign accountabilities and settle issues of turf, surface gaps, and illogical relationships, and bring to light questions about how a given business ought to be conducted. A BPA provides an end-to-end business view, if you will, versus a single process end-to-end view.

But is a BPA the highest-level view one could have of an organization? It probably shouldn't be. It should be part of a larger view that encompasses all aspects of an organization. That is, an 'enterprise architecture' would make sense as the top-level view, the 'architecture-of-architectures'. So, I do subscribe to the notion of EA. But I've never seen a good one.

There are lots of EAs out there, starting with Zachman's; but they are biased by their makers, largely in attempting to demonstrate the primacy of technology. In all the ones I've seen, processes are a thin layer, or a cell, amidst many others—and that is surely a distortion, as processes are about how a business does its business, which means it should not be relegated to a support or enabling role. In the most recent renditions of EA—in which capabilities are the leading element, derived from strategy, and labeled as 'what' an organization does versus 'how' it does those things (i.e. its processes)—we find another transparent attempt to make technology important and processes less important. Tell me why that's a useful idea.

So please somebody, build an EA in which a BPA appears prominently as a multi-layered engine of accomplishment in the center of the organization and enabled by all sorts of useful things, and I could buy that as the grand framework.

....

PHIL SHORT

IT Director, Mars Canada

Just as the blueprint of a building defines the layout of rooms and passageways to be built and maintained for optimal use, the blueprint of the business processes in an organization defines 'how work gets done' at a high level; also, how those processes collectively deliver value. This blueprint is the business process architecture (BPA) of an organization.

In my early work on business process, I was introduced to the Process Renewal Group's hexagon, which has evolved to the BPTrends 'Burlton Hexagon' (see Fig. 17 in the previous article). This put business performance in the middle surrounded by a business process layer; and then, outside of that, components that make up the enterprise, such as people, systems, infrastructure, policy, rules, etc. The power of this model, to me, is that it shows that to deliver business results, all aspects of the organization exist to guide and enable the organization's business processes. What this means is that the business process architecture is fundamental and key to understanding and managing the organization.

The other architectures define aspects of the organization, be they systems, information, capabilities, services, etc.—but, as I refer back to the Hexagon, the only one that effects the entire organization is the process architecture. The only possible exception to that statement is the enterprise architecture, which puts together an entire blueprint including process.

The problem with the enterprise architecture (EA), in my opinion, is that it is so complex that explaining it to senior business leaders to get buy-in for any initiative is almost impossible, and that any business case to introduce EA must consists of a team of enterprise architects that cost money with no obvious return. That being said, use of EA in the IT arena can make a lot of sense to connect the different layers of the organization together in a cohesive IT solution. The one thing it must have, though, is a business process layer, and one that the business leaders understand and can relate to—not one that resonates only with the IT function. So, this leaves me with the view that BPA is king.

The first use of the business process architecture is to provide the high-level view of how work is done to deliver value to the customer. Fundamentally, the enterprise process architecture, which I consider to be two levels deep, provides a common definition of the organization's business processes that is understood and agreed to by all the senior leaders. At its highest level, all functional heads can look at it and, irrespective of their functions, they can say 'this is how our organization works'. Just having this single view of the organization opens up a new dialogue and recognition that functions have to work together to deliver value. An additional benefit of this common understanding is that other supporting functions, such as HR and IT, are able to use it to drive their own activities, and it provides a common language between these functions and senior leaders.

The second use of the process architecture is in the strategic planning process. There are many functions vying for investment dollars, and having the ability to make investments that are directly impacting strategic objectives is key to success. Using the second level of the process architecture to assess current performance versus required performance of business processes to meet strategic objectives can be done using the Pain Gain Matrix (see the figure below).

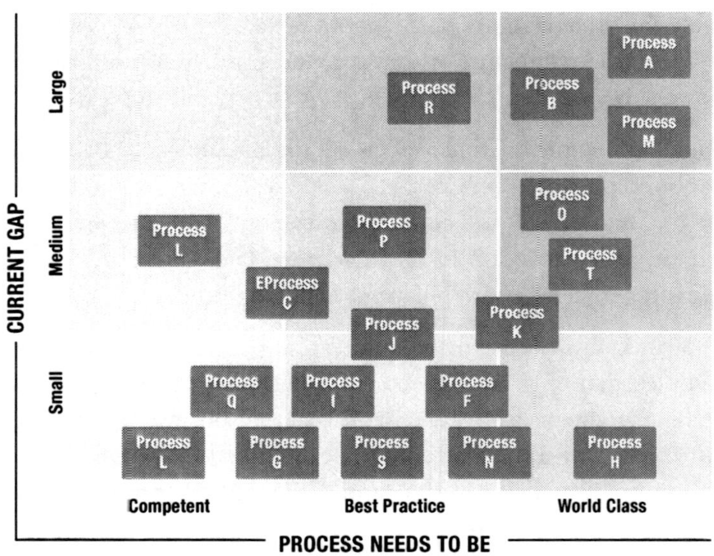

Figure 23: Pain/Gain Matrix

First, the processes are assessed to determine which need to be world class vs. best practice vs. competent to deliver the organizations objectives. After this, the gap between current performance and this required performance is determined. They are then plotted onto the pain/gain matrix. Investment focus should go to those processes in the upper right of the matrix highlighting those that need to be world class, but are currently a long way from that level.

A third use of BPA is to clarify project scope and to help coordinate a business change program. My experience in this area goes back to work done in deploying business systems over many years. Project interference was a big problem, where concurrent changes would take place in different functions of the business or parts of the same application without proper understanding of each other's scope and timing. This resulted in disconnects and rework upon delivery due to unknown interdependencies. Using the process architecture, an overall program of change can be established. It can be prioritized based on the pain/gain matrix, can clearly show the process scope of each change, and allow a discussion about overlap, interdependencies, and timing constraints before a project is launched.

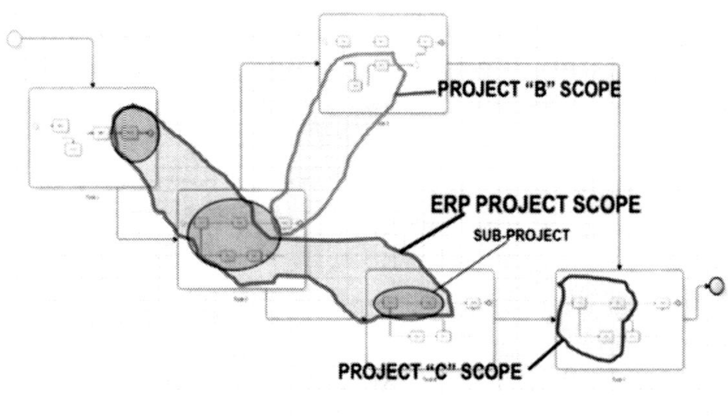

Figure 24: Project Process Scope

The program of change continues to evolve over time and, as new projects are identified, they are added to the program following the approach outlined above.

Additional uses for the process hierarchy that I have experienced only become apparent as process maturity increases. I do not believe that you can impose an existing hierarchy from another organization and expect to get true value from it unless you give time for your organization to adopt and evolve it. Every organization is unique; it has its own culture or ways of doing things, and has different stakeholder objectives—so, although an existing process hierarchy can provide a framework upon which to build, it takes time for people to understand and adapt it to be their own.

This 'ownership', along with a governance structure to support it, allows further benefits to be gained. One of these would be business resiliency, and the ability to plan for business disruption by focusing on recovery of critical processes first. Instead of planning to recover all aspects of finance, focus can be put on the cash collections process, which has an immediate impact on the business The process architecture is also very useful during an acquisition, since the business being acquired can be assessed and integrated process by process, rather than function-by-function, minimizing the impact to stakeholders. If it is a similar business, it almost certainly has similar processes. By analyzing the acquired business against the existing business process architecture, it presents the new business in the context of the existing business.

In summary, the process architecture is a valuable tool to the organization since it depicts the processes of the organization, which represent the work that gets done to deliver value. The process architecture has to be meaningful, and understood by everyone, to be truly effective. Notwithstanding the value of other architectures, it is the process blueprint of the organization defined in business terms that promotes a common language among enabling processes, senior leaders, and mangers.

ANDREW SPANYI

Founder and Managing Director, Spanyi International

THE VALUE OF PROCESS ARCHITECTURE

Process architecture, when properly defined and deployed, is instrumental in terms of establishing a common vocabulary in naming business processes, strategy execution, aligning performance measurement, and laying the foundation for process-based accountability. The process architecture for a company is comprised of two components;

- A high-level, one-page diagram or schematic that depicts the firm's main value creating processes
- A set of supporting documentation for each of the processes that

was defined on the high-level schematic.

To illustrate a high-level schematic, the figure below depicts a 'blueprint' developed by an insurance company.

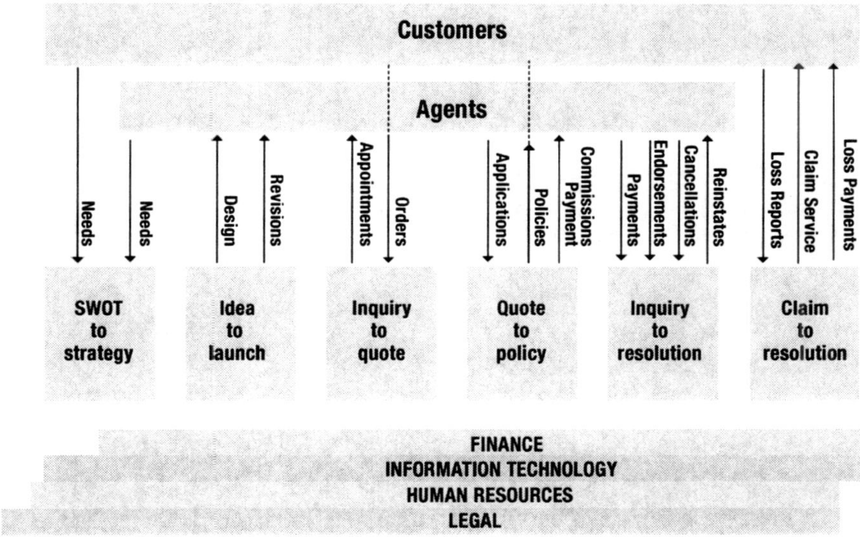

Figure 25: An insurance company enterprise process blueprint

In the case of this insurance company, each high-level customer touching process would have supporting documentation providing insight on topics such as the key steps in the process, the main end of process metrics, estimates of current performance, etc. While the high-level schematic or blueprint is mainly to facilitate organization-wide communication of the company's customer focus and process orientation, the intent of the supporting documentation is to stimulate discussion. The table below depicts the type of information that might be summarized for the 'idea to launch' process in an insurance company. Some companies also elect to include a 'swim lane' diagram as part of the supporting documentation.

Measures	Key steps	Departments involved
Value for money	Generate ideas	Customers, Product development, Sales, Marketing , Execs
Variance to promise date	Build business case	Marketing
Variance to budget	Develop Product	Product development, Underwriting, suppliers
	Test	Product development
	Prepare package for regulators	Marketing, Underwriting, Product development, Executives
	Launch	Sales, Marketing, Product development, Executives

Table 4: An insurance company enterprise process blueprint

When the process blueprint is backed up with solid supporting documentation, an organization is better prepared to execute strategy by answering the question: which of our business processes need to be improved by how much for us to achieve our strategic objectives? Further, the supporting documentation typically triggers these additional questions:

- How are we currently performing on the top priority metrics?
- Do our current information systems satisfy our operational needs?
- For example, do we have regular, easy to access data on the metrics that matter to customers—or must we collect this manually?
- Given that many of the steps in the process require cross-departmental collaboration, to what extent shall we consider some form of process governance?

The entire journey in preparing the 'blueprint' and the supporting documentation can be complex, and calls not just for senior leadership team (SLT) involvement, but also expert facilitation. In speaking with various process professionals on the topic of process architecture, the most frequently asked questions include: What are the best ways to develop enterprise level process architecture? What are some of the pitfalls to avoid?

There are two common approaches to developing process architecture at the enterprise level. Some companies prefer to start by examining one of the better-known process frameworks, such as the American Productivity & Quality Center's (APQC) Process Classification Framework (PCF), or the

Value Chain Group's Value Reference Model (VRM). Such frameworks are used to inform the leadership team on naming conventions for the major processes. These frameworks are best used as a place to start—not a place to end. APQC's PCF uses a phrase-based naming convention (Develop Vision and Strategy, Deliver Products and Services, etc.), while the VRM uses a one-word naming convention (Market, Develop, Fulfill, Sell, Support, etc.).

Some organizations, typically those who have more experience with process improvement and management, have their own framework in place. Whether an established framework is used or not, what's important is to ensure direct senior leadership team involvement in the validation of the one-page schematic or blueprint. This is needed to establish a common vocabulary for naming the firm's high-level processes. Then, the development of the supporting documentation for each process named on the enterprise level requires an iterative facilitated approach with ongoing involvement by the members of the senior leadership team.

Some of the major pitfalls to avoid:

- *Takes too long.* The entire cycle for the development of a process architecture, including the high-level blueprint, the supporting documentation, the identification of key metrics, and estimates of the current level of performance, and decisions around the company process improvement and management plan should not take more than three months.
- *Too detailed.* It can be problematic when process architecture drills below a 'level 2' view of business processes. The intent is to produce documents for decision-making—not for analysis or design. The modeling, analysis, design and implementation of target processes calls for a different and robust process improvement methodology.
- *Buried.* Once again, the objective is to create a common vocabulary for naming processes and a decision-making structure around a process improvement and management plan. This calls for ongoing involvement by the SLT. Little will be accomplished if the effort is buried deep in the organization, and limited to involvement by subject matter experts.
- *Too technical.* The perception of the development of process architecture has to be more about creating customer focus and cross-departmental collaboration than the technical aspects of defining business processes.

You know that the development of process architecture has been fruitful when:

- Members of the SLT ask questions about the timeliness and quality of process performance
- There is an increase in the frequency and efficacy of cross-departmental teams
- People can concisely describe the process they work within and understand what happens before and after their involvement in the process flow

....

QUESTION 7

WHAT'S THE RETURN ON PROCESS?

Taking an organization-wide BPM approach, however that is defined, requires a significant expenditure and considerable effort over a long period of time. Process analysis and improvement projects, BPMS implementations, change management, culture change, education programs—all of these things are a cost and distraction to 'business as usual'.

What do you see as the primary components of the ROI of BPM? What might be the compelling reasons for investment in BPM? What are the key variables that impact an organization's ROI on BPM?

OVERVIEW

Managers have been trained to always try to determine the return on investment (ROI) of their efforts. Unfortunately, while some aspects of process work are easy to analyze—where changes in processes save money—the more valuable, strategic aspects of process change are not. Consider developing a table of financial accounts. Every business needs it, but how do you cost the ROI? Or consider developing a new and improved software network to support your IT operations. It will improve the speed and efficiency of all your applications, but it's hard to say exactly what the ROI is.

Creating a business architecture is in the same category. If your organization is mature enough to use an architecture, then developing one will support a wide range of other valuable initiatives that will be hard to justify if only considered as a specific project. The problem, our authors suggest, is that so much depends on efficient process, one way or another, that traditional ROI can be difficult. Moreover, what you measure depends on things like how mature your organization is, and how critical specific changes are to support broader missions. In spite of all these challenges, and many qualifications, our respondents provide some rather good suggestions about how one might go about justifying process projects.

JIM BOOTS
Owner, Global Process Innovation

The primary components to consider about ROI when assessing an investment in BPM include: increased efficiency and reliability; fewer safety and customer-failure incidents; decreased on-boarding time for personnel to gain competence in a new role; a more impactful portfolio of improvement projects; reduced time by personnel spent looking for information or tools needed to perform their responsibilities; and increased satisfaction of personnel.

Why would an organization commit to BPM? Quite simply, to improve performance on whatever dimensions management considers important. Given that all work output is accomplished through processes, having a more rigorous approach to process design, collaboration, and improvement (including automation) can lead to better performance.

However, expectations for projected improvements in performance must be sufficient to justify the investments in BPM capability development that will be required. Not all organizations will find the ROI calculation equally compelling. The ROI of BPM will depend on several variables:

- The type of organization—for example, size, type of business (manufacturing, service, etc.), and complexity of the business.
- Whether an organization adopts truly strategic BPM or adopts some tactical form of BPM, such as a Lean Six Sigma program.
- The degree to which top management commits to learning effective behaviors that promote BPM as a cultural element of the organization.

Simplistically, larger organizations operating in more complex businesses will see greater benefits than smaller organizations in less complex businesses, Strategic BPM will yield a greater ROI than tactical BPM, but will require a longer timeframe to achieve it; and the greater management's sustained commitment is to BPM, the higher will be the ROI. Let's unpack these a bit.

Size and complexity are rather obvious factors in a BPM ROI calculation. When an organization is large and its processes are complex, there are inherently more opportunities for process coordination and improvement that can be influenced by BPM. That said, some organizations are so large and their processes so complex, that it may take some time for management to understand how and where to focus its BPM resources. In such circumstances, it is not unusual in the early days for false starts associated with non-intuitive framing of an organization's processes. But once an organization gets a handle on the top level of its process architecture, it should be possible for it to start directing resources toward improved process performance.

Regarding the effect of tactical versus strategic BPM: many organizations have implemented successful Lean, Six Sigma, or Lean Six Sigma programs. While the projects associated with such programs tend, almost exclusively, to have tactical impacts, the impacts from these projects can be quite large—that is, in the millions of dollars of benefits per year per project. The good news about such a program is that the internal capability development required is straightforward and well demonstrated, and the benefits for any given project can be pinpointed and estimated in dollar values so that an ROI can be calculated. The primary required capability is developing internal process improvement expertise—that is, in the form of Lean Six Sigma Black Belts—and having a way to point them to projects that will benefit organizational performance. In most organizations, Lean Six Sigma projects are expected to have a lifespan of a year or less, so the results of investments in such capabilities should start to be evident fairly quickly.

Likewise, development of a process automation capability can lead to a proliferation of cost-saving tactical improvements. As with Lean Six Sigma, an automation-focused BPM effort requires the development of a small group of experts—in this case, experts who know how to use automation software to implement useful automations.

On the other hand, commitment to strategic BPM implementation requires much more capability development and, typically, takes years before a full slate of benefits is realized. Strategic BPM requires training for multiple roles—BPM manager/coordinator, process sponsor, process advisor, process mapper, software support—as well as Lean Six Sigma Black Belts and automation programmers. Strategic BPM does not leave out process improvement or automation. In fact, they are important aspects of the totality of strategic BPM, but they are only part of a larger concept. The *strategic* change that is required is a change in culture, which will be exhibited in the behaviors of managers and employees. The ultimate focus of a strategic BPM effort is for all personnel to learn and collaborate much more effectively through the language of process. By implication, this means that there must be online access to compelling, intuitive representations of processes that personnel use as a communications platform.

In the strategic BPM scenario, it will take time to build the representational process architecture, to train those people performing key support roles that keep the process architecture up-to-date and effective, and to instill in all personnel the modes and methods needed for effective use of the process architecture—for learning, collaboration, deployment of improvements, and execution assistance.

Fortunately, undertaking tactical process improvements can be done even as strategic BPM capabilities are developed. Indeed, if the BPM program is properly framed, an organization gradually will experience synergies between tactical improvement efforts and strategic BPM. Gains from improvements will be baked into the process architecture, and deeper understanding of the entire process architecture will lead to selection of more powerful improvement projects.

This leads to the last point about management's commitment level as a key factor—probably the most important factor—in the ROI of BPM. Although it is not a decision to be made lightly, it is relatively easy for management to commit to the development of a process improvement (e.g., Lean Six Sigma), or automation capability. The key actions are to invest in the development of a few expert personnel and to set expectations with regard to the implementation of improvement projects throughout the organization (or where performance improvement needs are greatest).

It is not uncommon, however, for management commitment to falter, even to these modest investments. As a result, many Lean Six Sigma programs have failed to achieve expectations because insufficient time was given to developing capabilities that efficiently and effectively deliver improvements.

Long-term management commitment is an even bigger issue with strategic BPM. There are more roles to introduce, train, and reinforce; there is software to buy; there are many standards and methods to put in place; and, most importantly, there are behaviors to change, starting with management behaviors. For example, when there is a performance issue or an incident, managers should immediately focus the conversation around the process that produced the undesirable results. It will take a bit of practice for managers, and those reporting to them, to become skilled at using the process architecture to conduct a robust discussion and to develop a corrective action plan.

An additional challenge associated with the ROI of strategic BPM is that not all the benefits are easy to measure. Unlike measurement of tactical improvements associated with a Lean Six Sigma project, strategic BPM benefits are often dispersed across the entire organization in the form of people spending more time on higher-order activities because they spend less time re-doing things, resolving process disconnects, looking for key information, or just being downright confused. Taking the very big picture, the ROI of strategic BPM might be measured in terms of market performance versus competitors (e.g. based on a stock's price-earnings ratio), as well as an organization's reputation with customers and employees. But, admittedly, it will take some patience to perceive such gains. This bolsters the argument for building a process improvement capability early in a BPM effort—so there are enough tangible gains to maintain the organizational enthusiasm necessary to develop the full slate of strategic BPM capabilities.

In reality, there have been very few organizations with top leaders who have a clear vision of what they want to achieve with strategic BPM *and* the fortitude and positional longevity to see the vision realized. By clearly explaining what is meant by strategic BPM, we can only hope that more leaders will make the necessary commitment.

....

PETER MATTHIJSSEN

Managing Consultant, BiZZdesign

Of course, BPM tooling, expertise and products cost money, so it's a legitimate question to ask for the ROI. For some BPM practices, the question is quite simple. Process improvement initiatives, for example, should have a valid business case by themselves.

But what is the ROI for a process diagram? Or for process ownership, or thinking in processes? I think many of us feel that it is important, but for many BPM practices it is hard to build a good business case. But do we really need this business case?

Let's ask ourselves some other questions: *What is the ROI of our HR-department? Or the ROI of our IT-department?* Also, for these practices, the business case is often hard to build. But this doesn't mean these departments are not important; they are involved in making and keeping our assets in good condition (for HR our people; for IT our IT structure). BPM is aimed at another important asset: processes.

By treating processes as assets, there can be no dispute that these assets should be well designed, managed, and improved when needed. The alternative, not investing in process fitness, is eventually more expensive. Similar to neglecting HR or IT, poor processes will result in poor performance in terms of quality, speed and costs.

Of course, investments in BPM, just as in HR and IT, should be done wisely. Investments in suitable tooling and techniques can improve the efficiency and effectiveness of your BPM practice.

....

MATTHEW J. MORGAN

Head of Process & Metrics Excellence, Bridgewater Assoc.

BPM, in the broad scope I defined in Question 1, has many compelling reasons for organizations to make the investment. I will give a narrower description of process modeling more specifically in Question 14, but will provide this broad overview here. Hopefully this overview can be helpful for readers to develop business cases on their own.

We can broadly think of a business case on a spectrum from the more tangible and measurable (cost savings and operational improvements) to the more intangible and qualitative (revenue and culture). The Balanced Scorecard gives another framework that could be helpful in addressing a business case from multiple dimensions (whose four main components are: financial performance, customer satisfaction, internal business process efficiency, and organizational capability).

BPM provides the clearest quantifiable benefits along the lines of cost savings (through improvement in capacity utilization, reduction in head count, and reduction in inventory and backlog) and operational improvements (reduction in error and rework, improvement in quality scores, etc.). Clear process transparency allows for better process design and the elimination of waste.

Process improvement initiatives can also achieve less tangible benefits, either directly targeting these topics, or by these being second-order consequences that occur as results of the more tangible benefits in the preceding paragraph. While revenues are a financial (and, therefore, quantifiable) metric, I classify them in this category due to uncertainty and ambiguity of what could happen the future. Measurements such as market share, competitive advantage, and growth would comprise the revenue benefits of BPM. In addition, benefits to organizational capability and human capital can occur as it becomes easier to do business with the organization, and people's quality of life improves due to more predictable and more motivating, higher-value work.

I would like to acknowledge Don Harder of Arc Partners with thought partnership in developing the taxonomy below that provides a holistic view of various business objectives that would be optimized by BPM:

Table 5: The business case for BPM

Theme	Typical Metrics	Representative Business Questions
Cost	Headcount Personnel costs Contractor costs Service costs	Is our staffing higher than it should be? Are we exceeding our budget? Are our costs higher than triangulated benchmarks?
Quality	Process defect rates Repeat activity Performance vs. SLA Issue logs	Is our accuracy where it should be? Are we having too many issues logged? Are we meeting SLAs
Cycle time	Execution time Throughput	Are we efficient? Can we improve our productivity / speed?

Capacity	Process throughput per time period Backlog Aged backlog Performance vs. SLA	Are we managing our backlogs? Are our backlogs growing? Are we meeting SLAs?
Satisfaction	Survey results over time	How satisfied are clients with the services provided? How has the picture changed over time? How well is the business performing against external benchmarks?
Reliability & resiliency	Recovery point objective (RPO) / Recovery time objective (RTO) Risk assessment rating / audit items Performance vs. SLA Unplanned downtime	Are our recovery point and time objectives achievable? Are we meeting SLAs? Is our level of risk acceptable?

The categorization or decomposition of these benefits is helpful for the development of business cases. However, the different types of benefits are not causally independent or mutually exclusive; they often have inter-relationships and reinforce one another.

GILLES MORIN

Founder, BPMPlus Inc.

This is obviously a top-mind issue, and the first question any CxO would ask. And there are many answers to it. Let's review the key ones using three dimensions: the process lifecycle, the BPM maturity, and the BPTrends pyramid.

PROCESS LIFE CYCLE

- *Discovery phase*: Exposing—documenting—process by itself generates 10 to 20% efficiency gain. Just getting the right people in one room, discovering the reality of each other, and agreeing on how the process really works uncover quick wins that can be readily implemented.

- *Analysis and design phase*: agreeing on the right scope, collecting real-life performance data of process, defining how it could and should work, simulating impacts of different options, eliminating wastes, increasing visual based management normally increase efficiency, quality, and customer value by more than 25%. Just look at the average gains from Kaizens. And we have not yet talked about automation!
- *Automation phase*: In this case, ROI depends on all-too-well-known factors related to project management, BPMS project delivery, competencies, technology complexity, team readiness, sponsorship, scope, etc. In some cases, it is even advisable to automate an as-is process just to expose it and collect benchmarks performance data. Generally speaking, ROI may depend on using the right approach that aligns BPM maturity and capability of an organization with the tool or BPMS technology. ROI materialization is usually larger when both of these dimensions are in sync. At this point, we do not need to differentiate between case management project and structured process automation. In both situations, ROI can be significant, but materializing it is a bigger challenge in case management. Here again, we talk about double-digit gains than can approach three digits.
- *Real time performance management/monitoring*: This is the stage at which we can claim to have reached continuous incremental ROI, provided that the organization has implemented BPM capability to sustain business process management. Obviously, we talk about diminishing return over time, and new sizeable ROI may require us to redesign or reinvent a given process.

Using the BPM maturity model based on CMMI, we can make the case between a low BPM maturity organization struggling in materializing double-digit ROI using overly complex technology, and a higher-process management maturity organization having institutionalized benefits management to a point where the value goes way beyond a project based ROI. This is to say that ROI will depend on getting the right mix of BPM capability to fit your organization's BPM and process culture maturity. This where we shift from efficiency driven ROI to organization-wide and effectiveness-driven ROI, which is more enduring and at a much larger scale than the 20% to 30% ROI related to a project.

Using BPTrends BPM pyramid (see figure below), we can associate BPM ROI to each of the four dimensions:

- *Project level*—increasing ROI from project-based siloed project to transversal process project; from incrementally improving a process to redesigning it.
- *Technology level*—adding a completely new dimension of ROI related to the acceleration of the delivery of higher-quality business solutions using new solution delivery platforms, like iBPMS, is key. There are few metrics presented by vendors, but this dimension is not as well documented as the precious one (business project). Nonetheless, this is key and should not be overlooked. In this case, IT might be too often be the worst enemy, piling up constraints over constraints that end up killing ROI for every business project.
- *HR level and culture*—this is a key sustainability part of realizing ROI, and often missed by many organizations. This is even more important when talking about materializing case management ROI. Again, it is not a question of adding ROI, but sustaining benefits realization.
- *Strategy level*—this the part where we shift from project and efficiency based ROI to organization-wide and effectiveness-based ROI.

There is no doubt about BPM ROI and the fact that we talk about sizeable and sustainable ROI. It is more a question of execution strategy and leadership.

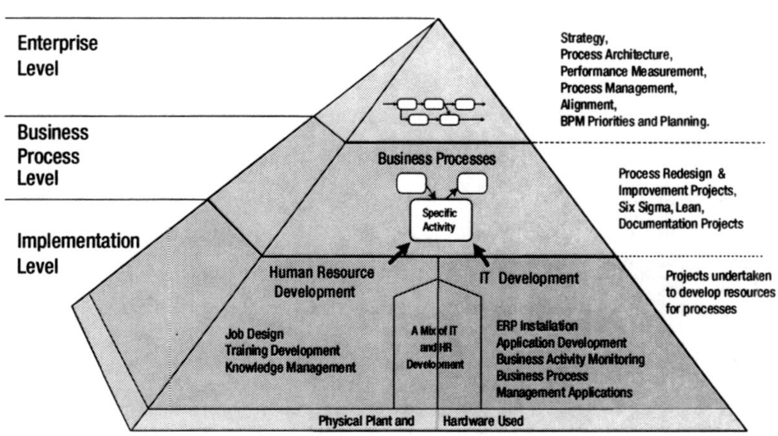

Figure 26: BPTrends Pyramid

•••

PROFESSOR JAN VOM BROCKE

Hilti Chair of Business Process Management, University of Liechtenstein

Reasons for investment in BPM differ; so do the variables that impact on the organization's ROI. It is, thus, important to enable organizations to assess the ROI of BPM according to their own parameters. Such an assessment allows us to systematically compare design alternatives in BPM and to optimize the BPM project portfolio.

While BPM has primarily focused on the evaluation of running processes for a long time—as operationalized by key performance indicators—the research stream of so-called 'value-oriented BPM' has contributed to the development of tools that enable the evaluation of alternative process and process management design (vom Brocke, Sonnenberg, 2015).

The 'return on process transformation' (ROPT) may serve as an example. The ROPT is a profitability measure, which is calculated based on all payments related to a process' (re-)design in view of a longer planning horizon (of, for example, five years). Payments related to the investment relate to the effort to be taken to conduct the (re-)design, while payments related to the return relate to the benefits anticipated with it. Such benefits can be cost savings as well as revenue increases, for instance, which are estimated by comparing different design alternatives—such as a process in t=0 and t=1 (and t serving as a time index). The schema for calculating the ROPT is presented in the figure below.

In calculating the TFPO, different levels of detail can be applied, and multiple examples are available to study the measurement in more detail (vom Brocke, Sonnenberg, 2015). In practice, a two- staged approach is often useful: (i) a rough assessment based on expert opinion can be conducted; ((ii) based on such first results, selected aspects of the calculation can be detailed on demand. For such a detailed calculation, process models can also serve as a basis to further analyze resource utilization and frequencies of certain process branches (vom Brocke et al., 2010; vom Brocke, Grob, 2008).

For rough assessment based on expert opinion, the ROPT can be assessed in three simple steps:

- The top five benefits decision-makers would expect from a process (re-)design are named.
- The five most important efforts decision-makers would expect from

a process (re-)design are named,.

- Values as decision makers would estimate them are planned for annual payments related to both benefits and efforts.

Based on this data, the series of payments related to the process (re-)design can be computed, and financial measures can be calculated according to standards from financial accounting (vom Brocke, Sonnenberg, 2015).

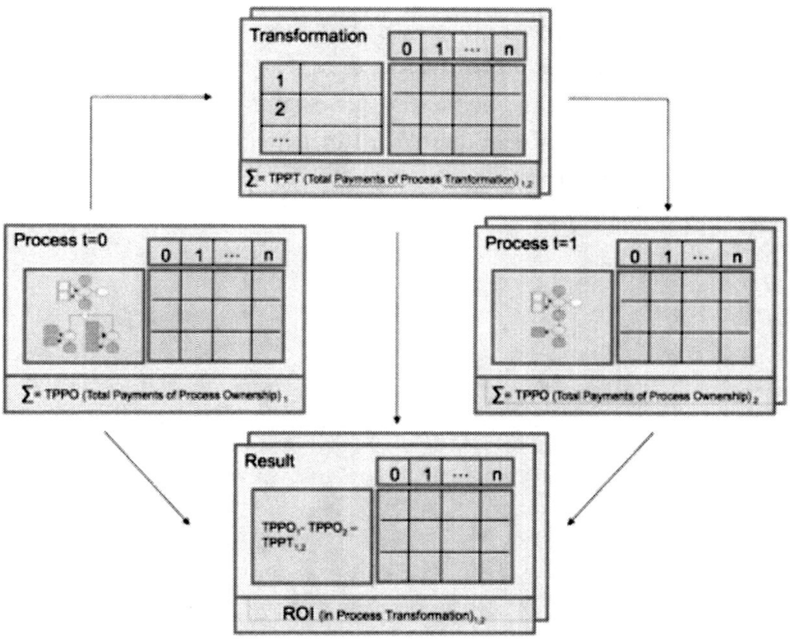

Figure 27: Framework for calculating the Return on Process Transformation

For decision-making, different scenarios can be calculated, such as a best, worst, and average case scenario. Also, further qualitative assessments need to be conducted to comprehensively evaluate process (re-)design alternatives. In combination with such additional information, the ROPT serves to put a 'price tag' on process related initiatives that take into account the company specific situation, and which is formulated in a way that it is meaningful from an investment accounting perspective.

References

vom Brocke, J., & Grob, H.L. (2008). "Profitability of Business Processes". In J. Becker, M. Rosemann & M. Kugeler (Eds.), Process Management. A Guide for the Design of Business Processes (pp. 491–520). Berlin, et al.

vom Brocke, J., Recker, J., & Mendling, J. (2010). "Value-oriented Process Modeling: Integrating Financial Perspectives into Business Process Re-design". Business Process Management Journal (BPMJ), 16(2), 333–356.

vom Brocke, J., Sonnenberg, C. (2015). "Value-orientation in Business Process Management". In J. vom Brocke & M. Rosemann (Eds.), Handbook on Business Process Management: Strategic Alignment, Governance, People and Culture (International Handbooks on Information Systems) (2 ed., Vol. 2, pp. 101–132). Berlin et al., Springer.

QUESTION 8

QUALITY OF PROCESS OR PROCESS OF QUALITY?

Even a cursory comparison of quality management and process management principles and practices shows there is considerable overlap between the two; both are ultimately focused on the consistent, cost-effective delivery of appropriate products or services to customers and other stakeholders.

How do you see BPM and quality management being the same and/or different?

OVERVIEW

Our authors took several divergent approaches to this question. Some suggested that quality concerns were a subset of a broader BPM approach. Others suggested they were different, but complementary. Most suggested that the response to this question would vary, depending on what you are trying to accomplish. Stepping back, one might have wished that someone had provided a bit more history. Early in the last century, most process work was termed 'work simplification', and associated with Taylor's work on defining the 'one best way to do a task'. This type of analysis focused on production lines, and sought to define each job in a production line.

In the U.S., this work became associated with industrial engineering, and later with quality control, which put a special emphasis on examining the output of processes to determine that they had been correctly assembled. Later, led by the American Society for Quality, a variety of specific techniques was developed to monitor and assure consistent quality. There is a sense in which Lean was simply a Japanese effort to apply quality control and work simplification to production lines. This very brief history suggests that the two have always been connected. On the other hand, today's BPM covers many things that were never included in traditional industrial engineering. The emphasis on the management of processes or the emphasis on using business rules to define the knowledge used in processes play a major role in BPM. Clearly BPM and quality control share a lot and, equally, it is clear that many Lean and Six Sigma people regard their work as distinct from BPM. It will be interesting to see where all this stands in another ten or twenty years.

....

ROGER ADDISON

Performance Architect, Addison Consulting

CAROL HAIG

Principal, Carol Haig & Associates

Performance architects work in a variety of functions in a broad spectrum of organizations. Most probably think of themselves as whatever their job title says they are, and have never considered that they are also performance architects. However, if they rely on a body of experience, proven approaches, and documented successes to help workers meet and exceed performance goals, then these folks are, indeed, performance architects.

Viewed through the eyes of a performance architect, *quality management* 'ensures that an organization, product or service is consistent. It has four main components: quality planning, quality control, quality assurance and quality improvement.'[1]

Quality planning is captured in one or more documents that together state quality standards, practices, resources, and specifications. These documents describe the required activities related to producing a product, service, project, or contract. Quality plans define:

OBJECTIVES TO BE MET

Steps in the processes that establish operating practices or procedures:

- Allocation of responsibilities, authority, and resources
- Documented standards, practices, procedures, and instructions
- Testing, inspection, examination, and audit programs
- Documented procedures for changes and modifications
- A method for measuring the achievement of the quality objectives
- Other actions needed to meet the objectives.[2]

Quality control consists of procedures to ensure that a product or service follows a defined set of quality criteria or meets the requirements of the client or customer.

Quality assurance, sometimes confused with quality control, is a set of procedures that ensure a product or service, while in development, meets specified requirements.[3]

Quality improvement is the analysis of performance and systematic efforts to improve it. Many models are used, such as Six Sigma (DMAIC) and Total Quality Management (TQM). These models, and others, focus on the ongoing effort to make performance better.[4]

To the performance architect, quality management sets the standards that an organization's products and services must meet consistently to achieve business goals.

Business Process Management. Think of BPM as a large umbrella under which all performance architects in all organizations "… share an interest in thinking of the(ir) organization as a system, of linking activities into processes, of measuring processes, and organizing people and support systems to make business processes more efficient and effective. All have best practices and everyone would benefit if they shared their knowledge and skills."[5]

Quality management. A system in its own right, sits under the all-encompassing Business Process Management system umbrella. The performance architect sees the need for these two systems to operate together to ensure quality standards are met. It is helpful to think of the relationship between these two critical systems and one of checks and balances.

The purpose of the *Checks and Balances Matrix* below is to assess how effectively an organization's quality management system is aligned with its BPM System.

Does your quality management system match your BPM System? Complete each cell with Yes, No, DK(don't know), or NA(not applicable):

Table 6: Checks and Balances Matrix

		Quality Management System			
		Quality Planning	**Quality Control**	**Quality Assurance**	**Quality Improvement**
Business Process Management System	Organization as a system	Yes No DK NA	Yes No DK NA	Yes No DK NA	Yes No DK NA
	Linking activities to processes	Yes No DK NA	Yes No DK NA	Yes No DK NA	Yes No DK NA
	Measuring processes	Yes No DK NA	Yes No DK NA	Yes No DK NA	Yes No DK NA
	Organizing people and systems to make business processes more efficient and effective	Yes No DK NA	Yes No DK NA	Yes No DK NA	Yes No DK NA
	Share BPM best practices, knowledge and skills	Yes No DK NA	Yes No DK NA	Yes No DK NA	Yes No DK NA

If all your cells say "Yes", congratulations! Your organization's quality management and BPM systems are synchronized and are enabling workers to meet and exceed their goals while providing products and services to quality standards. If there are "No" answers, you may want to develop an alignment plan. Any "DK" answers are signals that further analysis is probably needed to achieve alignment of the two systems.

Notes and References

[1] Retrieved July 2015 from: https://en.wikipedia.org/wiki/Quality management

[2] The Certified Manager of Quality/Organizational Excellence Handbook, ASQ Quality Press, Fourth Edition, 2014, Pages 266-268.
Retrieved July 2015 from:

http://asq.org/learn-about-quality/quality-plans/index.html

[3] Rouse, M. (May 2015) Quality Control Definition

Retrieved July 2015 from:

http://whatis.techtarget.com/definition/quality-control-QC

[4] Duke University Patient Safety Training—Quality Improvement module. Retrieved July 2015 from: http://patientsafetyed.duhs.duke.edu/module_a/introduction/introduction.html

[5] Wolf, C. (June 11, 2010). Once More: What is BPM? Retrieved July 2015 from: http://www.bptrends.com/?s=advisor20100615

....

AHMAD ALIBABAEI

Assistant Professor, Shahid Beheshti University of Medical Sciences

All organizations use business processes in order to create and deliver their products and services to customers. These processes are more or less effective. If they were not, the organizations using them would quickly go out of business. The world is not static, however, and customer and employee expectations are constantly changing. They want quality products and better services at reduced costs. Under these difficult competitive conditions, any lack of attention to quality or cost will lead to wasteful processes, poor products and services, and dissatisfied customers.

Achieving success in organization requires both a well-designed process and the management of quality.

Strategies in organizations are modified and improved continuously to optimize utilizing human resources, processes and technologies. Problems that derive from wasting resources, reworks, or poor customer satisfaction are hidden in the current processes of many organizations. If there are no standards, or if organizations lack monitoring tools, the identification of these issues will be very difficult. Often, organizations focus on symptoms, and undertake projects that make small improvements but do not really address the underlying causes. It's important that the root cause of problems be identified and that improvement projects are defined to actually eliminate the root causes of process problems.

Quality management, as such, does not solve the root causes of problems, but focuses on identifying and monitoring outcomes of underlying problems. Business process management is also an approach that focuses on process improvement to increasing quality; therefore, BPM can be seen as a part of quality management. There are different methods to build quality management systems in organizations. Methods, such as ISO or EFQM, try to assess organizations and, based on the results, verify the level of quality being achieved.

These approaches, however, do not provide process change tools. For instance, ISO tends to focus on documentation as an evidence for maturity. However, improvement in an organization needs a dynamic procedure based on the on-going monitoring of actual performance. A business excellence approach, like EFQM, focuses on assessment models rather than process improvement methodologies and procedures. Therefore, these models help highlight problems, but don't provide the means for real quality improvement.

Business Process Management can be used as a tool or methodology to implement changes identified by a quality management system. BPM is a tool to solve the organization's quality problems through specific improvement in processes. BPM is a comprehensive approach that has been affected by many of standards, methods and procedures. It can provide different methodologies and procedures, and can be used at various levels of an organization.

BPM considers dynamic factors in organization, and concentrates more on the current operation rather than static documentation. A performance measurement system that considers different aspects of the business is necessary for a successful quality management program. BPM includes a measurement system to evaluate and monitor business processes to achieve more efficient and effective processes and to satisfy customer needs. Therefore, BPM can be used as a procedure for implementing a quality management system in organization. It can help an organization achieve the following goals:

- Streamlining business processes for increasing efficiency and effectiveness
- Creating repeatable and reliable procedures for analyzing and managing the process
- Optimizing the utilization of resources to decrease operational costs
- Creating a better alignment between strategy and processes to improve productivity and agility
- Improving process performance reporting, with continuous improvement as the result.

BPM defines a collection of actions that align with an organization's strategy—and, by modifying business processes, improves the quality on an organization's products and services. Increasing process quality can affect product quality, and it can satisfy customer needs. In other words, stable and reliable processes can assure that organization products and services would be based on the specifications and customer expectations and, as a result, a better quality can be achieved. That's the goal of BPM, and it satisfies the needs of quality management.

PETER MATTHIJSSEN

Managing Consultant, BiZZdesign

Again, there are many definitions of BPM and visions on the scope of BPM. Similarly, there are different visions on the scope of quality management. Depending on these definitions and visions, quality management could be included in the BPM practice or positioned next to BPM. For sure, there is a strong relationship between quality management and BPM.

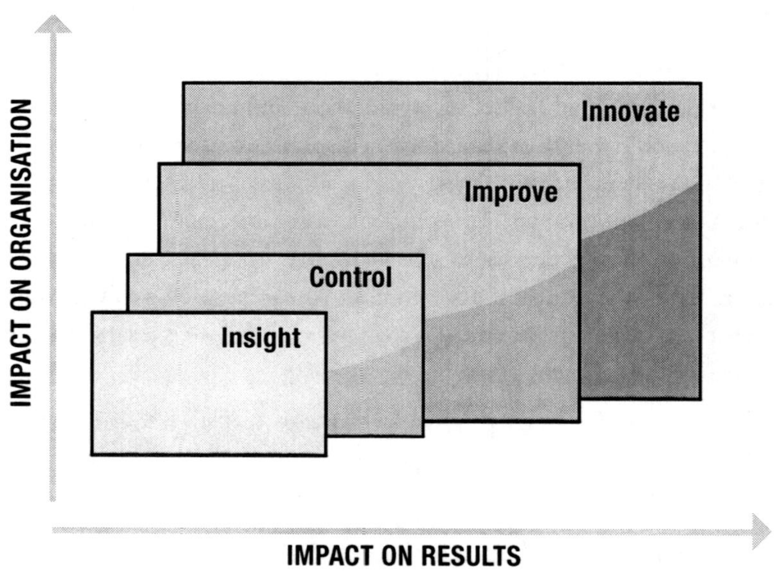

Figure 28: Scope of BPM

The control-approaches in BPM have a strong relationship with quality management. Controlling is not about change, but is about a predictive performance of processes. A best practice approach for process control follows the seven steps below:

- Step 1: *Thinking in processes*. Which end-to-end processes are present in our organization?
- Step 2: *Investing in process Ownership*. There is one contact point for the results and performance of the process.
- Step 3: *Capturing processes*. A good process document is 'fit for purpose!' It reflects the daily use and the objectives of the organization.
- Step 4: *Work!* The results of the previous steps are secured here.
- Step 5: *Measuring process performance*. To gain insight into the current performance, we evaluate the process.
- Step 6: *Controlling the process*. When performance of the process is insufficient, we use control instruments to make the process perform better.
- Step 7: Continuous improvement of the process.

Quality management frameworks can support several of these steps—for example, in mapping and standardizing processes (steps 3, 4). Also in selecting and implementing performance indicators (step 5, 6), quality management frameworks give direction.

....

GILLES MORIN

Founder, BPMPlus

Quality management might suffer from the same disease as BPM, being one of these all-inclusive terms that mean different things to different people. Quality management can be associated to Lean (quality defined by our customers), to ISO (certification required by our clients, or seen as a marketing plot), to continuous improvement, or to QA-quality control (be internally defined and focused).

Let's be clear, Lean and BPM are complementary, one aiming at improving cycle time, customer satisfaction and reducing waste of operational processes, the other aimed at managing processes as critical assets—as Roger Burlton would say, "process to manage process." Lean is a good way to accelerate the organization's process culture, the 'organizational software' part of BPM. BPM deals with process management capability, and does not deal with culture. BPM covers the organizational hardware side of BPM. You need both, the challenge being more about finding the right way to do it in your organization. Both are required to keep the BPM program in the sweet spot to realize maximum benefits.

In the case of ISO—even more so if ISO is a marketing plot—BPM has nothing to do with it, and should not have anything to do with it. However, in an organization wanting to maximize resource utilization to increase value of its BPM program, the quality/ISO team is a good place to recruit and build up BPM competencies. On a team of ten, I would dare say that you could shift 30% of them to the BPM program, leave 30% for compliance and marketing requirements, and you might be forced to relocate 30%, given that not all ISO team members have the required genetic code to contribute to the BPM program—this is not a scientific view, but more of an observation from the field.

I would associate continuous improvement to the Lean view. Quality control or compliance and BPM are different if your quality controls are product driven and not process driven. In the case of service, the lines are not that clear, as service can be seen as a customer-driven packaged process. In that sense, quality management and process performance management overlap.

RON ROSS

CEO, Business Rules Solutions

Everyone wants high quality from their business processes. But what exactly does *quality* mean these days? Let me tell you a quick story that recently got me thinking.

I like to eat toasted raisin bread in the morning. I even have a favorite brand. Every morning, when I'm at home, I eat several pieces. Over the years, I've become so experienced with the brand's quality, that I can spot defects. I know when they've laid on the cinnamon a little too heavily, or when the dough didn't rise quite enough. Every morning, I look forward to doing my little AM taste test.

But one morning, recently, I suddenly realized the large majority of client processes we've worked with over the last decade are not ones for which I can perform any taste test. There's nothing *physical* from the process I can taste, hear, or touch. There's nothing whatsoever by which to directly assess quality. That's because some clients simply have no physical products at all—for example, insurance, finance, or taxation. On the other hand, a good number do—electrical equipment, trucking, railroads, and so on. For these latter clients, the processes of immediate concern didn't directly involve those physical things, however—only just *white-collar stuff.*

So, the question becomes how do you assess quality from a business process when there's no physical product? How do you identify defects when there isn't any physical result?

My conclusion: *When there isn't any physical product from a business process, quality and defects are purely a matter of business rules.* If you're not documenting and managing business rules as part of your BPM or quality management approach (or elsewhere) you're missing a crucial part of the picture.

Quality must be viewed very differently in the white-collar world. The traditional view simply does not fit. In Henry Ford's day, for example, central to the concept of mass production was standardization of parts. That idea leads directly to the notion of manufacturing tolerances—that is, upper and lower limits for parts in three-dimensional space. The goal is to ensure *physical* interchangeability of *physical* parts. That idea is now standard practice, of course, across manufacturing and production sectors.

But what are the 'parts' in white-collar work? White-collar processes simply do not deal with physical things. How can you identify tolerances for them in three-dimensional space? *You can't!* In a very real sense, the 'parts' in white-collar work are literally just bits and bytes. If not tolerances as a basis for quality, then what's the proper focus? My answer: *consistency and reliability of results.*

For example, if I visit ten different branches of the same bank about getting a mortgage for my dream home, shouldn't I get the same answer on my application from all branches?! Let me tell you, that's *not* the way it works in many banks today. So, one aspect of quality in white-collar work is the consistency and reliability of *operational business decisions.*

Another concerns compliance. Every one of our businesses is subject to ever-growing numbers of (take a deep breath here) acts, laws, statutes, regulations, contracts, MOUs, agreements, terms and conditions, deals, bids, deeds of sale, warranties, prospectuses, citations, certifications, receipts, legal notices ... and the list goes on. Shouldn't I expect consistency and reliability of results with respect to all those obligations and commitments? I certainly believe so. If it's not about quality, then *what?!*

My expanded conclusion: *When there isn't any physical product from a business process, quality and defects must be measured by consistency and reliability of results, which are, in turn, always purely a matter of business rules.*

QUESTION 9

PROCESS GOVERNANCE—CONTROL OR LIBERTY?

The term 'process governance' has many meanings. For some, it is about the strict control of process change, and ensuring that process models reflect an accurate picture of current activities. Others will see process governance as a much lighter application of control allowing the maintenance of no more than a high-level view of an organization's processes.

What role, if any, do you see for process governance? Do you discriminate between process governance and process management? Where do you see the optimal balance between control and liberty in the management of business processes?

OVERVIEW

These process governance and management topics provoke quite a diversity of views. The differences are not in whether process governance is important, but in how and when it should be exercised. There is general agreement that, in a process-centric organization, some form of control needs to be exercised across the spectrum from high-level strategic management to low-level tactical operations.

A distinction is made by several authors between governing and managing individual processes, and applying those controls to the overall practice of BPM.

The need to balance the level of governance with the BPM maturity of the organization is raised. Should governance be imposed right from the start, or should it grow organically to meet developing needs?

While a variety of process governance models are discussed, there is consensus that process governance mechanisms need to be designed to meet the requirements of the particular environment and be integrated with other management systems.

Some authors challenge the need for heavy-handed governance arrangements, and remind us that there is a need to prove the business benefit for the costs and effort required to create and sustain process governance arrangements.

....

JIM BOOTS

Owner, Global Process Innovation

It is useful to distinguish between process management—which is the big umbrella—and process governance—which is an aspect of process management. Additionally, it is worthwhile to consider a higher level of governance—that is, governance of the BPM capability itself.

But first, let's start with an understanding of what we mean when we say governance and management. Online inquiries into the terms 'governance', 'management', and 'governance versus management' shed some light. In general, governance is more removed from day-to-day activities than management is. Governance is about establishing goals, behavioral policies, and frameworks of accountability; monitoring performance against goals and policies (typically at a monitoring frequency of a month or longer); and then holding managers accountable for their organizations' achievement of goals and compliance with policies. Common instruments of governance include governing bodies, boards, auditors, and regulators.

In contrast to governance, management is about organizing, deciding about, directing, monitoring, reinforcing, and holding accountable those personnel who perform the actions intended to produce expected outputs (and, in so doing, achieve the goals of the organization). Management engages with daily operations. Management reports to one or more governing bodies, providing performance information and making recommendations about big decisions that impact organizational goals and policies.

In short, governance is more concerned with 'what', and management is more concerned with 'how'.

In speaking about BPM, there are two forms of governance and one form of management to consider. At the highest level, there should be governance over the BPM capability itself. A BPM governing body might best be established soon after a top management team decides to adopt BPM. The responsibilities of the BPM governing body might wisely include:

- Clarifying the vision and key goals of the BPM initiative.
- Selecting a key manager or coordinator who will put in place the system of roles and responsibilities, software, and an array of standards and methods designed to facilitate achievement of the BPM vision and goals. (The governing board may or may not choose to insert itself in the approval process for such decisions that the BPM manager/coordinator will need to make. It may be that greater discretion is allowed over time as the BPM manager/coordinator proves his or her good judgment.)
- Monitoring performance of the BPM initiative and holding the BPM manager/coordinator accountable.

The point is this type of governance is associated with the BPM initiative as a whole, and not with the governance of individual processes. BPM governance helps the leaders of an organization ensure that the investment it is making in BPM is maximized.

The other type of governance associated with BPM is process governance. Process governance is a component within BPM that helps those who steward and interact with processes by providing process-related policies, standards, and guidelines. These governing elements are typically decided, documented, and deployed by the BPM manager/coordinator or his/her assistants. They include (but may not be limited to) the following:

- BPM software and rules of use for process modeling or automation.
- Notational standards for depicting process representations (i.e. within the software user interface).
- Process naming, role naming and other terminological conventions.

- Methods and rules for process change and for changing graphical process representations.
- Measurement expectations.
- Audit protocols.

In other words, the person accountable for developing the BPM capability and delivery of overall BPM goals will establish the governance framework so that those who steward, model, or improve processes, and those who use process content (i.e. all employees), will have a consistent set of expectations, and the organization will be efficient and effective in its process management activities.

Not every element of process governance will be anticipated and produced at the outset of a BPM initiative. The BPM manager/coordinator will need to anticipate process governance needs wherever possible, and be prepared to continuously monitor, add to, and improve the portfolio of useful governing elements. Lessons from a number of implementations suggest it is a good idea to start with fairly tight standards, while maintaining a willingness to adapt if more effective options emerge.

An alternative to this approach under-invests in governance and leaves it to individual process advisors, process modelers/mappers, and others to 'make up the rules as they go'—which is certain to lead to inconsistencies in approach that make the representation of an integrated process architecture nearly impossible. It would hamper universal adoption of a common process language intended to be the core artifact of a process-enabled culture.

In short, (a) governance over the BPM capability, and (b) governance over processes and process-related artifacts are both important for an organization to smoothly build BPM capability to a position of high maturity that delivers significant value.

Returning to the question of process management and how it is distinguished from process governance, consider again that process governance is one important aspect of BPM. In addition to process governance, other important elements under the BPM umbrella include process architecture, process stewardship, process modeling/mapping, process engagement, process execution, process analysis, process measurement, BPM technology, process improvement, process simulation, and process automation. Together, these comprise process management. The fact that most organizations have very low or no maturity in some of these elements does not change what BPM is. For example, if an organization has a mature Lean Six Sigma practice, then it has some BPM capability—since process improvement is part of BPM—but the organization may be quite immature in other BPM elements.

And, why do we need to manage processes? Using the discipline of BPM, what are processes being managed for? Processes are being managed so they are maximally effective in operational use by the organization's personnel. As with other management capabilities that a leadership team oversees—for example, performance management, business planning, project management, financial management—business process management is meant to assist the organization in the delivery of its mission. To be effective—that is, to deliver expected value—BPM must be done right. The likelihood that BPM will be done right—that processes will be sustainably well managed—will increase when adequate governance is part of the initiative.

ROGER BURLTON
President, Process Renewal Group

There is always some form of governance in place in organizations. Most of it, however, is applied in a traditional hierarchical setting. Governance being the management of management means that you have to be clear on what you want managers to do. Is it by organization chart or process? The best way to gauge a response to this challenge is to understand the level of process maturity of the business. There is no place in BPM more misunderstood that this topic. Everyone seems to want to introduce level-4 maturity governance on a level-2 mature organization, and it is too much too soon. Governance has to mature along with capability and cultural readiness. From most immature to highly mature, there are mainly three types of process governance: governance of compliance; governance of change; and governance of performance. Each of these commands a notch up from the previous level.

For compliance, the concern is about artfacts and standards such as:

- Modeling notations
- Process/capability change methodology
- Deliverables (output) definitions, including formats and level of detail

- Templates
- Tool usage guidelines
- Techniques to be applied
- QA checkpoint checklists.

For change, the concern is about process alignment, prioritization, and integrity, with other architecture capability components to decide on what process changes are to be done but without the benefit of accountabilities for process performance.

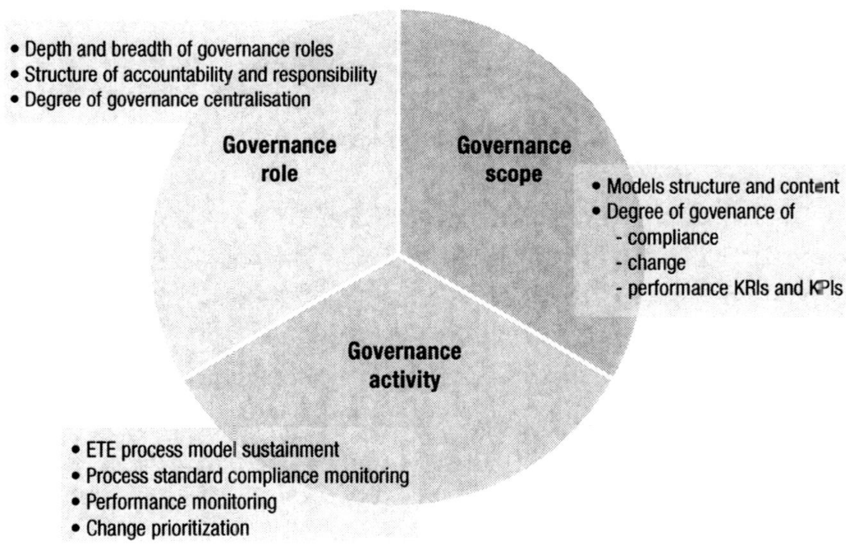

Figure 29: Three types of process governance

For performance, the concern is strategic performance alignment, and performance traceability through a robust measurement and accountability framework for full end-to-end processes. It requires process/capability-driven portfolio planning, and a robust CoE in support. This governance level is executed by the chief process officer, process council, or the management board with support from the architects and CoE members:

- Assures communication among all process leaders
- Resolves escalated resource issues
- Makes decisions regarding intra process conflicts, SLAs

- Keeps track of portfolio prioritization
- Assures process performance is in range and makes appropriate changes
- Authorizes process capability change budgets

The last level of governance should not be adopted until the organization is ready. Having process ownership in place prior to having the commitment, measurement tools, and cross-functional culture in place and expecting results is a myth. It is not sustainable.

....

MELISSA DOHERTY

Process and Innovation Manager, Brisbane City Council

Governance. No matter what the context, it's not a topic that makes many people particularly enthusiastic, even seasoned BPM practitioners. Well, there are probably a few people who love it! So why is it so common to see the terms 'process management' and 'process governance' inter-changed when governance is a term with so many negative connotations?

There is so much more to BPM than just the governance of process. And you don't have to look far to see or hear of the effects of overzealous approaches to process governance. Every BPM practitioner has seen that look of fear in people's eyes! Approaches to process governance, where any real value is not apparent, have given BPM a reputation of being an overly regimented, non-contextual practice that cannot be scaled or applied in differing ways depending on an organization and its objectives. It has made many organizations and executives run for the hills at the sheer mention of BPM. And, clearly, this is not the case. BPM can and is applied very differently, in different organizations.

There is a role and need for process governance in all organizations that practice BPM; there is, however, a need to find the optimal balance. It needs a balance that challenges the current maturity of an organization without pushing and driving BPM too hard so as to send any process practitioner, project, or business area scurrying for cover. Two of the critical success factors for sustained BPM are to have people collaborating, and to make the business process visible. Driving any process activities underground defeats the purpose.

Of course, striking this balance depends on so many different factors. Having significant process transformation activities in progress with large IT or organizational change budgets attached means that regimented approaches to process governance are almost welcomed. Process governance and the practice behind BPM can be used to manage project risk, as well as a means to incorporate disciplined business decision-making to support the achievement of project timelines. This sort of approach requires a huge commitment and investment by an organization and, as such, cannot be sustained longer term.

In a business-as-usual environment, process governance becomes much more complex. Organizations with low levels of BPM maturity require more regimented approaches to process governance until capabilities improve. But proceed with caution! Low levels of BPM maturity usually mean low levels of BPM capability. And there can be nothing worse than having no projects or business process changes proceeding because of an inability to get approval from the process governance gatekeepers. BPM will have a very short life in an organization with this sort of approach.

It is, therefore, essential to articulate the value of process governance, and determine an approach where you are likely to achieve incremental improvements in process quality, and support the development of BPM capability, while also achieving the organization's objectives. In some organizations, that may mean starting with a small subsection of the organization or project; in others, it may mean implementing governance across the breadth of the organization—but it means being *realistic* about how much process will actually be governed initially.

The ultimate goal for a mature organization would be to have almost indefinable process governance—and to have the practices of BPM and the governance of process change embedded into the existing organizational structures and practices. This would resemble the existing governance bodies having 'business process' as an ongoing topic, and practices such as project management integrating BPM approaches and methodology on relevant projects.

Formal governance in a mature organization would resemble more of a certification that the practice of business process has been followed, and that the business unit or project which has been assigned responsibility follows the agreed approach and methodology. This would include ensuring appropriate consultation on changes had in fact occurred.

In such a mature organization, BPM should be embedded through all layers in the organization—from the strategic layers to the operational with few specialized BPM roles, but business process capabilities and skills given to all people throughout the organization.

It sounds fantastic doesn't it?

The ultimate goal for process governance in an organization should be to embed BPM and process governance into existing organizational structures and practices—wherever possible and practical. While this is the goal in a mature organization, it is important to keep these goals in mind when establishing process governance initially, to ensure that process governance is not so disruptive to an organization's rhythm that it becomes the reason for opposing BPM as a practice.

••

IAN GOTTS

Founder, CEO, Q9 Elements, Nimbus

Digitalization is transforming everything we do and how we do it. Digital transformation does not just mean converting physical assets to digital counterparts, but rather about creating new business models and forms of customer engagement, leveraging digital information and knowledge worker abilities. The digital enterprise is a new way of interacting with customers, partners, and employees, enabled by technologies that allow the creation of new ways of doing business. Seizing the opportunities, and managing the risks that emerge, demand a range of capabilities across the enterprise. A digital enterprise requires a laser focus, or centricity, on four key areas: customer, knowledge, process, and innovation.

Customer centricity reorients business models to optimize customers' experiences in achieving their goals. Knowledge centricity boosts knowledge workers' effectiveness by surrounding them with a contextual, information-rich environment that presents them with the right information at the right time to support their decision-making. Innovation centricity fosters an atmosphere of innovation within the organization, which is essential to constantly reinventing business models and maintaining a competitive edge. But by far, process centricity is the most critical. Why? Because business processes are the fabric from which customer centricity, knowledge centricity, and innovation centricity are woven. Process centricity focuses the digital transformation efforts on end-to-end business processes that include: the customer's journey and goals; supporting customer centricity, which provides an information-rich context to knowledge workers for making the right decisions; enabling knowledge centricity, which offers the core fabric to reinvent the business models at will; and fostering innovation centricity. Business processes are the key enablers of the speed and agility necessary for digital success.

By now, you probably understand that we take a very holistic view of what 'process centricity' means. Process centricity takes its roots in the long-honored practice of finding efficiency and effectiveness in how things get done within an organization. It means different things to different constituents, and so it has long been the subject of much definitional rhetoric. What has become apparent is that as we shift from a more mechanical view to a more social view of process centricity, new paradigms or models are required.

Over the past few years, the concept of case management has been offered as a solution to processes that are very dynamic or complex in nature. Case management encompasses a wide range of work patterns that share some common traits: non-routine; unpredictable events; involves interactions and decisions by knowledge workers; and often requiring many types of data, information, and knowledge to move work toward desired outcome. Coincidental to the rise of case management, we have witnessed a growing interest in intelligent process management and adaptive case management. The quest to introduce effectiveness and efficiency using artificial intelligence is not new, but the rapid communization of machine learning and cognitive computing now brings the goal of intelligent adaptive business processes within our realm.

Multiple models are needed to better capture the various perspectives of how an organization achieves it goals. The future of process centricity, and thus Business Process Management, will encompass all these new models and technologies. Organizations, along with the business analysts and architects that are tackling the digital transformation, need to be versatile and proficient at integrating both process and case management perspective along with intelligent and adaptive technologies. The challenge is not with selecting the method or technique to adopt, but rather on how to integrate them all in a solution that meets the organization's desired outcomes.

The key deliverables of a business-led BPM project are documented processes in a format that the end user can understand and follow. Process diagrams have activity steps with links to documents such as procedures, work instructions, training videos, checklists, and links to the automated systems (CRM, ERP, finance, HR) that support the processes. Together, all of this information comprises a critically important company asset: 'process knowledge'. It's the electronic operations manual for the company.

A senior executive at Nestlé made the comment, "If only Nestlé knew what Nestlé knew, we would be so effective." He was referring to process knowledge.

Processes are not static. Different areas of the process knowledge will iterate—activities and flows on a diagram might change; the linked documents might be updated; the supporting applications might have new releases. Changes may be driven by major top-down initiatives or by iterative bottom-up process improvement suggestions from the field.

Therefore, it is important to have some level of process management. At a minimum, that means there must be a master version that everyone is working to, and a draft, or work-in-progress copy, where changes are developed and refined. Then there is a formal mechanism for overwriting the master version with the draft copy. This is process management.

Many companies now operate under a level of regulatory scrutiny: financial services have the FCA; food and life sciences companies have FDA regulations; energy and construction have Health and Safety. And over a million companies maintain ISO certification. Many companies have multiple different regulatory frameworks to satisfy—and all of these can be satisfied by a SINGLE managed body of process knowledge.

But to satisfy the external and internal auditors, there needs to be a more rigorous level of governance with an auditable chain of sign-offs, and the ability to go back to see prior versions of the process knowledge. And that means not only the process diagrams, but also the versions of the supporting documents—wherever they are stored. Ideally, it should be easy to see which processes support each of the clauses of a regulatory standard, because this is how an auditor views the business. But there is another benefit. If an area of the regulatory standard is updated, it is easy to pinpoint the processes that need to be changed.

The challenge is to be able to rapidly capture the process knowledge and make it available to the end users, provide them with a mechanism to suggest improvements when they see them, and be able to rapidly adopt those changes—while, at the same time, maintaining compliance with the regulatory standards. This is process governance.

With the right approach, culture, and process management solution, process governance is possible. This is not just a theory; it has been proven in companies ranging from small, nimble start-ups through to multi-national Fortune 500 companies.

In client organizations, we see different levels of process maturity as measured against the five-stage CMMI (Capability Maturity Model Integration). At the lowest levels, there is chaos—a culture of heroes. At the next level, there are some defined processes. But it is not until Level 4 that process management is formalized, and Level 5 until strong process governance is in place. And it goes without saying that the benefits that a client at Level 5 is getting are orders of magnitude higher than at Level 1. So, it worth the effort to climb up the maturity curve.

....

LEANDRO JESUS

Co-Founder & Director, EloGroup

Managing processes and, more broadly, running a process-based management system, are both concepts that do not involve only a single role. We need to think of a structure of responsibilities for all management actions required. Therefore, we need to establish a proper governance structure.

Governance concerns the definition of guidelines and rules for conducting management actions—and the consequent definition of responsibilities and authorities for those actions. It is important to emphasize that a process governance structure should complement existing structure, ensuring greater ability to customer needs without making this structure more complex, and without creating a redundancy of attributions.

A governance model that puts emphasis on processes must, therefore, optimize and eliminate deficiencies of the functional management structure, without creating a parallel structure. In general, an effective governance model involves the definition of:

- Who does what in regard to the management of each process and, more broadly, to organizational management (i.e. what the roles and responsibilities are)?

- What are the management actions to be performed?
- What are the standards for execution of management actions?
- What are the impacts on organizational structure arising from the defined roles and responsibilities for management actions?
- What are the goals associated to management actions?
- What are the required control mechanisms to ensure management goals are achieved?
- What are the evaluation and reward mechanisms associated with management goals?

It is relevant to emphasize, therefore, that governance is not just about the definition of roles and responsibilities; it involves the creation of a whole structure to ensure these roles are performed effectively. In any case, a simple and pragmatic process governance begins with the demystification of the role of a process manager (or owner). We believe the manager responsible for a process should be simply an existing manager, or group of managers, from the business (by the way, every manager should be responsible for one or more processes). That means, in general terms, that:

- For a typical functional process, existing functional manager should be understood as process manager.
- For a cross-functional process, this role should be performed by a set of functional managers responsible for achieving results, based on the establishment of shared goals and routine meetings.

The indiscriminate assignment of process managers only makes a governance structure more complex. We must focus on raising awareness, and preparing existing managers to this collaborative and integrated approach to management. This simplifies and gives agility to the current structure, strengthening process orientation and value creation.

One knows, however, that educating and preparing managers is not an easy task and, therefore, some additional roles may help building an adequate process governance structure. We will then emphasize two major roles that could be formalized—process guardians, and BPM Offices—as well as the role of senior management (see the figure below).

A process guardian is nothing more than a part- or full-time professional dedicated to support managers in improving and sustaining process performance. This role is also often quoted in the market as a process leader, focal point, internal consultant, transformation agent, among others.

Figure 30: Governance structure with process guardians and BPM Office

We chose here the name 'guardian' to help explain it's not just someone who conducts projects (as it would be an internal consultant or Six Sigma belt), but also someone who continuously promotes process culture among managers and executors. However, the name here is not what matters most, but the characterization of the role.

In fact, we believe that this is the role that needs to be effectively formalized to support process-based management. Managers do not always find enough time to think about changes, nor are they accustomed to managing their routines based on a vision of shared responsibilities and goals. There has to be some structure of professionals, full or part time, to support them in this regard.

It´s a process guardian who ensures changes are made in a process to improve its performance. Typically, it also participates in day-by-day management meetings with managers, and monitors the implementation of corrective or continuous improvement actions to sustain performance on a daily basis. Below we list a summary of its usual responsibilities:

- Lead transformation projects
- Analyze, propose solutions and manage the implementation of process improvements
- Estimate and determine performance gains to be obtained from a project
- Monitor process performance, risk and compliance on a daily basis, reporting to managers
- Propose suggestions for continuous improvement or correction of

deviations in process execution on a daily basis

- Maintain process normative documentation and process models.

Guardians must be few and qualified. The introduction of this role must be gradual, emerging from the awareness of managers to the need of this figure. Guardians can even be part of a professional development program, aimed at preparing future managers.

Guardians are usually trained by a central unit that seeks to support process-based management, which we call BPM Office. The BPM Office provides methodology and standards, as well as disseminates process knowledge. It supports transformation projects and day-by-day management, besides giving greater emphasis on behavioral change and training of managers and executors, so that they can all become aware of the benefits of a process-based management system. Some of its usual responsibilities are:

- Maintain the process architecture and repository
- Manage transformation projects portfolio
- Disseminate BPM culture and results
- Train and provide support to guardians and managers in projects execution and day by day management
- Maintain BPM standards.

Besides process guardians and the BPM Office, senior management obviously has a key role in a process governance structure, defining priorities, sponsoring projects and tracking overall process goals. This role can never be neglected.

Finally, it's important to point out that the presented governance structure is only a reference and usually evolves over time, as maturity increases. Organizations with low maturity, for instance, usually do not have guardians; instead, the BPM Office itself conducts most activities related to this role.

....

MATTHEW J. MORGAN

Head of Process & Metrics Excellence, Bridgewater Assoc.

Process governance or ownership is an essential component of process management. Processes must be defined in order for them to be managed and improved. A process description provides an operational definition of the major components of a process. The description specifies, in a complete, precise, and verifiable manner, the requirements, design, behavior, or other characteristics of a process. It also may include procedures for determining whether these provisions have been satisfied. Process descriptions can be found at the activity, project, or organizational level.

Processes may (and should) be improved to make them faster, less wasteful, cheaper, or produce better quality outputs. Process improvements respond to objective measures of current process performance, set objectives for characteristics of the process that need to be improved to meet specific goals, and then build plans to design and implement the improved process.

Process owners have responsibility for defining the process (i.e. owning the description of it), monitoring its performance, and carrying out improvements. Specifically, I would consider the process owner to be the person who has immediate supervisory responsibility for the process and who is responsible for the process's accuracy and performance. Many organizations will have processes with a varying degree of standardization across business units, or processes that are cross functional and, thus, without a clear supervisory authority.

In these cases, process ownership is appointed based on factors beyond the person's role responsibilities, which could include experience, knowledge, or other contextual factors. The process owner will likely delegate some responsibilities to others, including document ownership, which includes the creation and editing of process documentation, and review and approval, which (although typically the same person as the process owner) would be delegated authority. For document management purposes, we seek to avoid document authorship and approval being vested in the same person.

The method by which owners accomplish this is through governance or control, which exists in two levels. Governance committees can establish design decisions in both standardizing processes across an organization, or in making changes over time. Control systems are managed through attributes, such as: version number, type of revision, approval data, review cycle, and access restrictions. In a control system, the process's version number is often expressed in an x.x format, with the first number indicating the number of major revisions (with initial publication being 1.0) and the number after the decimal point indicating the number of minor revisions. The revision type, thus, could have two or more possibilities, such as a major revision, or significant process change, or change in process ownership and a minor revision, or change in format, verbiage, or new step that does not materially affect the process.

The approval date is the date at which the process owner (or his delegated approver) authorizes the process document. The review cycle defines the maximum time before a process must be reviewed and approved to be considered 'updated' in the control process. In a low-maturity environment that experienced turbulent and rapid process change with a low level of process stability and management, I established a maximum review cycle for any process document of one year. In more mature environments, our governance process established a two-year revision cycle. Last, access restrictions should define any limitations to access of a process due to security controls.

QUESTION 10

IS BPM DISRUPTIVE OR DISRUPTED?

Significant and disruptive technology developments are having profound effects across all types of organization, indeed, in life generally. They are changing the nature of work and redefining the human-machine boundaries.

What impact do you see theses disruptive technologies having on the management and optimization of business processes? Which technology changes will be the most disruptive? What will be their impact on BPM?

OVERVIEW

All agree that disruptive technologies will be…disruptive. From a BPM point of view, processes themselves will fundamentally change along with process management, process design, process execution, and every other aspect of process-based management.

Chasing incremental improvements in process cost-efficiencies becomes meaningless when disruptive technologies and business models are in play. There will still be cross-functional business processes and they will still be the way value is created and delivered, but their management will be disrupted. Processes, and those that manage them, will need to be disruptable. Will old

BPM survive in a disrupted world?

For the most part, authors have themselves chosen which of the 15 questions they wanted to answer for this book. Of the 109 answers that make up this book, only four are on this question. Could it be that those who deal with these issues were too busy disrupting to submit an answer? Others may not be sure about the impact—is the detail of disruption predictable? Or might it be that we process practitioners, the *processerati*, are stuck in a loop of arguing 'what BPM really is' and are about to be disrupted ourselves?

....

PETER FINGAR

Managing Principal, Meghan-Kiffer Research

The 'perfect storm' of emerging disruptive IT technologies like mobile, cloud, social media, big data (the new MoSAIC), and smart systems are causing a shift from a 'command-and-control' to a 'connect-and-collaborate' system. Do not think your organization will not be affected. It will. The shift will mean organizations will 'organize value'. This means working together in multi-company industry networks, being intimately connected, having common goals. The underlying structure that brings it together? It's the business process.

These are crazy times for change, threatening to disrupt so much of what we've worked so hard to achieve over the past decades of information technology and business process management. The disturbing part of disruption is knowing that what took so much energy to figure out, can be so quickly plowed under by something smarter, faster, and more adaptive. It's great fun to be the disruptor, but we all know in the back of our minds that the disruptors, too, will lose ground to the next great idea.

The complexity of BPM initiatives have grown exponentially since publication of the definitive book *Business Process Management: The Third Wave*. As Jim Sinur, James Odell and I wrote in *Business Process Management: The Next Wave,* intelligent agent technology is required to harness the complexity of today's business ecosystems. Technology marches on, bringing new dangers—and new opportunities. As cloud computing, social, mobile, big data, predictive analytics, and the Internet of Things are baked into more and more business processes, they will rapidly reshape how business gets done, today and tomorrow. Today, companies are struggling to come to grips with these forces that introduce unprecedented complexity. Business Process Management (BPM) has delivered benefits over a long time, and continues to do so. But as process scopes expand to meet the nexus of these forces, BPM needs to be enhanced and extended in order to harness the exploding complexity and to gain competitive advantage.

The idea of having all the intelligence centrally managed and delivered is outmoded and challenging, if not impossible. What's needed are insights and strategies for transforming current centralized BPM approaches by exploiting decentralized, distributed intelligence in the form of intelligent agent technology. Agent-oriented BPM (aoBPM), steeped in cognitive computing, will allow BPM to take on all of what is expected of it going forward. The *Next Wave* book provides a starting point that will help you know what is coming, and how to think about addressing it. It's about your organization's journey toward the future.

And as William Gibson wrote in *The Economist*, "The future is already here: it's just not evenly distributed." The time is ripe for cognitive computing and aoBPM. We point out that business process management has, until now, been mostly about tactical improvements—limited in scope, and largely focused on specific business functions. Getting beyond the tactical and into the strategic use of BPM will require an enterprise focus that cuts across functional lines and classic management silos and on to inter-enterprise business ecosystems.

We argue for moving process from an engine of execution to, "...any number of engines executing any number of processes..." We call for process being the grand choreographer of the value chain rather than today's common composite applications that interact with scattered processes. The answer to today's complexity and demanding business environment will come through intelligent agents powered with cognitive computing capabilities. With cloud, social, mobile and big data, there's really no choice but to take a new approach to business architecture.

....

GILLES MORIN

Founder, BPMPlus, Inc

We are living in interesting times, as several major disruptive technologies penetrate the markets at a speed that most organization cannot deal with. iBPMS, as ERP were, can be a game-changing technology if leveraged properly and incubated with the right culture. We can say the same for cloud, big data, cognitive systems, mobile, et cetera.

Case management is probably one of the next 'big thing' areas, as it focuses on the knowledge workers, the last value-creating island in most organizations. iBPMS, as it matures and evolves, makes the business analyst's role, as we know it today, obsolete—it creates a new space for a merged business / process / performance analyst. It will profoundly change the relationship between IT and businesses. Process-driven requirements and iBPMS allow the functional analyst to work directly with business people and generate new solutions in an agile mode. Traditional solution delivery methodology cannot accommodate iBPMS. I am certainly not saying that all iBPMSs are alike. Some have been built with architecture to ease this transformational change; others have been built using old paradigm and technical architecture and only add complexity, fueling the business perception about IT being disconnected from the business.

Provided that IT showcases the power of these disruptive technologies via the right incubation strategy to business people, we can expect these technologies to:

- Force a major transformation of the IT leadership and service delivery model.
- Challenge the thinking and behaviors of middle management.
- Accentuate expectations of business towards IT value creation.
- Change the way solutions are designed, delivered, and operated.
- Increase business autonomy to handle the business rules and process changes.
- Increase intelligence and feedback to knowledge workers on how best to deal with cases—a self-learning environment.
- Challenge traditional organization models based on hierarchy, command and control, and the 'boss knows it all'.
- Reshape the relationship between the organization and its customers, partners, and employees.
- Force a review of the organization's staffing plan to account for new competencies and genetic codes that will be required to fully leverage the new capabilities.
- Realign its key HR levers to fully access the potential, including the

performance management system.

- Change the way we design and build products and services.

This is even truer in older or more mature industries. If you are in a slow, clock-speed service industry, watch your back—someone is already moving. Embrace and incubate using a process-based approach.

....

PROFESSOR MICHAEL ROSEMANN

Head of Information Systems School, Queensland University of Technology

Disruptive technologies will have an impact on BPM in three ways. They will: (i) enable new forms of process management; (ii) enable new forms of processes; and (iii) require new process design objectives.

The first impact of disruptive technologies will *unlock new ways of managing processes* in the various stages of its lifecycle. Examples include:

- Advanced visualizations of process models, including 3D-environments for process modeling, and large-scale process visualizations (e.g. QUT's Cube).
- Virtual environments (e.g. Oculus) facilitating process experiences for process design, process testing, and educational purposes.
- Augmented reality solutions allowing the visualization of process models close to physical real world objects (e.g. showing an invoice verification process model triggered by identifying an invoice).
- In-memory technologies allowing rapid process analytics and increasing the frequency of process mining, leading to improved process models.
- Machine learning will allow improved recommender capabilities, leading to BPM systems able to guide users in their design decisions.
- Video analytics leading to improved process monitoring of non-automated processes (e.g. crown counting used for process performance management in environments like airports or shopping malls).

The second impact of disruptive technologies will be in the form of entirely *new forms of process possibilities.* Each and every disruptive technology will enable process transformations, leading to an opportunity-rich landscape of process design possibilities. Selected examples are:

- Voice will enable the triggering of business processes, as already supported in the form of Amazon Echo or Google Handsfree.
- Data science and advanced big data capabilities will allow new forms of process analytics and process predictions, leading to improved resourcing along a business process based on machine learning-informed algorithms.
- Robots and other smart devices will increasingly take part in business processes, either in the form of devices triggering a process (a car requiring fuel, a pipeline with a leakage), or as resources enabling new forms of process executions (drones for inspections, robots in contaminated areas, or cars receiving parcels).
- Location-based services will allow triggering processes based on spatial information (e.g. streaming advertisements, requiring health and safety training, approaching customers in competitors' stores (e.g. Meatpack Hijack).

The third, and maybe most profound, impact will be on the overall design paradigm. Disruptive technologies have a fundamental impact when they bring an end to an entire business model. The classic process design paradigm of cost-effective, highly efficient process executions is no longer the ultimate goal when disruptive technologies can question the *raison d'être* of a business process. As such, disruptive technologies will require not such cost efficiency, but revenue-resilient business processes.

Revenue resilient processes are characterized by the ability to remain relevant and revenue generating, despite a disruptive environment. This will demand BPM capabilities going beyond eliminating inefficiencies in a business process. Instead, process designers need to be able to protect the relevance of a business process by creating new lock-in effects, or continuously modernizing the value proposition of a business process. This requires the proactive use of disruptive technologies, a strong design, and comprehensive environmental scanning capabilities so that emerging technologies and their design affordances can be identified early.

....

PROFESSOR JAN VOM BROCKE

Hilti Chair of Business Process Management, University of Liechtenstein

The management of business processes naturally takes place in a given technological frame. The existent technology affords specific process-related action, and we need to be able to identify such affordances as well as act upon them. Against this background, digital technologies also bear the potential to allow new process-design and process-management practices (Schmiedel, vom Brocke, 2015). Sensor networks and the Internet of Things, for instance, enable us to capture data from running processes, and techniques of data analytics allow us to process such data and to feed it back to the process in real time.

In a number of studies, the impact of in-memory technology (Plattner, Krüger, 2015) on BPM has been investigated based on empirical data (vom Brocke, 2015), and these findings may serve well to further illustrate the affordances of digital technologies in BPM. In-memory technology enables a remarkable increase in the information-processing capacity of organizations' application systems. For example, SAP has reported increases in transaction speed by factors up to 100,000 for its in-memory computing appliance, HANA (High-performance ANalytic Appliance). This increase in speed is comparable to shortening the flight time from New York to Paris to 0.28 seconds, or that of circling the world to 1.5 seconds (SAP, 2012).

The effects in-memory technology can have on process work as identified in a number of cases are summarized in the figure below.

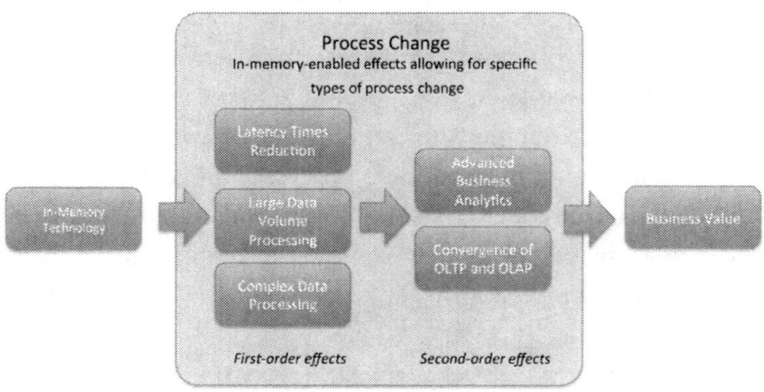

Figure 31: Model for Generating Business Value through In-Memory Technology (cf. vom Brocke et al. 2013)

The model shows, how in-memory technology generates different effects that build on each other. The increased information processing capacity, offered by in-memory technology, can allow for processing large data volumes, for instance. This, in turn, allows for new design principles of business processes, such as a convergence of transactional and analytical information processing (vom Brocke et al., 2013). This means to capture large volumes of data from a process and its environment while it is running, to analyze this data, and to use the results for process control in real time. For example, colleagues have referred to such mechanisms as: embedded analytics (Nijkamp & Oberhofer, 2009); operational business intelligence (Marjanovic, 2007); real-time business intelligence (Chaudhuri et al., 2011); or context-aware business process management (Rosemann et al., 2010).

The model also shows some important boundaries of the disruptive power of in-memory technology. The action possibilities are restricted by the capabilities of the overall socio-technical structures and processes. For instance, latency times may be reduced through a reduction of data latency and analysis latency, while the decision latency and the implementation latency may involve people in a great number of cases.

A mature IT landscape—including high-quality data, harmonization of diverse internal data sources, and information sharing along the supply chain—is required to realize the full potential of in-memory technology. In that sense, the increase of automated information-processing needs to be supported by the structures and processes (including people) throughout the entire value chain.

The results from the in-memory studies show how digital technologies may impact process management, in more general.

- First, digital technologies will contribute to further overcoming boundaries of time and space in process design. Processes will be smarter in that they are sensitive and responsive to their environment.
- Second, the disruptive power will be limitations by the capabilities of the socio-technical eco-system of processes. It will be important to look beyond technology, and to understand the dynamics of people interacting with technology. We need to be able to create a comprehensive picture of socio-technical ecosystems, in order to further develop these utilizing digital technologies.

In essence, this is what BPM has been very successful in doing over the past decades, and this is why BPM should contribute more to business innovation and digital innovation in particular (vom Brocke, Schmiedel, 2015).

REFERENCES

Chaudhuri, S., Dayal, U., & Narasayya, V. (2011). "An overview of business intelligence technology". *Communications of the ACM*, 54(8), 88–98.

Marjanovic, O. (2007). "The next stage of operational business intelligence: Creating new challenges for business process management". *Proceedings of the 40th Hawaii International Conference on System Sciences.*

Markus, M.L., and Silver, M.S. "A Foundation for the Study of IT Effects: A New Look at DeSanctis and Poole's Concepts of Structural Features and Spirit", *Journal of the Association for Information Systems* (9:10) 2008, pp.609–632.

Nijkamp, E., & Oberhofer, M. (2009). "Embedded analytics in front office applications". *Proceedings of BTW* (pp.449–459).

Plattner, H., Kürger, J. (2015), "In-Memory Data and Process Management", In J. vom Brocke & M. Rosemann (Eds.), *Handbook on Business Process Management: Introduction, Methods, and Information Systems (International Handbooks on Information Systems)* (2 ed., Vol. 1, pp.105–122). Berlin et al., Springer.

Rosemann, M., Recker, J., & Flender, C. (2010). "Designing context-aware business processes". In R.H.L. Chiang, K. Siau, and B.C. Hardgrave (eds.). *Systems Analysis and Design: People, Processes, and Projects. Armonk*, NY: M.E. Sharpe, Inc., pp. 53-74.

SAP. (2012). The "One Hundred Thousand" Club. http://www.experience-saphana.com/blogs/experts/2012/02/06/the-one-hundred- thousand-club

Schmiedel, T., & vom Brocke, J. (2015). "Business process management: Potentials and challenges of driving innovation". In J. vom Brocke & T. Schmiedel (Eds.), BPM—*Driving Innovation in a Digital World* (pp.3–16). Heidelberg: Springer.

vom Brocke, J. (2013). "In-Memory Value Creation, or now that we found love, what are we gonna do with it?" *BPTrends*, 10, 1–8.

QUESTION 11

INCREMENTAL IMPROVEMENT OR RADICAL INNOVATION?

Airlines and airports are moving beyond incremental improvements in queue management to eliminating queues completely. They will use innovative solutions like waving a card, providing a fingerprint, or the proximity of a smartphone. The problem (check-in-process) is solved, not by incremental improvements, but by radical innovation.

Are the common approaches to incremental process improvement able to deliver innovative solutions? Is the 'incremental mindset' the enemy of innovation? Can innovation be a consequence of taking a BPM approach, or is BPM a handicap? If there is value in incremental improvements, how does an organization strike the right balance between incremental and innovative thinking and change?

OVERVIEW

Our authors tended to suggest that BPM could encompass both incremental improvement and radical innovation. Some suggested that one used whatever was appropriate for the task at hand. At the organizational level, when managers are trying to make a major advance, innovation is called for. At the process level, when the process is already performing well, incremental improvements are more appropriate.

At the same time, most authors suggested that business change, and even radical change, is more common all the time, and that organizations didn't have the leisure they once had to make gradual changes. In fact, everyone knows that any large organization has many processes—some changing rapidly as technology changes, and some evolving more slowly. Smaller organizations may have limited resources and will decide to increment at one point and to focus on innovation at another. For larger organizations, it's usually a matter of combining both incremental and radical change.

....

JIM BOOTS

Owner, Global Process Innovation

An organization's specific BPM vision is an important factor in whether it sacrifices innovation in favor of incremental improvement. However, with the right messaging and behaviors from an organization's leaders, a BPM approach can foster both continuous, incremental improvement, as well as innovation. Indeed, synergies between improvement and innovation can be exploited. Points to support this contention are as follows:

- *Apply incremental improvement to the manage innovation process.* Under the broad context of the BPM umbrella, continuous (incremental) process improvement—such as might be typical of a Lean Six Sigma practice—can be applied to the innovation process itself (or, more correctly, the *manage innovation* process). As Larry Keely, respected innovation expert, has written, "Organizations that rely on repeatable processes to pursue innovations have impressive success rates between 35 and 70 per cent, as compared to industry averages of only 4 per cent for companies without structured innovation programs." In other words, applying BPM to innovation-related processes will strengthen an organization's innovation capabilities.
- *The process architecture serves improvement and innovation at every level.* If a mature, sustainable, strategic BPM initiative builds and maintains a well-articulated, 'living' representation of its process architecture,

all process improvement efforts will be more efficient, because the current state process will be readily available—to project teams as well as to all employees—for review, consideration, and recommendation for improvement. Furthermore, when improvements are deployed—especially larger ones that might qualify as innovations—key behavioral changes are more easily pinpointed, explained, and reinforced. Finally, the graphical representation of the process architecture will enable many perspectives on the work of the organization, fostering change considerations at every level—from individual and intra-group incremental improvements, to inter-departmental re-alignments to strategic outsourcing or insourcing of major functions.

- *Leaders can use BPM to foster an innovation culture.* Although the following statements could be associated with the same BPM initiative, there is an important difference in them:

  1. We want to standardize processes so we can be as efficient as possible.
  2. We want to standardize processes so the time of our workforce is freed up to do more productive activities—such as learning, researching, collaborating with colleagues, and consulting with customers—which will foster more generation of innovative ideas.

- If leader words and behaviors reinforce the second message, the organization's culture will form around innovation as a core value.

It is fashionable for leaders to talk about their employees as their most valuable assets. Also, in the news, we can read about good employment prospects and salary premiums commanded by knowledge workers. BPM, framed correctly, taps into the vision of an enabled and empowered worker, who can be seen most often doing high-order activities and occasionally performing necessary routines with confidence and competence. Autonomous, connected to the mission of the organization, passionate about performance—such employees provide the discretionary efforts and innovative insights that separate an organization's performance from competitors.

Whether an initiative is called 'operational excellence', 'fostering a culture of innovation', or some other phrase with aspirational intent requiring development of organization-wide capability, Business Process Management should be a core component of the initiative. It can provide a collaborative platform that elevates organizational intelligence around the initiative's points of emphasis, including innovation if so desired.

Perhaps it is worth mentioning where devoting resources to strategic BPM is probably not worthwhile. It will be difficult to sustain a living process architecture within a function, or other narrow organizational units, because there will be too few cultural benefits to sustain the required support and governance infrastructure. Therefore, investments in BPM that don't span large organizational entities will probably be best directed toward tactical BPM efforts—which still can be valuable, but will likely not be strategically impactful. Tactical BPM efforts would include activities such as implementing a portfolio of Lean Six Sigma projects, and automating information flows to increase procedural ease and reliability.

In summary, *tactical BPM* efforts can produce a stream of incremental improvements. Such efforts need not conflict with a desire to foster innovation, but tactical BPM efforts alone probably won't be viewed as central to an innovation initiative. In contrast, *strategic BPM*—which invests in a living process architecture—has the potential to supercharge the type of rigorous and creative collaboration that is the hallmark of an innovation culture.

....

PETER FINGAR

Managing Principal, Meghan-Kiffer Research

Isn't innovation an episodic event? The light bulb. The steam engine. The airplane. Innovation isn't just about some star in the R&D suite delivering a radical breakthrough, a home run, every now and then. What's wrong with hitting singles and doubles with regularity? Isn't it time that we stopped just talking about out-of-the-park innovation and got serious about developing the capability required to manage the complete innovation lifecycle? And companies had better manage that lifecycle because, in today's wired world, competitors can catch up to your innovation in an instant. Just look at the glitzy new Apple iPhone. Hackers broke the code requiring the exclusive use of AT&T; a Chinese company has a clone under development; and Google is pursuing the gPhone. In just weeks after its introduction, Apple had to cut $200 off its price due to competitive pressures. Today, it's not a single innovation; *the challenge is to set the 'pace of innovation'*—once you innovate, then you really have just begun and will need to run hard to outpace your competition.

As Dell's Chief Innovation Officer and I write in the book *Business Innovation in the Cloud*, setting the pace of innovation means going beyond inward-focused process efficiency programs such as Six Sigma, and on to energy maneuverability methods and techniques, such as OODA loops. During the early 1960s, John Boyd, together with Thomas Christie, a civilian mathematician, created the energy-maneuverability theory of aerial combat. Their E-M theory was a mathematical equation that calculated an aircraft's ability to change direction, altitude, or speed under specified conditions, and allowed systematic comparison between different aircraft for the first time.

In the 1970s, Boyd applied his understanding of energy maneuverability to help design the F-16, bringing together everything he knew about the competition. Then he focused on something even grander: a unifying theory of this thing we call agility. Boyd's key agility concept was that of the decision cycle, or OODA Loop (observe, orient, decide, act), the process by which either an individual or an organization reacts to an event in real time, or at least in time enough to make a difference. According to this idea, the key to victory is to be able to create situations wherein one can make good decisions more quickly than the opponent. The construct was developed out of Boyd's earlier E-M theory and his observations on air combat between MiGs and U.S. Sabre jets in the Korean War. The chief designer of the F-16, Harry Hillaker, said of the OODA theory, "Time is the dominant parameter. The pilot who goes through the OODA cycle in the shortest time prevails because his opponent is caught responding to situations that have already changed." Boyd hypothesized that people and organizations undergo a continuous cycle of interaction with their environments.

Bob Lewis, co-author of *The Cognitive Enterprise*, brings some balance to the discussion of OODA Loops, "As generally conceived, an OODA Loop is used to win the battles you fight, but not necessarily the way to choose the wars you wage. And in fact, one way of understanding what went horribly wrong in the second Iraq war is that the folks who decided it was a good idea were focused on their OODA-driven ability to win it, leading them to ignore the question of whether it made sense to fight the war in the first place. Had they allowed some of that analysis paralysis to take place they'd have figured out that removing Saddam Hussein from power would eliminate the main counterbalance to Iran in the region."

Isn't innovation just about great ideas? There are certainly no lack of great ideas in today's hyper-connected, wired world. But companies report a 96% failure rate on their innovation attempts. What's up with that? It's largely a result of innovation being approached in a haphazard fashion. Today, however, leading companies are taking the haphazard approach to business innovation and turning it into systematic, repeatable, business processes (think innovation process management or IPM). IPM can be compared to the rise of the total quality movement in the 1980s, where leaders such as Toyota taught the lesson of 'quality-or-else'. It turns out that quality is all about process.

Ditto for innovation.

Regardless of the specific innovation process chosen, there are two parts to successful execution—doing the right thing, then doing it right. The doing the right thing part would be an innovation architectural model; the doing it right would be the OODA loop model (always adjusting). Below we present an adaptation of the OODA loops, presented earlier in the book, which focuses in on an innovation process lifecycle.

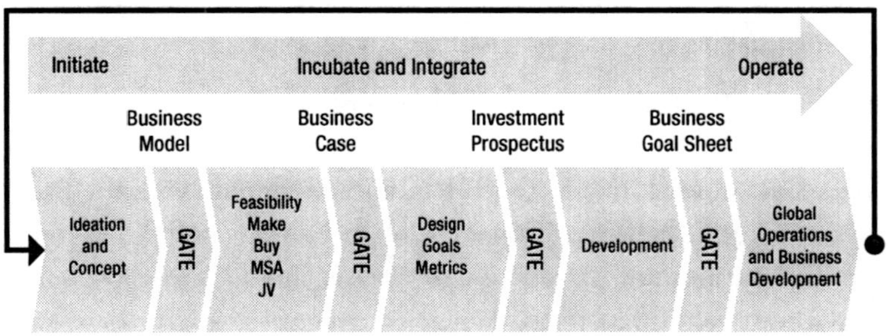

Figure 32: Innovation as a repeatable business process

Some companies have already implemented systematic approaches to innovation process management. GE calls it CENCOR (calibrate, explore, create, organize, and realize). The Mayo Clinic calls it SPARC (see, plan, act, refine, communicate).

A caution: Some companies, in pursuit of efficiency in their current business processes, have almost killed their ability to be innovative. 3M is an example. At the company that has always prided itself on drawing at least one-third of sales from products released in the past five years, today that fraction has slipped to only one-quarter.

Those results are not coincidental. Efficiency programs like Six Sigma are designed to identify problems in work processes—and then use rigorous measurement to reduce variation and eliminate defects. When these types of initiatives become ingrained in a company's culture, as they did at 3M, creativity can easily get squelched. After all, a breakthrough innovation is something that challenges existing procedures and norms.

....

ALAN RAMIAS

Partner, Performance Design Lab

This question actually surprises me a little. I suppose that's because it never occurred to me that someone might think BPM can't include innovative thinking. Such an assumption may be a consequence of Six Sigma, at least in those renditions that focus tightly on eliminating single defects—and maybe also Lean, if seen as mostly just about streamlining a process by taking wasteful stuff out. Such incremental improvements are certainly valuable, but could be justifiably viewed as not particularly innovative.

But, in my own experience, the goal of process improvement is often about radically rethinking how work should be performed. Starting with the process work I did at Motorola in the 1980s, and continuing with the Rummler-Brache Group and then Performance Design Lab, my colleagues and I recognized that the amount of redesign a process should undergo ought to be based on a combination of its inadequacies, customer expectations, and business requirements. Some processes need only to be tweaked; others need a complete makeover.

We would challenge design teams to come up with breakthrough ideas by using a technique we called 'could-be designs'. We generally use this approach before getting into the task of redesigning the process level by level. Instead, team members are asked to come up with wild ideas that might entirely eliminate a host of related problems, or completely change the way a business is run. Some ideas would eventually be baked into the final redesign, while others would be discarded as impractical.

The 'could-be' technique has sometimes proved to be the most powerful thing in our toolkit. In one memorable case, I sat in on a top executive meeting where funding for the upcoming year was being discussed, and the president asked about the status of an innovation he especially desired—and he used the name of the 'could-be' design first dreamed up months earlier. To him, that idea completely transformed a particular part of the business and he had put it at the top of his priority list.

And there are plenty of other techniques for encouraging process designers to dream up new ways of doing things. Benchmarking, bringing in outside speakers, field trips, research, and contests can all spark creative thinking. And much depends upon the mix of people you have on a design team. If they are all analysts, or relatively inexperienced, or a mite passive, it may be tough to get any new ideas. What works best is a mix of the disgusted and the eager, the cynical and the outlandish, the thoughtful and the persistent—along with few limits on their ideas and their range of exploration. They may start with a process, but they should be allowed to navigate to other, broader things (e.g. corporate policy, organizational structure, management practices, cultural norms) that might be connected yet, presumably, out of their scope. I've watched as design teams, given the freedom, have started by trying to resolve a specific timeliness issue with a given process, and ended up suggesting an entirely different service offering.

THE THREE PERFORMANCE NEEDS

THE THREE LEVELS OF PERFORMANCE	PLANNING	DESIGN	MANAGEMENT
ORGANIZATION LEVEL	Organization plans	Organization design	Organization management
PROCESS LEVEL	Process plans	Process design	Process management
JOB/PERFORMER LEVEL	Job plans	Job design	Job management

Figure 33: The nine performance variables

THE THREE PERFORMANCE NEEDS

PROCESS PERFORMANCE

THE THREE LEVELS OF PERFORMANCE	PLANNING	DESIGN	MANAGEMENT
ORGANIZATION LEVEL	Organization plans	Organization design	Organization management
PROCESS LEVEL	Process plans	Process design	Process management
PERFORMER HUMAN TECHNOLOGY LEVEL	Performance plans	Performance design	Performance management

Figure 34: The nine performance variables, revised

So, can BPM produce innovative change? Of course, if practitioners stay out of the weeds and instead ask questions about what customers want, what the business really needs, "Why can't you…?" and "What if…?"

……………………………………

RON ROSS

CEO, Business Rules Solutions

Perhaps in the traditional sweet spot of BPM—manufacturing and production of physical products—this question can be answered. For white-collar work and the digital economy, it cannot—at least as posed. In these latter areas:

- The key to incremental change is business rules, not process improvements. If you change the business rules, the results of processes will adjust.
- The key to innovative change is strategy, not process. Simply not the same thing. Sun Tzu figured that out three or four millennia ago.

……………………………………

QUESTION 12

HOW SHOULD BPM KNOWLEDGE BE MANAGED?

We have a growing number of academic programs training BPM specialists. Some organizations leave BPM to IT, while others regard BPM as a business management task. Some organizations have formal Six Sigma, Lean, or BPM groups, in some cases integrated and in others completely independent. Other architecture and project management groups are sometime co-located with BPM teams.

Who should be responsible for the process work of the future? Should they be specialists with academic degrees, or individuals who are certified; and if so, how? Should there be a central BPM Center of Excellence, and if so, where should it reside in the organizational structure, and what should be its scope of work?

OVERVIEW

Not surprisingly, our authors generally answered, "All of the above." However, they do so with important caveats. Wherever the 'BPM journey' has its source, it needs to be integrated, supported, and 'of the business', if it is to be successful. The close collaboration that is the hallmark of effective cross-functional process management must also be clearly demonstrated in the design and operation of a BPM CoE. BPM support systems must be designed to be fit for purpose, reflecting the particular organization in which they live.

The three authors responding to this question agree that, while there is a clear requirement for ubiquitous BPM skills of a generalist nature, there is also a requirement for specialist skills. Given a broad definition of 'process' and 'BPM', many competencies are required spanning the spectrum from 'soft' skills related to engagement with people and creative analysis, through to expertise in the 'hard' process, IT and data sciences.

This is one of the questions that received little response, just 3% of all answers received, and we wonder what, if anything, that might tell us. It is problematic, of course, to draw conclusions from an absence of data, and there may be many reasons why this question lacked appeal to most of our authors. However, one of those reasons might be that the importance of the topic and the need for active management in this area is underestimated. Might it be that the questions that attracted the lowest responses mark out areas of potential difficulty born of that lack of interest?

....

MELISSA DOHERTY

Process and Innovation Manager, Brisbane City Council

The practice of BPM is commonly initiated in an organization from within the IT group. It's easy to understand why, as CIOs and IT projects recognize that an understanding of business process is required to ensure that IT projects are successful and deliver on business need and requirements.

IT driving BPM is not necessarily a bad thing, but it is generally driven by a singular goal—to deliver an IT solution. The project gets enough of a view of the business to inform the project and solution design and, if it's done well, the solution will meet enough of the business's needs. But, commonly, the business doesn't actually get their business processes documented or handed back to them. Or, if they do, they aren't suitable for ongoing management. The business is also unlikely to have any capability to continue to manage them if they were developed as part of a project. IT projects generally focus on system process and siloed functions and modules that most likely don't reflect how the business really works, or the outcomes that they actually deliver.

I'd suggest this is why, in many organizations, BPM never progresses beyond IT, and continues to have a project-delivery focus and little emphasis on what happens to business process after a project is delivered. This certainly does nothing for maturing business process in an organization, or building capabilities to better manage processes and the business. I see it as a lost opportunity.

There are exceptions to this. Some IT areas are able to make IT-driven BPM work through their ability to source the capabilities and leverage technologies, such as SOA, to make process automation real to the business. These are key capabilities that all organizations need in their BPM toolkit.

Some organizations also have other teams that are focused on business-process, maybe in addition to an IT/BPM group, perhaps with Lean or Six Sigma approaches. They generally focus on process improvement or re-engineering projects, again with little consideration as to what happens to process after the 'new and improved' process is delivered.

For BPM to grow as a practice and for business process capability to mature beyond a few people in an organization viewed as specialists, and for BPM to be more than just 'that thing you do when you have a IT project, or a big problem', BPM must be owned by the business—that is, by the people who execute it and manage the delivery of process outcomes. BPM must be integrated into how the organization operates.

And why shouldn't it!? Business processes need to be managed; they need to be monitored to ensure they are meeting targets, efficient, worthwhile, and delivering the outcomes originally intended. This is not the job of just a few. People in an organization need to understand their responsibilities, their roles in the organization, and what value they contribute and deliver. The capabilities to do this need to be given to everyone in the organization—everyone in an organization needs to become process aware and capable.

However, just like any other business management practice, there will always be a need to have BPM specialists. While we expect that business managers must understand how to manage a budget and how to manage their people, they must also understand how to manage their processes—the work that they're responsible for every day, and the way that they deliver value, products and services to their customers. Business managers need to be able to call in the BPM specialist when they need one, just like they'd call in an accountant if they couldn't resolve their budget issues.

A BPM specialist is highly skilled at BPI, process re-engineering, process management, process execution and automation. These capabilities do require experience and training, whether through an academic path, or certification in business process. But these capabilities alone do not make a BPM specialist. For an individual to deliver on these capabilities in a real and practical way, they need to be skilled in other practices, and they need to integrate with other capabilities in an organization, such as: enterprise architecture, project management, change management, business improvement, and corporate strategy.

The soft skills required to ensure a person can be truly qualified as a BPM specialist make the search for BPM specialists difficult. These skills are often overlooked, but are critical to enabling success in BPM. These include stakeholder management, facilitation, and exceptional communication skills that ensure engagement by business areas.

If an organization is committed to BPM, and wishes to achieve a high level of maturity where the practice of business process provides maximum value, it should consider the following from a capability perspective when determining its approach:

- Everyone in the organization should be process aware and capable.
- The business must lead and own BPM in an organization for capability to mature.
- The practice of BPM must be integrated wherever possible, and practical about how the organization operates.
- Specialist BPM capability must be developed and provided to support the business.

....

GILLES MORIN

Founder, BPMPlus, Inc.

There is no unique model to support a BPM program via a BPM CoE. Having a BPM or process performance CoE, however, makes a difference in the success of BPM. It is, in fact, a must have. Similar to organizations establishing a Lean CoE to enable, grow and sustain its continuous improvement program, an organization that is serious about BPM ought to adopt some form of BPM CoE—and it needs to fit the organization specificities culture and BPM maturity.

The first question often asked is: where should it sit? In fact, the real question at low BPM maturity stage is more about which CxO wants it? Which one believes that it is a must, or will give it the means to start and deliver its first success? And, what strategic vision or corporate-wide pain will drive it. In more than 40% of the cases, the CIO incubates it, while in the other situations the COO or a business line leader is the key sponsor. It's simple—who wants it and why?

The second question is about its structure: should it be centralized or decentralized? In this case, it depends on its service model and the organization's culture. Generally speaking, though, centralization is a good thing when starting as a low BPM maturity organization with limited resources. Services models vary, and there is no unique or best model. The model must fit the organization's BPM maturity and scope of business projects, or change programs that will drive its *raison-d'être*. It's a real balancing act between being project driven (i.e. delivering process performance improvement projects), scaling up enterprise-wide BPM capabilities, fueling process culture change, and sustaining process governance. In most cases, at low maturity, a BPM CoE ought to be clearly focused on business solution delivery. The rule is simple—success breeds success.

One trap that many organizations falls into is to create multiple 'expertise driven' CoEs—a Lean CoE, plus an ERP CoE; a BPMS CoE, plus a BPM CoE, etc.—where the CoEs are means driven and not ends driven. BPM, Lean, ERP CoE are all about drastic and sustainable performance improvement, both incremental and leap frogging. BPM, continuous improvement, Lean are part of a same continuum and, in fact, we recommend to start, even at low maturity, by creating a performance improvement CoE. In certain cases, when it's more about a major strategic shift, organizations set up transformational office. Again, whatever formula you use, make it clearly 'purpose driven' and not expertise or technology driven.

Having said that, the role of the BPM CoE is to enable local teams to support local performance improvement projects. Process architecture and analysis, or optimization work, should be delivered through small teams located within business units. The CoE is there to incubate best practice, set standards and methodology; to ensure support for managing process as assets, and provide coaching, training, education, and tools—and directly support project realization where there are no local teams, or the project requires add-on resources.

There should now be enough knowledge, methodologies, and training curricula that the BPM CoE can have certified key practices leaders: green/black/master black belt, CBOK, BABOK, BIZBOK, ISPI—and these are examples of certification programs that might help solidify the practices. As these methodological guides or certification programs become mainstream, certifying key practices leaders is a good investment. However, these certifications, as with all other certifications, do not guarantee success. They are a means, not an ends.

Another important question is about the scope of work or the CoE services offering. The following figure is a simplified view of a typical process performance improvement or BPM CoE.

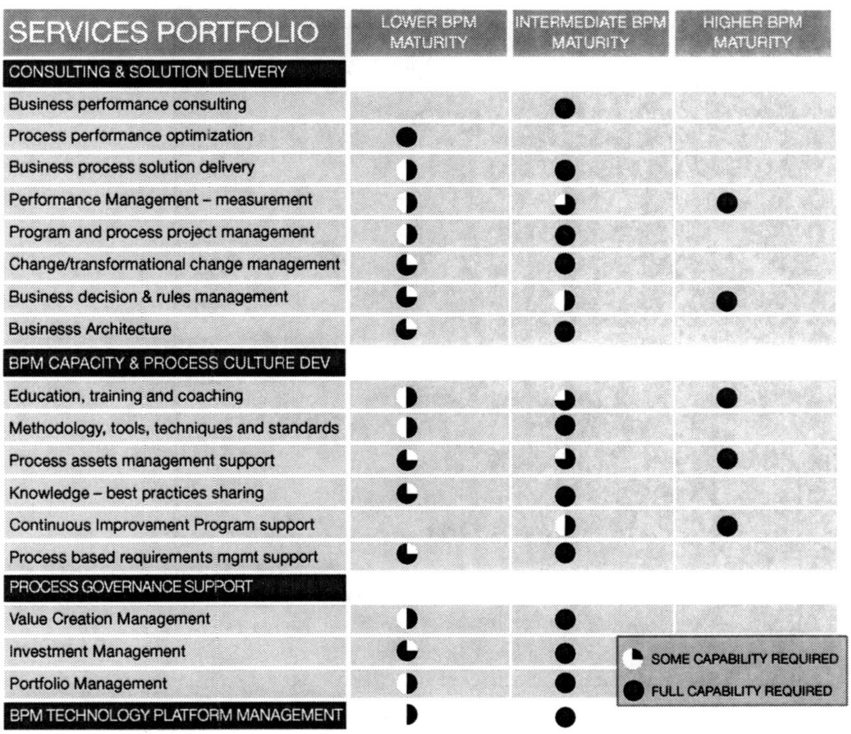

Figure 35: BPM CoE services

••

WIL VAN DER AALST

Professor, Eindhoven University of Technology

- BPM requires close collaboration between IT specialists, management, domain experts, and workers. Processes need to be modeled, enacted, analyzed, and managed. The figure below shows the four main types of activity in any larger BPM effort:
- *Model*—creating a process model to be used for analysis or enactment
- *Enact*—using a process model to control and support concrete cases),
- *Analyze*—analyzing a process using a process model and/or event logs
- *Manage*—setting goals, adjusting the process, reallocating resources, controlling, etc.

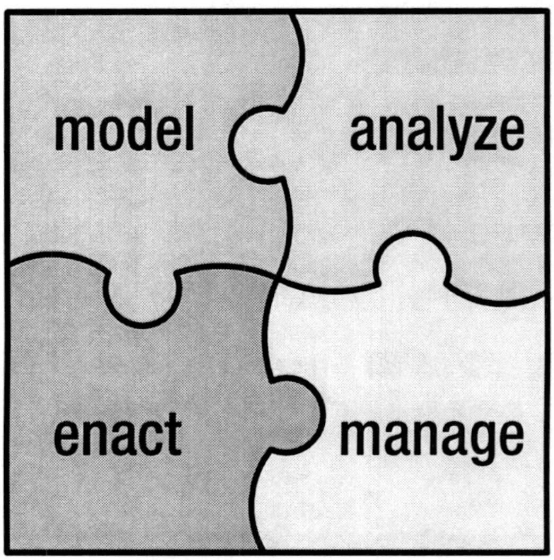

Figure 36: BPM professionals should be educated to fully understand the IT aspects with business/organizational aspects of the four main puzzle pieces of BPM

Each of these activities combines IT aspects with business/organizational aspects. One cannot expect all involved actors to be BPM experts. However, one would expect that self-proclaimed BPM professionals to master all the basics of process management. For example, it is remarkable that basic concepts such as the workflow patterns and the difference between process/activity instance and type are not well understood by many BPM professionals. Solid BPM education is of the utmost importance to improve maturity of our discipline.

In the context of BPM, we can identify at least three groups of actors:

- *BPM specialists*—the group of people, full-time involved in BPM and part of some central group (for example a Center of Excellence), and not connected to a specific process nor involved in the actual operational processes. Ideally, BPM specialists have an academic degree in computer science or industrial engineering, with a special focus on process management and business information systems.
- *BPM facilitators*—the group of people involved in BPM projects, but not considered to be BPM specialists (working only part-time on BPM). People in this group need to be able to model processes, define KPIs, use BI tools, and understand the IT-implications of process change. BPM facilitators are added to project teams that aim to improve existing processes or develop new processes. Certification or internal training programs can be used to ensure sufficient BPM knowledge.
- *BPM-aware managers and workers*—the group of people that use the fruits of BPM. These are workers performing the actual activities in the processes and the people managing them. People in this group just need to be aware of BPM concepts.

In terms of required skills, major changes can be anticipated due to the increased availability of process-related event data. Developments related to Big Data (in the broadest sense), will impact process management. BPM professionals will need to acquire more data-science skills. BPM will become more 'evidence based' and less subjective.

In recent years, 'data science' has become a common term to refer to the emerging discipline revolving around the abundance of data in modern organizations. We would like to match 'data science' with the umbrella term 'process science' which refers to the broader discipline that combines knowledge from information technology, and knowledge from management science, to improve and run operational processes.

The figure below shows some of the key ingredients of both data science and process science. BPM professionals should master the basics of both groups. For example, basic knowledge of large-scale distributed computing is needed when participating in Big Data projects. Knowledge of visualization techniques is beneficial when presenting the effects of process improvement projects. The figure below shows that process mining is the bridge between process science and data science. Data science approaches tend to be process agonistic whereas process science approaches tend to be model-driven without considering the 'evidence' hidden in the data. Obviously, both worlds need to be connected and integrated and process mining is one of the key technologies to achieve this.

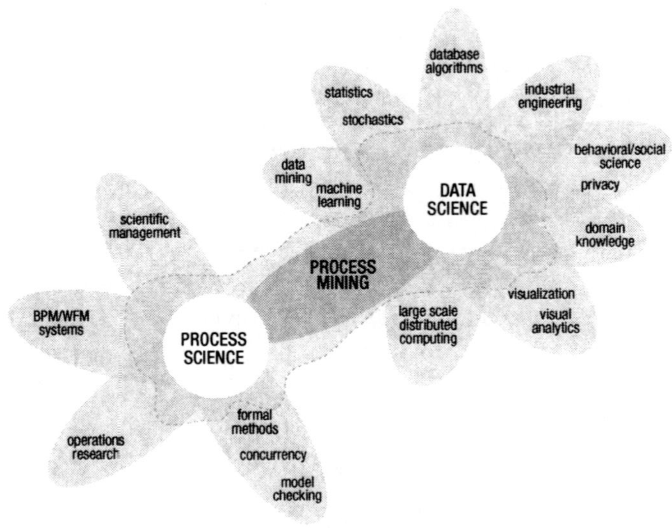

Figure 37: BPM professionals should combine 'process' and 'data' science' skills

Process mining aims to discover, monitor and improve real processes by extracting knowledge from event logs readily available in today's information systems. The starting point for process mining is an *event log*. Event data can be used to conduct three types of process mining:

- *Process discovery*—finding out what is really happing in the process and representing this as a process model ready for analysis
- *Conformance checking*—understanding where and why processes deviate and whether these deviations are harmful
- *Enhancement*—extending models with performance and conformance information and generating process improvement ideas.

Interestingly, process mining (and other data-driven BPM technologies) will help to improve collaboration between IT specialists, management, domain experts, and workers. The moment the *real* processes are properly visualized, discussion become more focused and fact-driven.

QUESTION 13

DOES THE DIGITAL ECONOMY NEED BPM?

Established business models are being overwhelmed by digital substitutes. New business models are radically different in relation to the assets that are of value, and interfaces with, and relationships to, customers. Old business paradigms are being discarded.

Is there any role for BPM in the digital economy? Has the very concept of 'business process' been so disrupted as to make BPM meaningless in the digital economy?

OVERVIEW

The digital economy does not cause business processes to disappear, but it does have the potential to change almost everything about how a process is designed, managed, executed, improved and experienced. Digital disruption causes radical and, for some, scary change. Inevitably, process change is either the intention of a digital transformation or one of its consequences. Effective management of business processes and related business rules therefore becomes critical in safely dealing with digital-enabled change.

Is the BPM toolset ready to deal with such changes? Will the process of process management survive its own disruption in the digital economy? Do events and rules become more important than activities? Will the traditional techniques of process analysis remain relevant? In their answers for this question, our authors give us compelling insights into the profound changes that will drive new perceptions of process-based management.

Change in the digital economy is qualitatively and quantitatively different, and process management needs to be reimagined as well.

....

PETER FINGAR

Managing Principal, Meghan-Kiffer Research

The digital economy is all about globalization, and globalization is the greatest reorganization of the world since the industrial revolution. And it's not just outsourcing or the search for cheap labor. It's about the globalization of *innovation*—not R&D driven innovation, but customer-driven innovation. This massive change is a huge challenge for BPM, as the comfortable confines of an enterprise are over—it's now demanding that BPM's reach is global, managing the processes of business supply networks and fully informed, demanding customers who don't bother coming to your fancy Web site, but collaborate among themselves via social networks. Indeed, there is something new being demanded of BPM.

WHAT'S NEW ABOUT NEW?

Here we go again with yet another hype curve: the Innovation Hype Curve. Why all the newfound interest in innovation? In short, it's globalization. Executives fear their companies becoming commoditized as a result of total global competition, and they desperately seek new ways of distinguishing their products and services so they can continue to earn healthy margins. But even though companies know they must innovate, it's not clear exactly how to go about it in the complex global markets of the twenty-first century. Is there more to it than just inventing some new gizmo or thingamajig?

And it is not just globalization in a geographic sense, but also in terms of how others can compete with you. The Cloud—the *technology* Cloud, the *business services* Cloud, the *information* Cloud—as it evolves eliminates so many economic frictions (costs, capital, resources, scalability, availability, reliability, survivability, time, etc.). Even the smallest least-funded organization anywhere on the globe can *appear and deliver* like the largest. That means less money to 'try an idea'. And that means more investors are able to create more innovations that can operate in smaller and smaller markets—challenging the twentieth century management assumptions about scale benefits.

AREN'T CUSTOMERS THE TARGET OF INNOVATION?

No, now they are the source! The Industrial Age was about mass production. Innovation was R&D-driven, from the inside out. It was about supply-push. The Customer Age is about mass customization. Innovation must now be driven from the outside in. It's now about demand-pull. It is about turning a company, and its entire value chain, over to the command and control of customers.

This new reality demands a shift in our thinking about innovation. Winning companies will be so close to their customers, they will be able to anticipate their needs, even before their customers do, and then turn to open innovation to find compelling value to meet those needs. That, in turn, as pointed out by the late management guru, Peter Drucker, *means becoming a buyer for your customers.* That means 'business mashups', where your company joins forces with suppliers, sometimes even your competitors, to expand your product and services offerings, blurring industry boundaries. Because *your customers are your only true asset in the new world of low-cost suppliers,* your business model will likely need to be expanded so that you can fulfill as many of your customers' needs as possible. This is how smart companies are seeking true growth and avoiding commoditization—they are no longer in the product business; they are in the customer business.

ISN'T INNOVATION JUST INVENTION?

3M's Geoffrey Nicholson once described the critical point about invention versus innovation: "Research is the transformation of money into knowledge. Innovation is the transformation of knowledge into money." It was Dan Bricklin and Bob Frankston who co-invented the spreadsheet (VisiCalc) that launched the microcomputer as a mainstream business tool. Of course, it was Bill Gates who ultimately transformed this digital invention into real money—and that's 'business innovation'. So, one key aspect of innovation that's new is the changing focus from invention to innovative new business models and initiatives that bring compelling new value to the marketplace.

ISN'T INNOVATION ABOUT R&D LABS?

Secretive R&D labs used to be the main source of invention. In 1900, Charles

Proteus Steinmetz convinced the GE leadership that they would need a research laboratory, and the first industrial research lab in the U.S. was born in the carriage barn in Steinmetz's backyard. Today, GE Global Research consists of 2,500 employees working in New York (a few miles from the original barn), Bangalore, India, Shanghai, China, and Munich, Germany. But there's even more to this story; it's called Open Innovation. Open Innovation changes the game of where ideas come from; they are no longer the exclusive property of internal R&D, marketing, and product development organizations.

WHAT'S OPEN INNOVATION?

The new world of widely distributed knowledge has led to the business proposition of 'open innovation'. No longer can companies win the innovation arms race from the inside out (internal R&D). They should, instead, buy or license innovations (e.g. patents, processes, inventions) from external knowledge sources, turning the table to outside-in innovation. In turn, internal inventions should be considered for taking outside the company through licensing, joint ventures, spin-offs, and the like. Procter & Gamble, the poster child for open innovation, is determined to move to the position where half of its ongoing stream of innovation comes from outside the company. Don't confuse open innovation with open source, free software. Open innovation is all about the money to be made. In short, in today's wired world, *knowledge can be transferred so easily that it seems impossible for companies to stop it.* Instead, smart companies are going to the ends of the Earth in search of knowledge that they can transform into money.

....

IAN GOTTS

Founder, CEO, Q9 Elements, Nimbus

Technology is reshaping all industries. They are being transformed at a frightening pace, making it difficult for the established players to respond. The power is with the new entrants. They're the ones who get to develop new business models without the baggage—people, premises and processes—collected over the years. They are able to innovate and then iterate rapidly. It is a scary time to be a 'major player'.

Marc Andreesen summarized the current phenomenon with a simple phrase published in a *Wall Street Journal* article as far back as 2011: "'Software is eat-ing the world." In that article, he argued that every business in every industry would feel the disrupting force of technology, and that new entrants to the market would have a lasting effect. But recognizing the threat and doing something about it are two very different things. Changing the direction of a 10,000-, 100,000- or 1,000,000-employee company isn't easy. As one analyst put it, "the greatest challenge is staying relevant." The numbers tell the story: only 12% of the original S&P companies still exist.

This means that change and agility need to be core competences of every company, and that means mastering process management techniques. For some companies, it may be sufficient to simply iterate, improve, and harness technology. For others, complete reinvention may be required.

For industries with strong regulatory compliance, then change is even more difficult, because compliance is a huge inhibitor. But there are proven approaches for heavily regulated industries, so their difficulties cannot be cited as the sole reason for defending the status quo. Or, to put it another way: change is not mandatory—but neither is existence.

Back to start-ups. Just because they are starting with a clean sheet doesn't mean they have it easy. If your picture of a start-up is two guys hacking out an app in a college dorm and fueled by Red Bull, then your view is outdated. The start-ups that are changing the way industries operate are highly innovative, well-managed, lean operations that have enterprise scale technology with a compelling UX underpinning them. Nothing else will cut it anymore.

Examples are Uber, Airbnb, Netflix, Upwork, StitchFix and a host of others. If we look at those new businesses, they have a number of common themes. They are solving real-world problems and, possibly, coming at them from a different perspective. That's because they are not shackled by current industry thinking. They have a vision about how technology can help them deliver a better customer outcome, and still deliver profitable results.

They have designed a lean, highly efficient business model that is outside in. It puts the customer at the center of the business and the processes, procedures and systems are geared around delivering an exceptional customer experience. They have used the process-led business model to design their external application and internal systems around the customer. In other words, this isn't just cool, neat technology finding a problem to solve, but a technology-enabled business play.

Their mindset is one of innovation and agility. That enables them to iterate and pivot to find the optimum approach. They recognize that the chance of building the perfect business for the beginning is impossible, particularly when they are delivering a truly innovative solution. They will probably change to respond to customer behaviors, expectations and needs. Henry Ford is often quoted as saying, "If I had asked my customers what they wanted, they would have said a faster horse."

An upshot of this is that BPM still has a critical role to play in the new digital economy. Incumbents need to hone their process management skills to be able to become far more agile and to design new, lean operations so they can respond to the challenges. Start-ups need to develop process skills because they are scaling so quickly, and they can't fly by the seat of their pants for long. They need the disciplines of process management to be able to operate profitably and still deliver a consistent customer experience.

The irony is that the process management industry—the methodologies, training, tools and consultants—needs to adapt too, so it can be valuable in the new digitized world. This was said of other industries, but it's just as relevant to BPM: change is not mandatory—but neither is existence.

PETER MATTHIJSSEN

Senior Consultant, BiZZdesign

We live in interesting digital times. According to Gartner "… in 2017 every company will be a digital company." In which way does this change the position of BPM and the activities we perform in BPM?

Obviously, speed is an important theme. The typical lifecycle of processes is much shorter. There isn't always time to design, test, implement, and monitor processes in a waterfall-style. New processes and process changes are needed overnight, and flexibility in performing processes is necessary. Of course, this has a large impact on the way we do BPM.

But new developments in the digital economy don't make BPM obsolete. Processes were there a thousand ago; we have processes today, and there will be processes in a thousand years from now. Processes change, so BPM should change accordingly. Some interesting developments in the field of BPM:

- Process execution platforms, generating IT functionality based on process diagrams. For straightforward, basic processes, this is very powerful.

- Lean management approaches for process improvement.
- Process mining technologies. Based on (combined) data the process flow is generated. This is very powerful for governance checks and process analysis.
- Agile processes. Next to costs, quality and speed, the agility of processes is increasingly important. How can we design processes that are prepared for future change?
- Customer journeys. What is the real journey that customers follow through your processes?

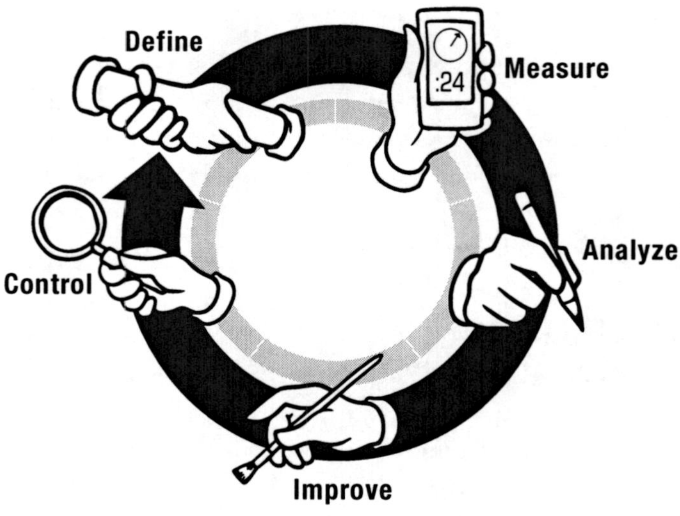

Figure 38: DMAIC cycle

So, the speed of BPM is increasing. BPM initiatives are becoming more and more short-cyclic. It is not about designing great processes that will last for the next decade—BPM is about ensuring performance over time, in a changing environment. For the BPM practitioner this means less (massive) process manuals that need to be written. Their work is more dynamic and short-cyclic; following a DMAIC-like cycle. What happens in the world (define, measure); what impact does this have on our processes (analysis); what change do we need to do (improve, control).

References

[1] *Thinking in processes, an introduction in Process Management*; second revised version; Peter Matthijssen; 2012

[2] *Working with Lean, an introduction in Lean Management*; Peter Matthijssen, Almar Jong; 2013

....

PROFESSOR MICHAEL ROSEMANN

Head of Information Systems School, Queensland University of Technology

Processes remain an essential artifact within corporations, and value chains will remain the blood vessels of economies. However, the digital economy is rapidly changing how we design, execute and experience processes. The old paradigm of a 'controlled business process' is disappearing as, increasingly, external stakeholders and their devices, data, and apps contribute to the way processes are designed and executed.

One very tangible impact that the digital economy has on Business Process Management is the increasing importance of events. Events used to be the 'poor cousin' of business processes, as opposed to activities, which are carefully studied in terms of their value contribution, their performance, costs, or the degree to which they could be automated. In the digital economy, events are becoming more relevant as emerging technologies facilitate the production of digital signals. These could be in the form of signals in social media platforms (e.g. a tweet can trigger a corporate response), status changes (e.g. a change in Facebook will trigger advertisement), or as automated signals from smart devices (e.g. a car involved in an accident might trigger an ambulance service).

This increasing availability of digital event information means processes can start earlier if corporations are able to identify and react to such events. The time between the occurrence of an initial event and the actual start of a process is called 'process latency', and is composed of the time it takes to identify the event occurrence, analyzing if this is a relevant event, and initiating the event. The shorter the process latency is, the sooner the process is made available. In competitive environments, short process latency might constitute a source of competitive advantage. An example in the digital economy is 'Amazon Dash'. This device facilitates retail shopping with Amazon, and allows customers to either voice record a demand, or to scan a bar code of an item they require. Process latency is reduced by making it possible to produce a digital signal when the demand occurs. The competitive advantage results from the fact that the 'competition waits at their web pages', while Amazon collects the demand 'in the kitchen'. Another example for reduced process latency is medical tracking devices that can be used to monitor physical well-being. Related data could be streamed to a medical professional or an automated system and, if needed, required support could be triggered.

Besides an increased focus on process latency and digital signals, the digital economy comes with a plethora of fast emerging, digital and often disruptive technologies. The inherent design opportunities will facilitate entire new business processes. However, the dominating set of tools, techniques, methods, and the overall body of BPM knowledge is severely under-prepared for these opportunities. The core of BPM so far has been an analysis-intensive approach dedicated to overcoming process inefficiencies.

However, the affordances of the digital economy will require a design-intensive proactive BPM approach. Instead of analyzing a problem and seeking solutions, the exponential growth of design options, will require improved environmental scanning capabilities and the ability to quickly assess which processes will benefit from new digital technologies. This will mean organizations need to re-train business (process) analysts to become business (process) designers and a dominating inside-out view needs to be complemented with a stronger outside-in view.

Both perspectives have to co-exist leading to what I call *'ambidextrous BPM'*—that is, the corporate ability to exploit existing business processes and explore new process designs at the same time. Most corporations have advanced process exploitation capabilities, but the digital economy will require new process exploration capabilities.

....

RON ROSS

CEO, Business Rules Solutions

I wouldn't go so far as to say that process and BPM are meaningless across the board. If you're manufacturing or producing a physical product, you still need to think in terms of a modeled and managed business process.

On the other hand, if your products are *non-physical*—for example, money, time, skills, information, meta-data, etc.—you'd better have a major re-think. The old rules of the game simply don't apply to white-collar work. Nor do they apply if your business model is about digitally leveraging other people's idle assets—*think Uber.*

You must still consistently satisfy contractual obligations and regulatory constraints in this new digital world, of course. But that's a business rules problem, not a process problem. A major characteristic of the new world is that activity is never static in any sense of the word. You simply get no points for hardwiring repetitive behaviors. You must:

- Continuously make informed operational decisions in the blink of an eye (actually, often faster than that).
- Selectively respond to changing circumstances with subtle adjustments.
- Be as dynamic as possible, yet still produce outcomes of predictable, consistent quality.
- Understand that business rules are a major part of the solution here too.

Whether market disrupters really 'get' these points about business rules, however, is an open question. To win in new digital markets, you pretty much must land first. Unfortunately, that perceived reality is likely to produce a lot of lousy legacy.

QUESTION 14

WHAT'S THE RETURN ON MODELING?

The 'M' in BPM stands for 'management', and yet it seems that the majority of process work is about modeling. Process modeling can be useful and insightful, and it is a necessary prerequisite for automation. It can also be a considerable waste of time and resources, creating unused and unreliable process documentation.

What should be the business purpose of business process modeling? How can organizations ensure a proper return on modeling?

OVERVIEW

The editors have long been involved in managing websites and producing industry conferences, and those experiences have shown time and again that process modeling is high on the topic wish list for almost any group of people with an interest in BPM. This proves to be true again here as well, with author responses to this question coming second in volume only to the first question that tested everyone's favorite question, *What is BPM?*

There is no disagreement among the authors that modeling is important, indeed fundamental, for effective BPM. Although there are differing views about how to model (standards, notations, tools, etc.), there is unanimous agreement that process modeling must have a well-defined purpose. No organization has a problem called 'we don't have enough process models', so true business benefits must be delivered.

The answers for this question discuss many different types of process models, but generally in two categories, the difference being their intended audience. A process model created for *humans* seeks to visualize and explain the process. A process model created for *machines* is about automating execution of the process.

Several authors identify benefits coming from the act of creating the models. Process models define the practical nature of collaboration, and shared modeling activity can be very powerful in breaking down barriers and sharing knowledge.

If there are hundreds—or perhaps just tens, or maybe even just three—modelers working all day producing many models, how does an organization know that was useful work? Our authors suggest many requirements for quality modeling, using words such as: accurate, up-to-date, relevant, understandable, accessible, consistent, practical, real, useful, and complete. That sets the bar quite high.

Modeling is not just about process activities, but also includes rules, decisions, events, resources, systems, and anything involved in the execution and management of processes. Can models use the same notations to include all such elements?

In the digital economy, where many processes are more dataflow than physical instance, does process modeling change? Where data defining a process already exists, albeit dispersed in space and time, will modeling become less about post-it notes in physical workshops and more about data science? To what extent will the process of modeling be automated? Is that how we will get over the high bar?

....

DR. WASANA BANDARA

Senior Lecturer, Queensland University of Technology

The visualization of business processes in the form of process models has increased in popularity and importance. The resultant prevalence and magnitude of process modeling projects demand appropriate means of evaluating such initiatives, yet realizing organizational value from process modeling has largely remained elusive. This was highlighted Indulska, Recker, Green and

Rosemann's [1] research, which looked at issues and challenges of business process modeling, and where the *Identification of the value proposition of business process modeling* was rated as the most challenging area of concern. This describes a process modeling success measurement model, which has been empirically tested (with 290 responses to a global survey of process modelers),[2][3] forming a firm step towards measuring the value of business process modeling efforts.

Business process modeling is fundamental not only to BPM, but it has become an established practice in a wide range of initiatives, including organizational improvement, business transformation, compliance management, and IT projects (such as enterprise systems and workflow management implementations).[4] Process modeling is not a trivial investment. Training, the actual conduct of modeling, and the maintenance of such models (which can be 1000s in larger organizations and needing well-developed modeling repositories), creating and maintaining conventions, and frameworks on how to apply and govern the modeling efforts can mandate substantial investments.[5]

Business process modeling often occurs as part of a larger organizational improvement initiative. As the figure below depicts, modeling takes place to support a target process change. A number of such (sustained) process improvements will contribute to enhanced organization performance. Hence, process modeling is not an end itself; it's a means to an end. Recognizing this is the first step towards an effective measure of process modeling success. The 'chain/network' in which the modeling takes place is important. One needs to identify the anticipated goals and purpose of the modeling effort, which is normally highly aligned and/or a part of the goals and deliverables of the larger initiative (as previously discussed) the modeling efforts resides in. The focus (as depicted in the figure below) of this discussion is on how to measure the success of the modeling phase.

There are three key things to measuring the success of process modeling initiative: (i) the model quality; (ii) the efficiency of the modeling process; and (iii) if the modeling has met its purpose. Let's refer to them as: (i) model quality; (ii) modeling efficiency; and (iii) modeling impacts—all three are important for an accurate measurement. For example, a model may be of high technical quality (semantically and syntactically flawless), but has not contributed to the goals and/or tasks of the larger initiative. Similarly, a modeling project may achieve high standards of quality and impact, but at exorbitant cost (for example, due to modeling for perfection over a long period of time).

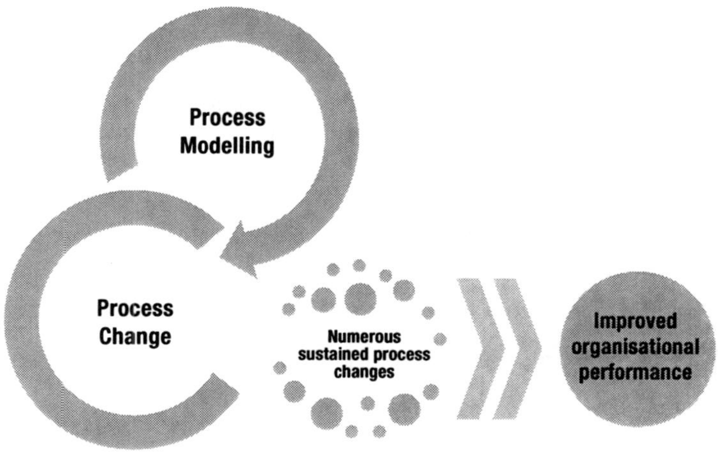

Figure 39: Process modeling is a step towards process change

WHAT CAN/SHOULD BE MEASURED UNDER EACH OF THESE ASPECTS?

There is a plethora of literature that discusses how to measure model quality. [6] These evaluate how well:

- The model users found the process models easy to use
- The process models met the model user requirements
- The process models accurately depicted the modeled processes
- The process models were easily modifiable
- The information available from the process models was important
- The process models provided relevant and complete information
- The process models were easy to understand
- The process models were concise … covers the most important and relevant aspects to look at when evaluating business process models.

Modeling efficiency can be measured by looking at how efficient the modeling project was in terms of:

- The invested person days of effort
- The overall project duration
- The overall resources required.

Measuring modeling impacts is the most challenging. To evaluate this, one needs to clearly understand the initial goal as to why the modeling work was called for (which sometimes is not 100% clear). Given that process modeling is used within BPM to improve processes, modeling impacts can be evaluated by looking at the degree to how the process modeling helped with:

- deriving cost effective processes,
- identifying improvements to the quality of products and services resulting from the modeled processes,
- reducing the processing time of the modeled processes, and
- resulting in improved business processes in general.

WHEN DO TO THE EVALUATIONS?

These three measures can apply to the different lifecycle stages of process modeling. Model quality can be measured from the start of the modeling effort with the progression of each set of completed models. Modeling efficiency is best measured immediately at the end of each modeling effort. Modeling impacts can only be measured after the process models have been put to use.

WHO WILL DO TO THE EVALUATIONS?

The best stakeholder to make the evaluation for each dimension will be different. For example, the model quality is best evaluated by someone with modeling and domain expertise—typically the modelers themselves and/or the model users. The modelers will be able to provide the most accurate input in terms of modeling efficiency. It is the sponsor of the modeling project (the one who called for the modeling to be done as part of the larger initiative) who can best evaluate modeling impacts.

In summary, this paper discussed the what, when, who and how of measuring process modeling success, by presenting: *what* should be measured (presenting the main aspects and how to best tap into them); *how* to measure; *when* to do the measurement; and *who* can best do the evaluation.

References

[1] Indulska, M., Recker, J., Green, P. and Rosemann, M. (2009) Process Modeling: Current Issues and Future Challenges, *in the Advanced Information Systems Engineering - CAiSE 2009* (Amsterdam, The Netherlands).

[2] Bandara, W., Gable, G. and Rosemann, M. (2006) Business Process Modeling success: an empirically tested measurement model, in the *International Conference*

of Information Systems (ICIS) (Milwaukee, U.S.A).

[3] Bandara, W. (2007) Process modeling success factors and measures. PhD thesis, Queensland University of Technology.

[4] Hjalmarsson, A., Recker, J., Rosemann, M., and Lind, M. (2015) Understanding the Behavior of Workshop Facilitators in Systems Analysis and Design Projects: Developing Theory from Process Modeling Projects, *Communications of the Association for Information Systems*: 36, Article 22.

[5] Dijkman, R. M., La Rosa, M., and Reijers, H. A. (2012) Managing large collections of business process models—Current techniques and challenges. *Computers in Industry*, *63*(2): 91–97.

[6] Gemino, A. and Y. Wand (2004). A framework for empirical evaluation of conceptual modeling techniques. *Requirements Engineering* 9(4): 248–260.

Acknowledgements

This paper is based on research conducted at Queensland University of Technology (QUT), Brisbane Australia, on process modeling success in collaboration with Prof. Guy Gable and Prof. Michael Rosemann.

JIM BOOTS

Owner, Global Process Innovation

First, let's be clear about what we mean when we say 'modeling'. For our purposes, let's include any representation of a process. This could include anything from a 'boxes and arrows' drawing on a napkin, to a carefully defined set of code that executes certain automated steps. While some practitioners may have a different perspective, this entry contends that there are generally two types of process models with specific business purposes:

- Process model type 1—A visual representation of a process that helps people explain, understand, and talk about steps in a process, including what the steps are, their sequence, who does them, and what their inputs and outputs are (e.g. for learning one's role in a process, for collaborating on improvement, for assisting human performers with execution of their responsibilities).
- Process model type 2—A visual and/or textual description of steps that

a computer can interpret in order to automate part or all of a process.

By and large, these process models are used independently and by different types of personnel; however, the second type—an automation model—may be informed by the type 1 model as a process goes from being generally understood to being rigorously specified so a computer can 'read' the steps it must do.

There is a rather long history of erudite people who have spent a lot of time trying to bridge the gap between the two types of process models mentioned above. Their intention was to establish one process modeling language that is optimally useful for both humans and computers. The result is the terribly inadequate notation known as BPMN (Business Process Modeling Notation).

The problem with BPMN is that it is not good for human understanding of processes (type 1), and may need supplementation for automation purposes (type 2). For many years, a broad industry and academic consortium has been working to define BPMN 3.0 so that it can be read by a computer and executed. However, the BPM software vendors that produce automation software have generally created their own supplemental toolkits containing 'smart objects' to accomplish complex tasks which, if rendered in BPMN, would take a lot more space to describe. In other words, BPMN has not proved to be especially efficient for the actual coding of automations.

However, because of its universality, BPMN has been useful to some organizations for specifying automations, even though the actual code may vary substantially from the BPMN models. Such consistent specifications can be useful to analysts and coders. Some might reasonably argue that this is a third purpose for process models. A case for BPMN might be made for this type of use; however, such automation specifications also could be captured in other notations, such as UPN, which is discussed below. Nevertheless, there are practitioners who have a great deal of trust in BPMN as the standard language for process automation.

When it comes to the human domain—that is, type 1 process models—BPMN is, quite frankly, a bad choice. There are many problems with using BPMN if one's objective is to help humans understand, explain, and collaborate. First, BPMN, even in its 'simplified' form, employs too many symbols; average people can't keep them straight. Second, processes in BPMN are shown in a matrix format (usually segmented by role or department); this is not the way people think, and it also is very inefficient with regard to the use of space on a sheet of paper or a computer screen when describing a complex process. As a result, BPMN diagrams often look like intimidating wiring diagrams on extra-large pieces of paper with arrows going all over the place. In practice, very few people have the patience to sort out the logic of the process and, because of the visual complexities of the diagram, a process diagram is frequently incorrectly rendered versus reality.

So, returning to the question of the value of process modeling: the answer is that process modeling can deliver a high ROI to an organization. But addressing each type of modeling need—human understanding and automation—requires the right tools for modeling to be successful.

In the case of automation (type 2 modeling), there is no need to spend a lot of time discussing modeling options. It may be that BPMN is used by an automation team to specify automated steps. The actual automation model itself may or may not be solely based on BPMN, but it also may use objects (or symbols or tools) that have been created by the automation software vendor. The key point with the notation used for automating processes is that the people writing the automation—most likely IT people—will be familiar with the selected notation or coding, so they can consistently and efficiently build, maintain, and change automations as business needs dictate. Essentially, every automation software vendor will provide guidance on how to effectively build process automation models in their software—whether mostly based on BPMN or not.

In the case of process modeling—so workers can best understand steps in a process and how they contribute to the process objectives—BPMN is not recommended. A much simpler notation is preferred. Universal Process Notation (UPN) is a good choice. (There is some information about UPN on the Internet and, for a deeper discussion, I cover it in some detail in my book, BPM Boots on the Ground: How to Implement Strategic Business Process Management.)

Why UPN rather than BPMN? Because we want an average worker to intuitively understand the process diagrams he or she looks at. It is under such circumstances, using a universally intuitive process language, that the 'Return on Modeling' has the potential to be large. Diagrams should not have to be explained by the modeler; they should be self-explanatory. When they are self-explanatory, everyone can use them as training and orientation tools, and as the basis for performance and improvement discussions. Furthermore, software that uses UPN can be used as a platform wherein an organization's entire process architecture is represented, and 'tools' (forms, templates, applications, policies, guidelines, etc.) can be linked into the UPN diagrams.

Such a process architecture, using UPN, can form the basis for development of strategic BPM capability—because it gives the workforce a new, powerful, intuitive way to communicate rigorously about work. Indeed, it is hard to imagine a successful broad-based BPM initiative that does not have process representations that workers find compelling. On the other hand, a BPM effort that only uses BPMN for its process representations is likely to remain trapped in the world of analysts and IT specialists. Although some significant improvements may be achieved, a BPM effort based on BPMN is unlikely to have ongoing strategic impact—because, it won't be embraced by the workforce as a common language.

In summary, process modeling is an essential component of a BPM initiative that is aiming for maturity. It is important to be clear about the purposes of modeling, and to select modeling notations and tools that best serve each modeling purpose. When this is done, the ROI on modeling can be high.

DENIS GAGNÉ

CEO, CTO, Trisotech

We all model. Some of us are aware, and others not. Our ability to manipulate mental models is one of the traits that defines us as a specie. We are, therefore, all modelers. Many are not aware of these mental models and, thus, they remain tacit and implicit in the way these individuals go about their business. Others work hard at communicating and sharing their mental models to achieve a common or shared one. Explicit models make for efficient communications and effective coordinated actions. Business process modeling is no different from any other modeling endeavor. Business process models help us decide, design, and strategize about our organization. But be mindful of fool's gold. Business process modeling is a means to an end, and not an end of its own.

So what are models? Broadly speaking we use the term to refer to any structured knowledge that accurately reflects—and helps us to make sense of—the world. Models exist both internally as 'mental models', and externally as 'cognitive artifacts'. These cognitive artifacts can take many forms: graphs, diagrams, spread-sheets, equations, etc. While these different kinds vary greatly in their form and function, they all share certain desirable properties.

- Salient: since no model can represent everything, it must selectively represent those things most relevant to the task at hand.
- Accurate: the model should precisely encode the actual state of affairs and not an erroneous or biased view.
- Complete, yet parsimonious: the model should be as simple as possible, but no simpler. It should concisely capture all the relevant dimensions of the problem without squeezing out the opportunity for insight.
- Simple to understand: Once we perceive the model, we must be able to make sense of it; it shouldn't be too complicated or unfamiliar for us to understand.
- Granularity: selecting the relative size, scale, level of detail, or depth of penetration that characterizes an object or activity (selecting what is atomic). Atomic is the lowest level of granularity of interest.
- Coherent: models do not exist in isolation, but in interlocking systems; thus, any particular model should be coherent with other related models.
- Flexible: they should be open to ongoing revision to reflect new data, our growing understanding, or our evolving needs.
- Useful: usefulness is the sum of the above properties and the degree to which they combine to promote understanding and effective action.

It is important to note that the most accurate, or the most complete, or the most elegant model is not necessarily the most useful. Selecting the right model for the right purpose is key. All models are incomplete. All models are a compromise. The art of creating useful models lies in making those shrewd trade-offs that will render the model most useful to the problem at hand. These properties all apply to business process modeling.

Once articulated in a model, business processes become assets. As like any other assets, they need to be managed. We have to decide how to obtain or discover them, how to accumulate or safeguard them, how to maintain them, and which one to transform to ensure their accrued value. We may even invent totally new business process models that will transform who we are as an organization, and that will disrupt the market we operate in.

It is our firm belief that the value of business process models as assets can be increased and made enduring by ensuring universality via open business process modeling standards. For the past decade, we have been contributing to various modeling standards (XPDL, BPMN, CMMN, DMN, and BPSIM) in an effort to create unambiguous process descriptions that are understood by everyone. The goal is to produce useful shared mental models of how business processes are achieved by the organization.

In conclusion, business process modeling is a means to an end, not an end itself. Business process models help us decide, strategize, and design our organizations to make them agile and adaptive to their external environment, while ensuring effectiveness and efficiencies in the way the organization operates. Many models are better than one. Descriptive models, analytic models, and models of automation all have different goals. Make sure to use the right model for the right goal. Use standards to capture models, ensuring universality and portability.

IAN GOTTS

Founder, CEO, Q9 Elements, Nimbus

The 'M' in BPM stands for 'management'. But the BPM software vendors have used their marketing dollars to make it stand for 'automation' in the minds of the IT buyer. So now, BPM is synonymous with workflow or automation technology. As has been discussed earlier in this book, BPM has a range of interpretations, but there are a couple of things we can all agree on. BPM is way broader than just automation. And, second, the only time automation comes before modeling is in the dictionary.

If you talk to process professionals—whether in companies or consultancies—about the objectives of BPM projects, they will talk in business terms: reducing waste, driving improvements, getting consistency, raising quality, satisfying regulators, and now, increasingly transforming business models.

Whether a company is able to benefit from a BPM project depends on two things: the format of the diagrams in the process model, and what happens to those process models after excitement and passion of the workshop dies.

The format of the process models is driven by their intended audience for the process models.

If the purpose is to define what needs to be automated and the audience is the IT team, then the modeling format is probably BPMN. The process models are for the project team only, and are probably discarded once the automated workflow is delivered. However, if the aim is to get all the business users aligned, and to identify improvements, or keep the auditors happy, then a very simplified, hierarchical modeling standard is the most effective. This format is called UPN (Universal Process Notation). It was deliberately designed to be easily understood by end users who were not in the workshop. The model will become the new electronic operations manual. The users will refer to it when a process has changed, if they haven't done an activity for a while, or they are new to the company or business area.

The process model also encourages a culture of collaborative process improvement. Suggestions are made in the context of the process that is a baseline on which the improvements are built. The best way to develop the process model is for the business users to capture the flows in a live workshop. This visualization of the key activities and the hand-offs often drives out huge benefits and exposes ambiguities. This is frequently the first time managers and staff in highly siloed organizations will ever have had a cross-departmental view of their end-to-end process.

The best way of locking in the benefits from modeling is to make sure the model is executed. This could be by simply by making the process model available to end users to access through a portal. It could be by automating the process flow in a standalone workflow application. Or, it could be by re-configuring the core enterprise applications (e.g. Salesforce, SAP). In the last two cases, it is still valuable to allow end users to have access to the process model and to be able to see the applications in an end-to-end process context.

Whether it is BPMN or UPN, the process models are a valuable asset of the company. Developing them has taken time and effort. Therefore, they should be managed properly. Just because the BPMN process model has been executed as an automated workflow, it doesn't mean the process model is no longer useful. The process model should be the starting point when any changes are required to the automated flow. It is far easier to go back to the BPMN diagrams, rather than start with a clean sheet or try to interpret the process from the automated application.

So, if the process models are valuable, then shouldn't they be captured in a process solution that is designed to develop, manage, and govern the content? You don't manage your customer contacts, financial accounts, or inventory in an Excel spreadsheet that's emailed around to different people to update. So, why use diagrams created in PowerPoint, Visio or another diagramming tool, stored on a hard drive or embedded in a Word document that no one will ever read for a process model?

It's time to take process modeling seriously. If you do, you will be staggered by the benefits you will reap.

....

ANDREAS HAVLIZA

Consulting Principal, Team Leader, Leonardo Consulting

INDRAJIT DATTA CHAUDHURI

Senior Consultant, Leonardo Consulting

CLEMENT HURPIN

Consultant, Leonardo Consulting

Process modeling is used to represent reality in a diagrammatic form. It is used for communicating with a larger set of people. It is also used to analyze the flow of work. The most common forms are as-is and to-be, with multiple could-be in between.

The as-is process is meant to represent the operational reality and, hopefully, highlights the issue areas in the operations. These models can be used to analyze and question each step and identify opportunities for improvement. The process models are also a good tool to identify the stakeholders involved directly in the execution. The to-be process model is a theoretical representation of the future state, which then is implemented.

Process modeling is one key aspect of Business Process Management. But, too often, Business Process Management related programs or projects concentrate too much on the process modeling, ignoring that the 'M' in BPM represents 'management' and not modeling.

BPM, though—if done properly—won't work without modeling. It's critical to embed the modeling activities in the overall BPM strategy to avoid shelf ware—that is, hundreds of process models stored somewhere without anybody utilizing them or even keeping them up to date.

The foundation of every BPM activity is the definition of a process architecture. And this process architecture is the starting point for any process modeling. The process architecture itself is modeled—ideally in some sort of BPM tool that allows reporting on the gathered data. All further modeling of more detailed processes should always start and be based on the processes defined in the process architecture.

It is very important to not just start modeling—even though it's tempting, as it's quickly done—but to review a couple of questions whose answers have, indeed, a big influence on the success of process modeling:

- Which goal is to be achieved by the modeling? Are we looking at a process optimization project that requires as-is processes as a basis? Or are we, for example, looking at process automation?
- The answer to the question above determines the modeling notation (event-driven process modeling vs. BPMN vs. simple flows charts, etc.) that is suited best to accomplish the set target.
- Once the notation is selected, a modeling convention workshop is required to agree on the artefacts to be modeled in the process models: to what level is organizational information required? Are organizational units sufficient, or is a role level required? What other information needs to be gathered in modeling workshops? Are risks and controls in focus? To what extend is input and output to be defined?
- Another question to be answered upfront is the level of detail to which the modeling has to take place. The leveling concept is ideally already defined by setting up the process architecture. If done so, modeling workshops can relate to the defined process levels that ensure that the process modeling is performed to the same modeling depth.

No matter what the reason for the modeling is, it is essential that the governance aspect is not neglected: to keep the process architecture up to date, process guardians need to be defined—people who are in charge to review the processes on a regular basis on to trigger actions, if required.

ERIC HERNESS

CTO & Chief Architect, IBM (BPM)

There are many ways to leverage process modeling in the grand scheme of running a business, and in the pilgrimage towards BPM enlightenment. Knowing up front why modeling is occurring, what the models are used for, and how the return on modeling will reduce disappointments and manage overall expectations.

WHY ARE WE PROCESS MODELING?

The primary purpose of modeling is to figure out what is going on, and then figure out whether or not there is value in automating a given process or set of processes. Modeling projects are funded and initiated with some intention. There is an assertion either that there are inefficiencies that must be addressed, or there are new business opportunities that demand new approaches to doing business that can only be implemented by figuring out what the current processes are doing.

The point is that we are not modeling merely to produce models of what the business does, or what is should do. That was a good idea, as outlined by some, at one point during the evolution of the business process management discipline. At this juncture, organizations do not have time to model every process to the nth level of refinement, and then declare that they know what the organization is doing and what it should be doing differently—all in the abstract. Modeling, in my view, is a means to an end. It helps us to get somewhere, and that somewhere is to become more efficient, support new business opportunities, and to run a chosen set of processes on a BPMS.

A detailed model of a to-be process is valuable. If the change from the as-is view of the process is significant, and the gains to be enjoyed are substantial, then automation is the only logical path forward. Just pronouncing the 'to be' model as the right way, and suggesting to employees that they proceed to use this model without the help of automation, probably won't yield the desired benefits. Even if it does, they would be hard to measure.

Tools, like IBM Blueworks Live (www.blueworkslive.com/), offer a modeling environment to help ensure that the modeling activity derives the desired results. A more subtle reason why we model is to gain consensus among the constituencies. This consensus includes agreement on how the current process works, how the new process should look, how it impacts various involved business stakeholders, and how the processes link to business goals. The Blueworks Live features for collaboration and review have demonstrable value when it comes to this consensus-building element. More consensus at this level is good, because it reduces churn and complexity in downstream automations.

How do we get the proper return on modeling (ROM)?

Modeling efforts must provide a return on investment. This means linking back to the purpose of modeling. It also means using a practical approach, having an automation plan, and thinking about modeling as a part of an overall BPM effort.

The first piece of guidance I would give to those wanting to get a proper return on modeling is to have a practical approach. Explaining this further involves a few things that should be done and a few things to be avoided.

A practical approach means a proper scope in terms of processes being modeled, and the level of modeling that is applied. Depending on the breadth of the organization being inspected, scope the processes to be looked at. If the processes of interest relate to customer relationships, then model those processes that are integral and near that part of the business. A scope that is too narrow can encourage sub-optimizations. On the other hand, customer relationships as a focus probably means that modeling the supplier part of a business, or modeling internal employee onboarding would be out of scope. It is too easy to slip into the view of modeling everything.

Do high-level process models across the chosen scope. Go deeper into modeling as the core area of interest is approached. But, even in this case, time box these efforts, and be willing to move forward before perfection is achieved. Analysis paralysis lives on in this space, and is easy to get sucked in.

Even if the task is a general modeling of an entire business, don't model every process down to the final level of detail. Go breadth first, and then go into depth on those that have high value potential. Figure out which of these processes are key to current business challenges and have long-term linkages to key value chains.

The next thing to have to get a proper return on modeling is an automation plan. Models created where no automation plans are in place become out-of-date paperweights, and those modeling efforts become sunk costs that can discourage future BPM exploitation.

An automation plan doesn't necessarily mean a plan to place all processes under BPM control. That happens in stages over a number of years. An automation plan needs to consider:

- Quick win automation projects. These projects can help all constituencies see the value of an end-to-end BPM approach, and can help keep proper funding coming.
- Processes that are hard to understand from just a model. Consider ways to automate the high-level process, and then begin watching how this process behaves and iterates the automation. This can often be much more cost effective than trying to get a completely detailed version of the process running for the first automated delivery.
- Providing guidance on which processes to not automate via a BPMS. This means that some processes just won't have a automation return on investment, or at least not via a BPMS. An automation plan that suggests some processes be handled via packaged applications, or SaaS offerings, is also part of the plan. For example, complex processes that are not core to the key value chains of a business, and not a source of key competitive advantage, are good candidates to automate via other means.

When I speak to large organizations about embracing BPM, I often hear things that make me a bit nervous. When I hear about 1000 processes and an intent to automated them all on a BPMS in 'as-is' format, I usually shudder and become restless in my chair. While I'm all for leveraging a BPMS for lots of processes, a lift and shift approach onto a BPMS will likely burn a lot of resources for a limited set of returns. In fact, IT-led efforts like the one I'm describing will almost inevitably run out of funding before achieving the goal, and probably will leave BPM with a tarnished reputation in the process.

SUMMARY

Modeling should be used to:

- Explore the feasibility of capturing new business opportunities
- Learn how the business is working today, and where efficiencies might be applied
- Seed automation efforts

Modeling will provide a proper return on investment if:

- Done with purpose and with a scope in mind
- Done only to a level of detail that is valuable to downstream efforts

- It has an automation plan.

Automation of processes is a step towards real BPM. Modeling is a prerequisite to automation. Once automated, the model that matters is the one running in the BPMS. It should be 'listened to'; meaning that automated processes are observed for metrics and KPIs. Trouble spots are identified, and opportunities for additional automation present themselves. Things like business rules and how to leverage them to augment or replace human decisionmaking are easily injected once we have that framework for an automated system. As the straight through processing goal is marched towards, more and more human interactions are questioned, more aids are provided to those human activities, and more business value is delivered.

This is all hard work and takes investment, stakeholder commitment, and perseverance. Do this for the processes that matter the most, and it will provide the largest return on investment.

....

PETER MATTHIJSSEN

Managing Consultant, BiZZdesign

Of course, BPM is more than just modeling. As explained before, we look at BPM as a management discipline to improve performances. However, of course, models play an important role in BPM. Models support in visualizing processes, communicating processes, performing analysis, and implementing processes. Different objectives require different models.

When talking about BPM and modeling, you cannot step by to BPMN (Business Process Modeling Notation). There is a lot of discussion about BPMN as the standard modeling-language for process diagrams. Many believers are happy with this international standard, which covers a wide range of modeling concepts, views and tools. When it's your goal to capture a process in detail, for example for process execution, BPMN will do the job.

On the other hand, many people are reluctant to use BPMN. For them, it's too complex to fulfill their BPM goals. They say BPMN is too hard to learn, and BPMN diagrams are too complex for communication. Some might even call BPMN a programming language.

In the end, it is all about the goals you try to achieve. Sometimes BPMN gives you the means you need for a goal. But, in my opinion, users should smartly choose from the large toolbox of BPMN. BPMN is no goal by itself; it's a means.

When I look at process diagrams in organizations, I see many diagrams that I think are too complex. Diagrams are not there for BPM practitioners to show off; diagrams should support in achieving a (business) goal. This goal should be clear first, and then the practitioner can decide on model type, model scope, model detail, and model visualization. I would always say, keep process diagrams as simple as possible, but no simpler than that. A good process diagram is fit for purpose.

In many cases, the biggest impact of BPM lies in a mental shift: 'thinking processes'. For this shift, you want to communicate a process from trigger to result, across organizational roles and departments. In this case, this aspect should be highlighted; you don't want to distract people with too much detail.

Below are two process diagrams that describe the same process. For the first, I used detailed BPMN, with specialized events, message flows and gateways. This diagram could be suitable for detailed analysis and possibly execution. The target groups would be experts.

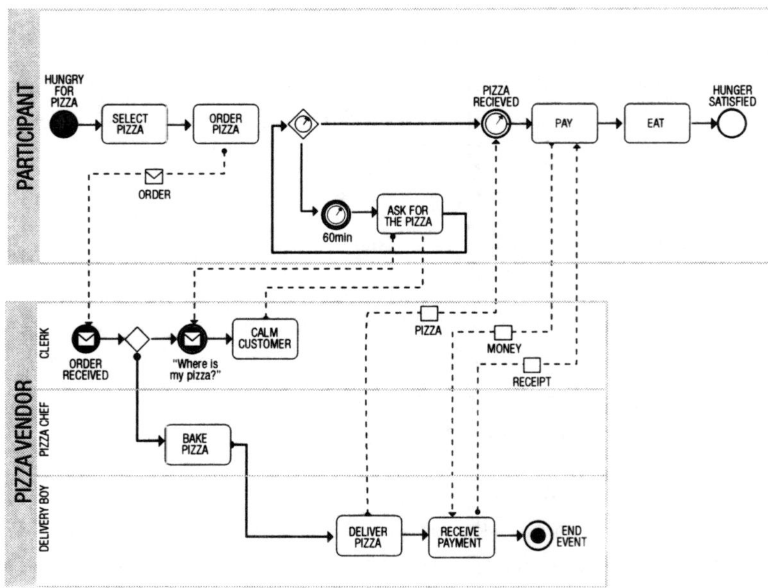

Figure 40: BPMN diagram—detailed level

The next figure shows exactly the same process, but without the details. The model holds less information, and is drawn a little bit more 'free format'—but, in many cases, this makes the model more powerful. Sometimes, 'less is more' applies. The target groups for these models could be shop floor users or management.

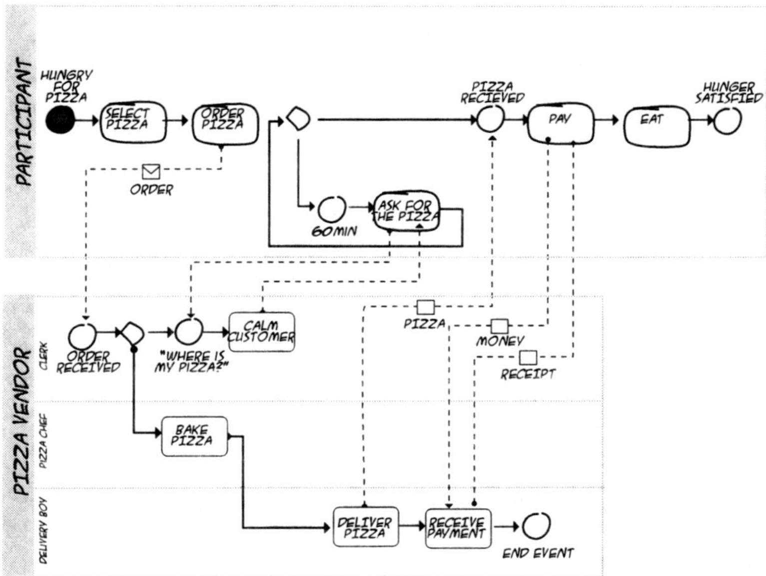

Figure 41: BPMN diagram—introductory level

My key message: choose the visualization that supports your goal best. This might mean that you need to toggle between different visualizations, for different goals and target groups.

MATTHEW J. MORGAN

Head of Process & Metrics Excellence, Bridgewater Associates

While modeling is a prerequisite for automation, it has many other business purposes. In my last two roles overseeing process management functions, our process modeling efforts were tied to document control systems to ensure documents were constantly up-to-date and in a single source of truth. So, the business purposes I outline below are defined in this context. I should also point out that modeling enables other parts of the broader BPM value chain to unlock value for the organization. I addressed such second-order benefits in detail in Question 7 on the return on investment of BPM.

Process modeling and document controls, first of all, reduce non-value-added work that occurs when business users and stake-holders must otherwise search for documents and duplicate documents that might already exist. The single source-of-truth provided by a document control system, and the process architecture that connects to and leverages other existing documents, both avoid this waste.

In addition, the maintenance of updated process models reduces various forms of risk. Key-person risk is mitigated by knowledge retention, and process models can be useful artifacts for transparency and awareness, communication, and training. In one of my experiences, the industry and company I worked for suffered from high turnover, so the process documentation service we provided both helped mitigate the flight of knowledge due to personnel attrition, and prevented new hires from needing to 'reinvent the wheel' by generating (or regenerating) exhaustive documentation right after joining. Process models also mitigate legal risk by having demonstrable and effective controls. This has the added efficiency benefit, and a further boost to controls, by facilitating external audit.

Process modeling also enables process improvement. Ongoing maintenance of accurate models allows for systematic diagnosis of root causes when problems arise. Process modeling, which enables the maturity and management of processes, will facilitate reduction of errors and improvement of throughput, and customer satisfaction. Finally, process modeling leads to reduced time and cost. In low maturity organizations, there is a risk of constant reinvention of processes; process modeling gives transparency into the process design—so, rather than constantly designing from scratch, it allows organizations to, instead, focus on the 'lean out' of processes to reduce time and cost.

JAMES TAYLOR

CEO, Decision Management Solutions

Do we need a separate modeling notation for decisions?

The Object Management Group has long had a modeling notation for business processes—the Business Process Model and Notation. This has recently been joined by a decision-modeling notation—the Decision Model and Notation or DMN (as well as the Case Management Model and Notation or CMMN). Why do those modeling processes need to know this new notation, and how should they use it alongside their process models?

First and foremost, it is worth reiterating that decisions are not processes. A process describes the coordination of various activities, their sequence and the roles that perform those activities. A decision, in contrast, is a choice made at a point in time with the data assembled at that point in time. It uses the data available to answer a business question. This answer impacts a process by driving the process down one path or another, or by being made available to tasks later in the process that need to know the answer. For instance:

- A decision to reject, approve or refer a claim typically precedes a gateway that routes the claim to one of three different sets of process tasks.
- A decision as to the rate at which tax must be withheld from a transaction is used by a task later in the process that transmits the appropriate payment, and another that prints an appropriate acknowledgement.

Because processes and decisions are separate business constructs, it is worth separating their models. This separation of concerns allows them to be discussed, modeled, evolved, changed and implemented independently. This separation does not explain why a separate notation is required—two separate models could be developed using BPMN, one that describes the overall process, and a second one that describes the 'decision process'. Individual tasks within this decision process would then, for instance, be described using business rules. Indeed, this is what many organizations have done to date. The limitations of this approach are several:

- The way a decision is made can best be described in terms of what needs to be known, and what is required to make the decision—the sequence is often unimportant. For instance, one can decide a claim is not complete if the claimant is not valid, the claim type is not covered by the policy, or the amounts of the claim exceed defined limits. There is no particular reason why one of these three sub-decisions should be made first. A modeling notation that is focused on sequence as BPMN is may not, therefore, best represent decision-making.

- Information is central to decision-making. What information is required for each part of the decision, and how that information is used in the decision-making, is critical. Where a process model can touch fairly lightly on the content of information being passed along the process, this is not true in decision-making.
- Knowledge is essential in decision-making. How each element of the decision should be made, and what guides or constrains it, really matters. A modeling notation for decision-making should make it easy to show where in the decision-making which policies regulations, analytics, etc., are used.

DMN was created as a notation specifically to support the definition of decision-making. It allows for the effective decomposition of decision-making to show the structure without imposing a sequence. It allows the usage of information within the decision-making to be expressed accurately. And it allows the knowledge required to make the decision to be shown.

A BPMN model can now be used to specify only the process, leaving a single task where a decision must be made. How this decision should be made can then be specified using a DMN model. A DMN model can represent purely manual decision-making, showing a decision-maker how the decision is best made and using what information or knowledge. A DMN model can also reach down to the specific business rules or decision logic required to execute the decision where the decision is to be automated. The models can easily be linked, allowing for both separation of concerns and effective orchestration.

One final note, DMN models also allow decision-making to be defined outside of the context of a process—in response to an event, say, or in a part of the business where processes have not yet been defined or formalized, even in a case management environment.

....

WIL VAN DER AALST

Professor, Eindhoven University of Technology

Process modeling can be a valuable activity. Often the activity of modeling is more important than the resulting models. Modeling forces people to elicit assumptions, requirements, and goals. Moreover, process modeling is a great tool to stimulate discussions on process improvements. However, too much energy is wasted on notational issues. BPM professionals tend to be almost religious about the process notations they use.

BPMN, Petri nets, Workflow nets, EPCs, BPEL, and UML activity diagrams are just a few examples of the many languages used. Debates on which notation to use are seldom productive, and definitely do not contribute to concrete process improvements. In recent years, BPMN has become the de-facto standard for process modeling, but people tend to use only a tiny subset of the BPMN language (the lion's share of BPMN modeling elements are unknown or deemed irrelevant). Moreover, many BPM professionals lack good modeling skills. This is reflected by the many errors in process models. Models have internal inconsistencies, such as deadlocks and livelocks, or different types of process instances are mixed in the same diagram (e.g. activities related to customer orders and orderline items are connected, thus, blurring the instance notion).

The return on investment of modeling depends on: (i) the quality of the team making the models; and (ii) the BPM maturity or ambition level of the organization. Flawed models have little added value, and will not be taken seriously. Moreover, organizations at one of the lower BPM maturity levels tend to use process models merely as 'wallpaper'. If processes are documented without a clear purpose and the models tend to be outdated, then modeling is a waste of time.

Models are most effective when they are used actively, for example to drive a BPM system or to project event data on. Models should also be used continuously. Models can be compared to (geographic) maps. There is no need to make maps without actively using them in day-to-day operations. The constant confrontation of maps with reality will help to keep them up-to-date. If organizations are not taking models seriously, the 'return on modeling' will be limited.

Compared to business process modeling, data-driven BPM approaches (such as process mining) are likely to provide a higher return on investment. In a time when organizations are drowning in event data, it seems foolish to model processes by hand while not considering the 'evidence' in databases, transaction logs, and audit trails. The growing importance of Big Data and Data Science signify a trend towards more data-driven approaches. Data should not just be used within processes, but also to learn more about processes. Recent breakthroughs in process mining research make it possible to discover, analyze, and improve business processes based on event data. Process mining results can be viewed as X-rays showing what is really going on inside processes. Such X-rays can be used to diagnose problems and suggest proper treatment.

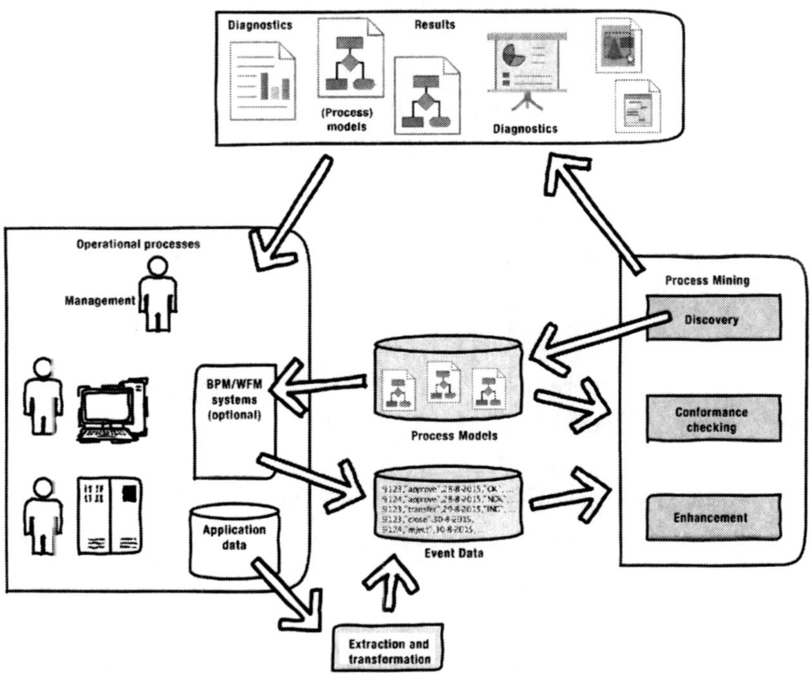

Figure 42: Positioning process mining as an alternative to pure modeling approaches

Process mining is likely to provide higher returns on investment than traditional process modeling approaches: the threshold to get started is low and process mining results are real. Unlike modeling, process mining provides insights and diagnostics based on facts. Through process mining, process models can be 'confronted' with the actual processes (through event data).

As a result, process models do not end up in drawers or serve as wallpaper. Visualizing detailed performance and conformance diagnostics on process models on a day-to-day basis is a potential key asset for any BPM initiative. It is a great tool to make workers aware of BPM. Unfortunately, traditional BPM professionals (the 'BPM dinosaurs') have difficulties transitioning to more data-centric forms of BPM.

....

DR. STEPHEN A. WHITE

BPM Analyst, BPM Advantage Consulting

Process modeling is a bit like racquetball (and many other sports). It's easy to perform the basics of racquetball, like hitting a ball against a wall—but, in a competitive game, the ball moves very fast and can come at you from many different angles, high and low, and with different spins. Thus, it takes a lot of practice, patience, and time to be good at racquetball.

Process modeling is like that. It is easy to string a couple of activities together and maybe put a decision in between. But when it comes down to creating process models that accurately represent the complex angles and spins of an organization and its behaviors, then there is a lot more to consider:

- Does the model reflect the reality of what it is trying to capture?
- Remember that Charles Box once said: "All models are wrong, some are useful." Thus, does the model reflect reality enough to be useful (more on usefulness below).
- Does the model have enough detail to fit the purpose for which it is being created?
- And does the model really work?
    - o Is the model constructed in a way that its behavior is valid? That is, if you were to simulate 'performance' of the process, would it behave as intended? Would it follow the appropriate paths under the proper circumstances? Would it get stuck while waiting for something that can't happen because of the way the model is laid out?

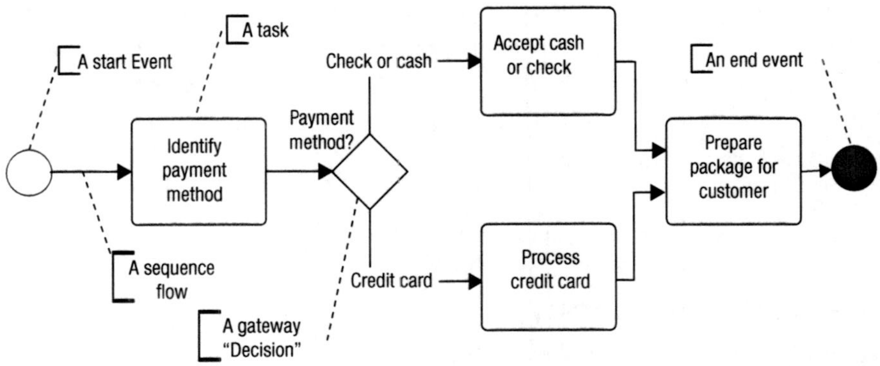

Figure 43: A simple BPMN process

If we accept that useful process modeling takes time and effort, then we can ask: "Is it worth it?" The answer to that question is very much, "Yes." However, there are some caveats:

- First, not every process that an organization performs needs to be documented.
- The organization should prioritize what really needs to be captured (e.g. customer-facing processes are important).
- Second, the amount of detail applied to the model should be appropriate to the purpose for creating the model—not every process that is modeled needs an excruciating amount of detail to make it useful for an organization.
- There are different purposes that process models will provide for an organization, and these determine the usefulness of the models for the organization. For a given process model to be useful, the level of effort to create the process and the level of details included in the model should match its purpose. Here are three purposes, for example, in decreasing order of effort and required details:

  o Detailed process models that are used within a business process management system (BPMS) to run the organization's processes in real time—these types of processes require a great deal of information about the process and how the process interacts with users, data, and services.

  o Mid-level detailed processes satisfy regulatory process documentation—these types of processes don't require as much detail as those intended for a BPMS, but they should provide enough detail so someone could track the real performance of the process with the model (but not in an automated sense).

o High-level documentation of an organization's procedures—usually as part of a catalog.

  i. These processes can be modeled with fewer details. For example, a high-level activity can represent a lot of low-level system activities, which would only clutter the model.

  ii. These processes do serve as a company repository of process information, and the individual processes could then be expanded upon if higher-levels of detail become required.

- It should be noted that the different purposes for a process model usually have a different set of audiences and modeling roles. An executive does not need to see the details of a process being run by a BPMS, but might see a simple, high-level process.
- With the proper modeling tools, process model details can be linked to other business models, such as decision models, or goals and strategy models. This will help the organization determine if their business operations (processes) are working to serve the business objectives.

QUESTION 15

HOW WILL PROCESS ANALYSIS EVOLVE?

There are a number of proposals for extending business process analysis to support modeling processes that are very dynamic or complex. This approach is sometimes called case management or iBPM, and is the subject of a new OMG notation standard, CMMN. IBM talks of integrating other advanced techniques to build cognitive solutions.

Does the future of process work lie with cognitive and dynamic techniques? Should new business analysts be focused on BPMN or on newer approaches like CMMN?

OVERVIEW

Every organization has a wide variety of processes. Some processes are concerned with more or less mechanical production tasks, whether they involve manufacturing a car or assembling a report. Other processes involve the use of knowledge and require decisions. To make matters even more complex, some processes are very dynamic, as when one handles an emergency, or interacts with a customer on the phone to try to resolve a problem. Historically, process work began in factories as an effort to define and then improve production line operations.

Today, most process practitioners are more focused on processes that involve knowledge, dynamic decisions, and complex interactions with partners or customers. Most companies still have lots of routine, procedural processes in need of improvement, but some are actively trying to extend process analysis and improvement technologies to handle more interactive, dynamic or knowledge-based situations. There are a number of techniques being promoted to extend the range and capabilities of process analysis and redesign techniques. Our authors review some and offer suggestions as to how process work will probably trend in the next few decades.

••

FRED A. CUMMINS

Business Systems Architect, Agile Enterprise Design, LLC

THE FUTURE OF BPM IS IN ADAPTIVE AND EMERGENT PROCESSES

In the future, process work should focus on all forms of collaboration, including BPMN *repeatable* processes, CMMN *adaptive* processes and *emergent*, 'unpredictable' or *ad hoc* processes. These are all collaborations among people and organizations working together to achieve a shared purpose.

Repeatable business processes continue to be relevant, but most of those are automated and only involve people where they are required for skills, analysis, judgment and planning. Most of these people-activities are candidates for support by adaptive process techniques, such as those modeled by CMMN. The benefit is flexibility, more timely action, better record-keeping, improved accountability and decision-support.

The full potential of CMMN processes is in supporting collaboration among multiple people and organizations, doing planning, adapting, advising and supporting the activities and interactions. These collaborations are supported with shared information, alerts for changing circumstances, coordination of activities, and guidance for planning and decision-making. They describe such endeavors as production operations, systems development, business transformation, problem analysis and resolution, product development, marketing, strategic planning, and business development.

The market for automated support of adaptive and emergent processes will likely be a multiple of the current market for management of repeatable processes, since most current work on repeatable processes is for improvements.

Most of current human business activities can be characterized as 'knowledge work', and most can benefit from development of automated support.

Rule-based inferencing and machine learning have applications at specific points in repeatable processes where decisions can be automated but are complex and may require modification as circumstances change. For example, rule-based inferencing or machine learning can support fraud detection—but fraud techniques will evolve, and business circumstances may create new incentives for fraud. Machine learning may recognize patterns not evident to humans to improve the fraud detection. However, machine learning requires repeated, relevant observations and feedback on the acceptability of results to learn the patterns. It cannot respond correctly for patterns of fraud that have not occurred (nor been simulated).

On the other hand, adaptive and emergent processes provide much more opportunity for machine learning techniques. The records of human activities, the initial and emergent circumstances reflected in the case records, the choices made and the outcomes provide a rich history of each case. The processes will vary with the circumstances and human judgment to support identification of patterns that support better or worse results under various circumstances. Machine learning techniques can improve the speed and reliability of implementation of pattern recognition for improved guidance, best practices or, in some circumstances, implementation of repeatable processes.

Systems that support adaptive and emergent processes should include the capability of individual users to capture, refine and save new process fragments and refinements to guidance in their personal toolkits—they need not wait for improvements to be made by specialists (or inferred from multiple occurrences by machine learning).

Venturing into the modeling and automation of processes that depend on human judgment and experience also requires consideration of why people make the choices they do. The motivations may be personal or driven by the cultural context. If automated support and guidance conflict with incentives and personal values, people will not perform at their best, or may work against the system. The developers of adaptive and emergent process supports will need a good understanding of the people doing the work, and the motivation to engage them and enhance their performance. Machine learning techniques may also contribute to adapting to cultural factors by correlating results with personal values of participants.

……………………………………

PETER FINGAR

Managing Principal, Meghan-Kiffer Research

In 2011, IBM Watson won the Jeopardy quiz show! Google recently made a $500 million acquisition of DeepMind. Facebook recently hired NYU professor Yann LeCun, a respected pioneer in AI. Microsoft has more than 65 PhD-level researchers working on deep learning. China's Baidu search company hired Stanford University's AI Professor Andrew Ng. All this has a lot of people talking about deep learning. While artificial intelligence has been around for years (John McCarthy coined the term in 1955), 'deep learning' is now considered cutting-edge AI that represents an evolution over primitive neural networks.

Taking a step back to set the foundation for this discussion, let me review a few of these terms. As human beings, we have complex neural networks in our brains that allow most of us to master rudimentary language and motor skills within the first 24 months of our lives, with only minimal guidance from our caregivers. Our senses provide the data to our brains that allows this learning to take place. As we become adults, our learning capacity grows while the speed at which we learn decreases. We have learned to adapt to this limitation by creating assistive machines. For over 100 years, machines have been programmed with instructions for tabulating and calculating to assist us with better speed and accuracy. Today, machines can be taught to learn much faster than humans—such as in the field of machine learning, that can learn from data (much like we humans do). This learning takes place in 'artificial neural networks' that are designed based on studies of the human neurological and sensory systems. Artificial neural nets make computations based on inputted data, then adapt and learn. In machine learning research, when high-level data abstraction meets non-linear processes, it is said to be engaged in deep learning, the prime directive of current advances in AI.

What's this got to do with adaptive case management and process analysis? Everything. Cognitive computing, or self-learning AI, combines the best of human and machine learning and essentially augments us. As Keith Harrison-Broninski taught us in his book *Human Interactions: The Heart and Soul of Business Process Management: How People Really Work and How They Can Be Helped to Work Better*, "there's a new breed of competitor on the block."

In today's uncertain global business world, these fierce new competitors are dominating industries by leveraging the universal connectivity of the Internet with a new category of business technology, Business Process Management (BPM). But the BPM techniques currently available are suitable primarily for activities carried out by machines. What about the many processes centered on the very foundation of commercial success—human-driven processes?

After all, processes don't do work; people do. Indeed, technology support for human interactions is the missing link in today's BPM systems. Even the early process-based competitors are eager to reinvigorate human-centered work processes, for they know that these are the heart and soul of performance improvement and innovation.

So, what is work? What does an information worker actually do all day? Read and write emails, create documents, make phone calls, attend meetings, talk to people, research, think, decide, agree, reject—this is the process of work; it's how real work works. But because little of real work is augmented by modern computer systems, how can it be properly managed for greater effectiveness? The solution is not to try to find systems that replace humans—to automate people out of the picture. We are nowhere near the (perhaps mythical) stage at which humans have become irrelevant to the daily functioning of the enterprise. To the contrary, we need to make the best use of human skills by facilitating how work actually gets done, by real people. Amplifying the work carried out by people not only benefits the enterprise as a whole, but also improves job satisfaction of the individuals who are its life-blood.

To amplify human-driven processes, we need to first understand how to formally describe such work, and then capture this understanding in a computer system. This calls for a change in kind in both business process modeling, and the BPM systems being proffered by today's IT vendors. This involves 'role activity theory' and 'role activity diagramming' where the process kicked off by a given role results in an emergent process pattern populated by new roles and sub-roles as work progresses, not a predefined machine-oriented process. This emphasis on human-oriented work is now gaining lots of attention via adaptive case management, CMMN, and cognitive intelligent assistants.

References

www.businessweek.com/magazine/content/07_24/b4038406.htm

DENIS GAGNÉ
CEO, CTO, Trisotech

Digitalization is transforming everything we do and how we do it. Digital transformation does not just mean converting physical assets to digital counterparts, but it is, rather, about creating new business models and forms of customer engagement, leveraging digital information and knowledge worker abilities. The digital enterprise is a new way of interacting with customers, partners, and employees, enabled by technologies that allow the creation of new ways of doing business. Seizing the opportunities and managing the risks that emerge demand a range of capabilities across the enterprise. A digital enterprise requires a laser focus, or centricity, on four key areas: customer, knowledge, process, and innovation.

Customer centricity reorients business models to optimize customers' experiences in achieving their goals. *Knowledge centricity* boosts knowledge workers' effectiveness by surrounding them with a contextual, information-rich environment that presents them with the right information at the right time to support their decision-making. *Innovation centricity* fosters an atmosphere of innovation within the organization, which is essential for constantly reinventing business models and maintaining a competitive edge. But, by far, *process centricity* is the most critical. Why? Because business processes are the fabric from which customer centricity, knowledge centricity and innovation centricity are woven. Process centricity focuses the digital transformation efforts on end-to-end business processes that include the customer journey and goals—to support customer centricity, that provides an information rich context to knowledge workers for making the right decisions—to enable knowledge centricity, and that offers the core fabric to reinvent the business models at will—to foster innovation centricity. Business processes are the key enablers of the speed and agility necessary for digital success.

By now, you probably understand that we take a very holistic view of what process centricity means. Process centricity takes its roots in the long-honored practice of finding efficiency and effectiveness in how things get done within an organization. It means different things to different constituents, and so it has long been the subject of much definitional rhetoric. What has become apparent is that as we shift from a more mechanical view to a more social view of process centricity, new paradigms or models are required.

Over the past few years, the concept of case management has been offered as a solution to processes that are very dynamic or complex in nature. Case management encompasses a wide range of work patterns that share some common traits: non-routine, unpredictable events, involving interactions and decisions by knowledge workers, often requiring many types of data, information, and knowledge to move work toward the desired outcome.

Coincidental to the rise of case management, we have witnessed a growing interest in intelligent process management, and adaptive case management. The quest to introduce effectiveness and efficiency using artificial intelligence is not new, but the rapid communization of machine learning and cognitive computing now brings the goal of intelligent adaptive business processes within our realm.

Multiple models are needed to better capture the various perspectives of how an organization achieves it goals. The future of process centricity, and thus Business Process Management, will encompass all these new models and technologies. Organizations, along with the business analysts and architects that are tackling the digital transformation, need to be versatile and proficient at integrating both process and case management perspectives, along with intelligent and adaptive technologies. The challenge is not with selecting the method or technique to adopt, but rather on how to integrate them all in a solution that meets the organization's desired outcomes.

....

ERIC HERNESS

CTO & Chief Architect, IBM (BPM)

This is an interesting and emerging topic without a doubt. There are many exciting things going on in this area. Let's break this into pieces so that some perspective can be provided, and work our way through this interesting and very timely question.

First, new business analysts should be focused on the business and the how problems are solved and decisions are made. There is usually a framework for this work, and it is a process. BPM and the process is then augmented and extended in leading-edge systems with unstructured work and case handling, as well as cognitive systems. Let's explore each and the role they can play and the impact that is possible.

UNSTRUCTURED WORK AND CASES MEET BPM

Business Process Management, in the sense of what business people are doing every day, includes fully structured business processes (as described by the BPMN standard), as well as additional aspects like business rules and case management. Case management adds two major facets, often referred to as *unstructured work* and *unstructured data.*

In my view, straight-through processing is the chosen end for many processes. However, this is one of those things that will often involve a journey that never ends. Exceptions will always occur, and humans will need to intervene. When you first create a straight-through process, exceptions are implemented by merely taking the exception data and presenting in a human service for someone to sort out. As time goes on, and the quest for continuous process improvement continues, the exceptions requiring human involvement are refined, modeled, and better understood. Sometimes, the mainline straight-through process is refined to handle more of the exceptions. Business rules are often leveraged to handle decisions that are repetitive and straightforward. That is good and adds value, but does not cover what might be an ever-changing set of exceptions. The ones left at this point are the really complicated ones, or those that require *ad hoc* thinking to solve.

Another angle on refining exception handling is to provide knowledge workers with a set of information to help them make the decision. In the more advanced processes that we see, advanced techniques to suggest next best actions, or to run a set of rules against the data and to present resolution options to those knowledge workers, are also becoming more prevalent. But, after all that, there are still exceptions that require human intervention, and there's often not a good way to refine the work that goes on to handle those exceptions—at least not using conventional and traditional BPMN modeling techniques.

So, what happens as that knowledge worker is figuring things out; when there is no easy way to consistently provide valuable information to that knowledge worker to expedite the work being performed and ensure the accuracy of that work? This is where the *ad hoc* case concept fits in. Here we see the task worker presented with something along the lines of what is shown in the figure below. Notice that the knowledge work is presented with the following:

- Information that is already available, generally meaning structured data and related documents.

- Zero or more tasks that can optionally be performed. Some of these are for gathering information about the work to be done, while other optional tasks can be seldom required, but necessary updates that are needed on a 'case-by-case' determination.

Zero or more tasks that are mandatory and must be performed. These are usually updates and, in fact, updates similar to that which the straight-through process would execute on the happy path.

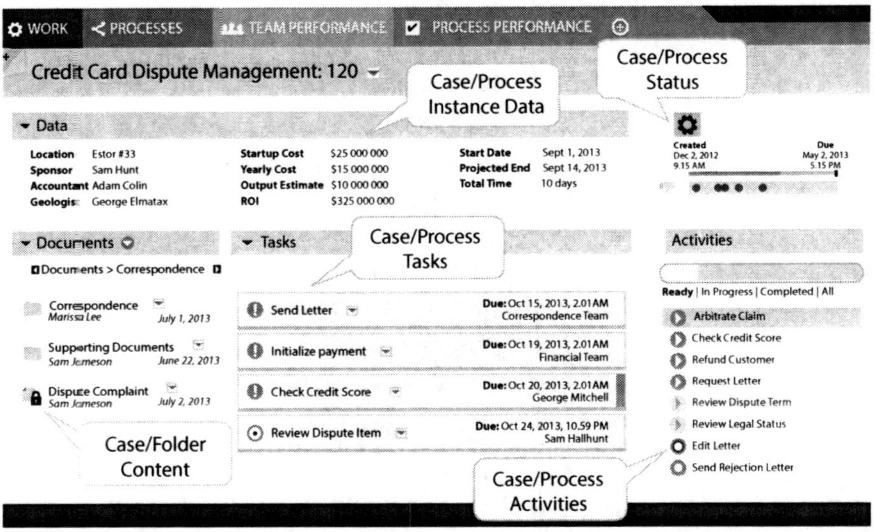

Figure 44: Knowledge worker view of case

Knowledge workers are empowered to make decisions about the sequence of steps while the process is running. As experts in the business domain, they act on new information and changing conditions, and are responsible for achieving a business goal. Knowledge workers have a 360° view of the overall case instance; they dynamically start activities as they are needed for the concrete case instance, or decide that certain activities are not needed in the context of the case instance.

That basic idea of providing the knowledge worker with this set of accelerators and capabilities to perform these unstructured activities is the core thought. We do need notational support for this, and CMMN provides some of that, as logical extensions to the BPMN that we know and love today.

BPMN 2.0 *ad hoc sub-processes* are a first step in the direction of *ad hoc work patterns* required by knowledge workers. CMMN 1.0 adds more concepts, such as: decorators (automatic vs. manual activities; required vs. optional activities; repeatable activities); entry and exit criteria (logical expressions); events (document added); or milestones. Most of the CMMN concepts would also apply to *ad hoc* activities in a regular process, such that the line between processes and case is really blurred. In some cases, a similar notation is used for different concepts—for example, a rectangle with dotted/dashed lines for BPMN event sub-processes, as well as for CMMN discretionary activities. As a result, the additional case management concepts could have (and should have) been added to BPMN in the first place.

Case management typically involves structured data (business objects) as well as unstructured data (documents). New case instances as well as *ad hoc* activities within a running case instance may be triggered or enabled upon arrival of a new document. A case folder (CaseFile in CMMN) represents the container for holding such documents, and each case is associated with exactly one case folder. CMMN does not make assumptions about the storage location for unstructured content, but mentions the possibility to implement it using folders and documents defined by the Content Management Interoperability Services (CMIS) standard. This may then be underpinned by an arbitrary Enterprise Content Management (ECM) product supporting the CMIS standard.

This explanation suggests a process on-top approach, where the case or *ad hoc* activities are within the context of some higher-level process. This is a pretty solid use case for this capability. However, there is another school of thought that suggests that the *ad hoc* or case activity is the primary and top-level abstraction, and that some of the activities performed underneath can, in fact, be standard structured BPMN processes. In the end, it doesn't really matter—as long as we mix these concepts together properly, we will do a better job of improving the overall business via applying the techniques afforded by our ever broadening and evolving definition of BPM.

COGNITIVE SYSTEMS MEET BPM

With the explanation of *ad hoc* and case concepts done, the next to explore is potential role of cognitive systems and how they will impact work. Cognitive systems, including IBM Watson technology, present great opportunity to mix in with BPM as we know it today. Cognitive systems need to be fed information, and they then learn from that information. They respond, as time goes on, with more and more relevant replies to an increasingly more complex set of questions. How we then blend that value within the context of BPM is the next part of the answer to this question. Three areas of synergy are mentioned here, each at varying levels of definition and refinement:

- Knowledge workers interact with cognitive systems
- Cognitive systems engage process participants
- Cognitive systems that find and refine processes.

KNOWLEDGE WORKERS AND COGNITIVE SYSTEMS

Let's begin by referring back to how we help the knowledge workers who are assigned various work items. We are trying to augment their understanding with whatever we can. Rather than just getting information, consulting scoring models and suggesting next best actions based on stateless and stateful rules, we should go even further to help. We can formulate and ask cognitive systems questions. We can open up a dialogue between the knowledge worker and those cognitive systems that can provide timely and context sensitive answers to questions that aid that knowledge worker.

The simplest form of this is merely to present the knowledge worker with an interrogation interface to a general advisor. A more advanced approach could be to take the information associated with the process and feed it to the advisor, let it add this contextual knowledge to the base that it already has, and then begin asking questions. That information includes all of that unstructured data that might have been gathered along the way. With so much of the world's data being unstructured, it seems logical that structured and unstructured work can be done more efficiently and effectively by getting more information from the unstructured data.

COGNITIVE SYSTEMS ENGAGE PROCESS PARTICIPANTS

Another approach to consider is that of having process participants, whether they are end users or knowledge workers, interacting with cognitive systems. Cognitive systems are generally interactive and work with written, spoken and visual techniques to communicate.

In the context of a process, there are many possible interaction points where this can make sense. It is easy to conceive a simple validation of inputs by asking process participants disambiguating questions. More advanced and hybrid scenarios, where the process engine and the cognitive system work together to guide a conversation with an end user, are also possible. The context provided by the process, combined with the knowledge and interaction capabilities of a cognitive system, open up a myriad of possibilities.

COGNITIVE SYSTEMS THAT FIND AND REFINE PROCESSES

Finally, let's visit the topic of process discovery, process evolution and process improvement with cognitive systems in mind. Everyone associated with BPM has probably thought about discovering and generating business processes from existing systems that are not running on a BPMS. Various approaches have been espoused over the years, but the value or the yield of those efforts has been limited at best. Sometimes, this was because an 'as-is' system was so complex that there was no easy way forward. Sometimes, it was because there was something missing—namely, the parts of the process happening outside of the realm of the IT systems within the human interactions.

Today, we have Big Data, and we have cognitive systems. Is it time to take another run up this proverbial hill? Perhaps it is. A cognitive system could be devised that learned from the more traditional systems of record or classic IT systems. What if it also observed the actual practices of humans (as evidenced by their vocal interactions with customers and peers, through their emails and texts, through their physical actions, through the triggers they pull in a variety of digital and analog forms, etc.)? Next, it could use the combined set of those observations to create a formal representation of that process.

There are some definite possibilities here that will get attention over the course of the coming years. There is a lot of room for a partnership that blends BPM and cognitive systems

PULLING IT BACK TOGETHER

To go back to the original line of questioning, my assertion is that a strong foundation in BPMN and BPM, as we understand it today, is essential. Remember, BPM provides context around business situations. That context then leads us to more clearly see where we can leverage both *ad hoc* case capabilities, as well as where and how to best leverage those cognitive capabilities which are emerging in the world of IT.

....

GILLES MORIN

Founder, BPMPlus Inc

New BPM technologies, like iBPMS, is forcing IT and business to rethink the way they plan, design and deliver business solutions. One of the key changes is the merging the jobs of the business analyst, the process analyst, and the functional analyst. The other key element is that as BPM and process architecture awareness grow, organizations discover that not all processes are equal (e.g. back office and administrative processes, customer experience processes, structured and predictable processes, and unstructured or case type processes). Dealing with case management, or knowledge worker processes, is a whole different ballgame to dealing with transactional, low-complexity processes.

This means that not only are business analyst jobs merging, but also that they will need to change–because organizations want to focus on case management and more intelligent platforms. Data and service management, rules and decision management, and intelligence management will become new key expertise areas.

Organizations will face two choices with regard to standards: selecting proprietary non-standard notation formalism; or select platform or tools that support three new basic standards, BPMN, CMMN and DMMN. This also means selecting a best-of-breed strategy, or a unique and 'integrated' platform solution.

Both directions have pluses and minuses—locked-in, or compounded integration issues, being a key disadvantage in either case. In all cases, even in situation where an organization is implementing case management, standardization and normalization will be required. In that sense, adopting these standards early will be a good decision. What will be a bad decision is misusing these standards—for instance, requiring that a process or business analyst be trained on full BPMN 2.0 when we know that only five to 10 notation elements are required when doing process analysis, and that you can get by with just 20 to 30 when designing an executable model. Fortunately, DMMN and CMMN do not show that same complexity…for now! Keep in mind that both CMMN and DMMN are not mainstream yet, which means they are not integrated in all iBPMS solutions.

Finally, no organization is ready or equipped to leverage a new generation of cognitive based technology, unless they already play in the technology innovation arena. There are no appropriate standards and methodology to deal with this. It's an unchartered land for trailblazers and innovators.

……………………………………

RON ROSS

CEO, Business Rules Solutions

Before I answer the question, let me make an important digression. To understand the real future of processes, you must dig a little deeper than many people do.

Process thinking goes back well over a hundred years, to the origin of modern iron and automobile production. The raw materials and finished goods of such manufacturing and production processes are literally spatial—three-dimensional. What can you do to significantly improve productivity in a three-dimensional world? The answer today is simple: you build robots. Robotization has literally changed the world during the past thirty to forty years.

Rather than manufacturing and production processes, however, the world is now increasingly focused on *white-collar* and *digital* processes. What three-dimensional presence do the raw materials and finished goods of these processes have? Well, exactly *none*. The raw materials and finished goods of these processes aren't physical, and simply have no spatial presence whatsoever (except maybe for paper artifacts). Robots (at least physical ones) aren't an option. That fact of life makes a huge difference in how you have to think about automation for such processes.

Instead, the raw materials and finished goods of such processes are all about your operational business knowledge, and your capacity to express and apply it. That capability, in turn, depends directly on your business terminology and business language. For white-collar processes, you have no choice—the world is *semantic*. So, you must deal with the subject matter *semantically*.

That takes us in a very different direction than most professionals currently foresee. For one thing, it takes us toward natural language and away from diagrams. That's a huge shift in mindset. Imagine having a business conversation with your smart phone about gaps and ambiguities in business policies, and in the meanings of the vocabulary you use to talk about subject matter knowledge. Don't think that's possible? Have you watched your kids talking to their smart phones lately?

Sooner or later, businesses will realize that operational business knowledge differentiates their product/services and enables their ever-more-automated processes to function. Capturing, managing and re-using that knowledge puts a premium on structured business vocabulary (concept models),[1] and on business rules expressed in structured natural language.[2] Those business rules are the *only* way you have to ensure quality from white-collar and digital processes. So now, finally, let me turn to the original question.

Many 'processes' people are looking to implement these days are clearly best viewed as *case-oriented*—patient care, mortgage applications, etc. Individual cases must be orchestrated through various states, often with undesirable or wayward transitions. There is significant variation in the paths that various cases take. Things just don't always move along as predictably as on a production line.

For such problems, you'll want a more case-oriented style of modeling. (For business practitioners, that technique may or may not prove to be CMMN.) You might not use traditional process modeling at all. Whatever your approach, you'll definitely want to be very clear about what milestones are relevant, and which business rules apply for each. That puts a premium on business rules.

People are also starting to ask why current processes *are so dumb*. For example, why can't they:

- Learn from experience?
- Be more goal-driven?
- Dynamically balance between conflicting goals?
- Self-adapt?

Some people suggest the use of cognitive computing to help make processes smarter. I doubt anybody today really knows how far this idea can be taken. I can, however, say two things with certainty:

- If you don't know what your business rules are (i.e. what rules guided previous executions), can you really expect *a machine* to figure them out? A machine can undoubtedly identify patterns, but that's a far cry from demonstrating compliance, guaranteeing consistent results, or customizing appropriately case-by-case.
- Suppose self-adapting processes do become reality. The question I have is *what will keep them from going out of bounds*? How do you avoid them doing things that are undesirable, self-defeating, or even illegal? These are critical questions that will always bring you right back to business rules.

References

[1] Refer to "What Is a Concept Model?" by Ronald G. Ross, *Business Rules Journal*, Vol. 15, No. 10 (Oct. 2014), URL: http://www.BRCommunity.com/a2014/b779.html

[2] e.g. in RuleSpeak®. Refer to http://www.rulespeak.com/en/

....

DR. STEPHEN A. WHITE

BPM Analyst, BPM Advantage Consulting

I've said this before, *a process is a process is a process*. For business processes, there is a range of process complexities and requirements.

To set the stage here, in the realm of business process modeling, there are two main kingdoms with their own modeling tool markets:

- Traditional 'process modeling', which tends to involve a very structured set of activities (such as a set sequence of tasks). Over the last few years, the relevant modeling tools have used the Business Process Model and Notation (BPMN) as the standard for notation and semantics.
- Traditional 'case management modeling', which tends to involve a very unstructured set of activities that can be done in any order and at any time (with some constraints). The relevant modeling tools have mainly used their own notations and semantics, but recently the Case Management Model and Notation (CMMN) standard has been developed, and some tools are now starting to use it.

But, underneath, the same set of process concepts apply across the spectrum of process types. And, even on the surface, the practical differences between 'process' and 'case' is not always clear-cut. This has been illustrated in my discussions with customers of BPM products, where there has been quite a wide range of opinions about what a 'case' is. For some, a case, as you might expect, is a very unstructured collection of activities and data—for example, a police investigation. But for others, a case is a well-defined, highly structured process, like handling a dental claim.

Furthermore, many other BPM customers want to mix and match the structured process with the unstructured activities without constraint. That is, they want the ability to create:

- One process that is only structured (e.g. a credit application)
- Another process that is only unstructured (e.g. a doctor's visit)
- Another process that is mostly structured, but has some unstructured elements (e.g. an auto claim that includes a fraud investigation)
- And another process that is mostly unstructured, but has some structured elements (e.g. an airplane crash investigation that has to deal with regulatory requirements).

A single organization may want to create any or all of these types of processes, across the range of possibilities with a single tool and common end users. This could be done now, but is technically complex with two overlapping process specifications (BPMN and CMMN) that each has different underlying models and some conflicting notations. Neither process specification, by itself, is sufficient to handle these requirements.

My hope is that the OMG will consolidate the BPMN and CMMN specifications into one comprehensive specification—presumably named BPMN (but I may be biased there). While there is some recognition in the OMG that this consolidation should occur, it is not clear when and if it will. I'll note that more than twelve years ago, the authors of the original BPMN 1.0 specification anticipated the inclusion of case-like processes with *ad hoc* sub-process element. This was only a placeholder, and now that CMMN has advanced the formal definition of unstructured process behavior, it is now a good time to fully integrate 'case' and 'process' behaviors.

In the end, the end users of process modeling tools usually don't care about the name of the standard that the tool they use supports. They just want a tool that works for the problems they have. The key is how process tool vendors provide smart tools for their general and niche markets. A well-constructed BPMN/CMMN specification will provide all tool vendors the flexibility and power they need to support their customers—across the spectrum of process types.

....

Companion Books from Meghan-Kiffer Press

Cognitive Computing
A Brief Guide for Game Changers

The Cognitive Enterprise

Business Architecture
The 21st Century business Platform Built on Cloud Computing

Business Innovation in the Cloud
Strategies for Executing on Innovation with Cloud Computing

Value Networks
And the True Meaning of Collaboration

Smart Process Apps
The Next Breakout Business Advantage

Human Interactions
The Heart and Soul of Business Process Management

Enterprise Cloud Computing
A Strategy Guide for Business and Technology Leaders

Extreme Competition
Innovation and the Great 21st Century Business Reformation

Business Process Management
The Third Wave

Business Process Management
The Next Wave

Mastering the Unpredictable
How Adaptive Case Management Will Revolutionize the Way That Knowledge Workers Get Things Done